Q&A

European Union Law

FIFTH EDITION

Cavendish
Publishing
Limited

London • Sydney • Portland, Oregon

Q&A Series

European Union Law

FIFTH EDITION

**Mike Cuthbert, BSc (Econ)
LLB, LLM, BA (Law)**
Principal Lecturer
University College, Northampton

Cavendish
Publishing
Limited

London • Sydney • Portland, Oregon

Fifth edition first published in Great Britain 2003 by
Cavendish Publishing Limited, The Glass House,
Wharton Street, London WC1X 9PX, United Kingdom
Telephone: + 44 (0)20 7278 8000   Facsimile: + 44 (0)20 7278 8080
Email: info@cavendishpublishing.com
Website: www.cavendishpublishing.com

Published in the United States by Cavendish Publishing
c/o International Specialized Book Services,
5824 NE Hassalo Street, Portland,
Oregon 97213-3644, USA

Published in Australia by Cavendish Publishing (Australia) Pty Ltd
3/303 Barrenjoey Road, Newport, NSW 2106, Australia

British Library Cataloguing in Publication Data
Cuthbert, Mike
European Union law – 5th ed (Q&A series)
1 Law - European Union countries – miscellanea
I Title
341.2'422

Library of Congress Cataloguing in Publication Data
Data available

ISBN 1-85941-733-7

3 5 7 9 10 8 6 4 2

Printed and bound in Great Britain by Biddles Ltd, King's Lynn, Norfolk

INTRODUCTION

European Union law is unlike any area of law that you may have encountered in your other legal studies. It does not follow the traditions and principles you have come across previously. It is different, and that fact, perhaps with the added importance given to it by the legal profession and business in general, is why it is increasingly attractive to students. However, although it may have different sources, traditions and terminology, it still requires the student to approach examinations with the same preparation as any other examination. One problem you will encounter is that the opportunity was taken in the Treaty of Amsterdam to re-number the EC Treaty. This will mean that the textbook or journal article references may be to Articles of the Treaty which are no longer correct. Obviously, the old cases, which are so important to the development of Community or Union law, will refer to the old numbering of the Articles but, if you are aware of the old and new numbering, this should not prove too much of a problem. I have referred to the new numbers in the text but there is a table of equivalences on p xxv to help you find your way between the old and current numbering.

Wide reading and a detailed review of both the syllabus and past examination papers is important for European Union law, just as it is for contract, tort, etc. Many topics in European law are interrelated, as you will see from the questions in this book. Some students have difficulties because, being so different from the common law tradition, they are unsure what is important. They cannot see the wood for the trees, in that they study particular topics but find it hard to see the connections. Then, it suddenly clicks. Hopefully, this happens before they enter the examination hall! It will happen sooner if you read one of the many basic textbooks on European law, making sure that it is the latest edition you can find.

The answers to the questions in this book are not the only possible answers. They have been written at a particular time. If I had to write them again I would probably change some of the contents, perhaps bringing in different cases, or changing the emphasis. However, the main points would remain the same. I hope that, by reading these answers, you will obtain a clearer view of European Union law and the relationship between different topics.

As you will see, there are some basic cases which are authority for a number of principles of Union law. They appear in answers to many questions. You should ensure that you are familiar with these and gradually build up your confidence with the topics. Start with the definitions and basic principles, looking for an authority either through a case or Article of the Treaty, for example.

This approach will help you when you come to the examination hall and read the questions for the first time. Don't panic! You should have grasped the essentials of the European Union law from your studies. In your preparation, you should consider the following suggestions:

- Read the question paper carefully. Underline or highlight what appear to you to be the key points. This is especially important for problem questions, which may be quite long.
- Write, on the question paper or one of the pages of the answer book, any ideas you have when you first read the question. This might be definitions, cases, Treaty Articles, quotations or other references. This is good practice, because it may help you decide the best questions to tackle, but more importantly, when you return to answer that particular question, these notes will help you to concentrate on the new topic. As you are writing other answers, ideas and cases may suddenly come into your mind. Write them down before you forget them! You can always put a line through these notes at the end of the examination, so that the examiner will not bother to regard them as part of your answer.
- When you start to answer a particular question, plan your answer carefully. This will help you to adjust to the topic, but it will also help you recover from those moments when your concentration lapses through some distraction. It may also help you find your next point in your answer when you ask yourself 'what shall I write next?'. Remember that you will get little credit for rambling, so planning and following your plan are very important.
- Make sure that you deal with all the parts of the question. This applies to all questions and not just those which have separate (a) and (b) parts. If you do not answer the question fully, you are limiting the range of marks you can obtain for your answer. When you are dealing with problem questions, remember that the examiner is not just looking for an answer which shows knowledge of principles. Your answer should show understanding of the principles and the ability to apply them to the facts in the question.

Lastly, make sure that the examiner can read what you have written. This may seem a very simple point, but examiners like to follow the logical thread of your answer. If it takes a while to decipher what you have written, the examiner might not appreciate your answer fully. In this context, I would like to thank Christine Blundell, who through much practice is able to decipher my handwriting and thus helped in the production of part of this book. You will not be so fortunate, as it is not common practice to have a secretary in the examination hall. However, like you, what I have written remains my own responsibility.

Mike Cuthbert
January 2003

CONTENTS

Introduction   *v*

Table of Cases   *ix*

Table of Legislation   *xix*

Table of Equivalences   *xxv*

1   Community Institutions   1

2   Sources of Law   23

3   EC Law and National Law   35

4   Judicial Remedies and Review (1): Direct Actions   53

5   Judicial Remedies and Review (2): Indirect Action –
     Preliminary References   73

6   The Free Movement of Goods   93

7   Competition Policy   111

8   The Free Movement of Workers   137

9   The Freedom of Establishment and the Freedom
     to Provide Services   153

10   Freedom from Discrimination   171

11   External Relations   189

12   The Internal Market and Beyond   201

Index   213

TABLE OF CASES

Note: Where recent cases have not been widely reported, it is possible to read the judgment on the ECJ website. Go to www.curia.eu.int, select 'Proceedings' and 'case law'. Use the case number to search for the case you want to read.

AGS Assedic Pas-de-Calais v Dumon & Froment
(Case 235/1995) [1998] ECR 1-4531 83

AKZO Chemie v Commission (Case 53/85) [1986] ECR 1965 ....113, 122, 124, 127

Adams v Commission (Case 145/83) [1986] 1 CMLR 506 120

Aerospatiale-Alenia and De Havilland OJ C280,
28 October 1991 134

Ahlström and Others v Commission (Wood Pulp) [1988] ECR 5193;
[1988] 4 CMLR 901; [1993] ECR I-1307; [1993] 4 CMLR 407 134

Airtours plc v Commission (Case T-342/99) [2002] 5 CMLR 7 134

Alfons Lütticke (Case 57/65) [1966] ECR 205 40

Amsterdam Bulb BV v Producktschap voor Siergewassen
(Case 50/76) [1977] ECR 137 30

Antonissen *See* R v Immigration Appeal Tribunal
ex p Antonissen—

Arcaro (Criminal Proceedings) (Case C-168/95) [1997] All ER (EC) 82 42

Arsenal Football Club plc v Reed (Case 206/01) (2002) 103

Auer (No 1) (Case 136/78) [1979] ECR 437 158

Barber v Guardian Royal Exchange Assurance Group
(Case C-262/88) [1990] IRLR 400 ....178, 185, 186

Bayerische HNL Vermehrungsbetriebe GmbH
v Council and Commission (Cases 83/76, 94/76,
4/77, 15/77 and 40/77) [1978] ECR 1209 71

Decker v Finanzamt Munster-Innenstadt (Case 8/81)
[1982] ECR 53 ....41, 45

Bela-Muhle Josef Bergman v Grows-Farm
(Skimmed Milk case) (Case 114/76) [1977] ECR 1211 ....26, 86

Berlin Butter *See* Rau v BALM—

Bilka-Kaufhaus v Weber von Harz (Case 170/84)
[1986] ECR 1607 ....47, 173, 176, 177,
179–81, 186

Blaizot v University of Liège (Case 24/86)
[1989] 1 CMLR 57 155

Bonsignore v Obserstadtdirektor of the City of Cologne
(Case 67/74) [1975] ECR 297 ....147, 150, 156

Bosman *See* URBSA v Bosman—

Bourgoin SA v Minister of Agriculture, Fisheries and Food
[1986] 1 CMLR 267 66

Brasserie du Pêcheur v Germany (Case C-46/93) [1996] 1 CMLR 889 . . . . . .47, 48, 51, 67

Bresciani (Case 87/75) [1976] ECR 129 . . . . .43, 190, 192

Bristol Myers Squibb v Parnova (Case 427/93) 106

British-American Co and Reynolds (RJ) Industries Inc
v Commission (Philip Morris Inc and Rembrandt
Group intervening) (Case Nos 142/84 and 156/84)
[1987] ECR 4487; (1987) The Times, 30 November 135

Bulmer v Bollinger [1974] 2 All ER 1226 . . . . .31, 79, 86

Burton v British Railways Board (Case 19/81) [1982] ECR 555 186

CAM SA v Commission (Case 100/74) [1975] ECR 1393 59

CILFIT SA v Ministry of Health (Case 283/81)
[1982] ECR 3415 . . . . .73, 76, 78, 80, 82, 88–92

CNPAAP v Council (Case 87/95P) [1996] ECR 1-2003 63

Calpak SpA v Commission (Cases 789/79 and 790/79)
[1980] ECR 1949 . . . . .58, 85

Camera Care Ltd v Commission (Case 792/79R) [1980] 1 CMLR 334 123

Cassis de Dijon *See* Rewe-Zentral v Bundesmonopol Verwaltung—

Centrafarm BV v Winthrop BV (Case 16/74)
[1974] ECR 1183 104

Centrafarm v American Home Products (Case 3/78)
[1978] ECR 1823 105

Centrafarm v Sterling Drug (Case 15/74) [1974] ECR 1147 . . . . .106, 109

Codorniu SA v Council (Case 309/89) [1994] ECR 1-1853 63

Cohn-Bendit (1979) Conseil d'Etat, 22 December 1978 . . . . .43, 45, 91

Colditz (Case 9/67) [1967] ECR 229 32

Commercial Solvents (Cases 6 and 7/73) [1974] ECR 223 . . . . .114, 115, 125

Commission v Belgium (Case 149/79) [1980] ECR 3881;
[1981] 2 CMLR 413 . . . . .145, 146

Commission v Council (Case 81/72) [1973] ECR 575 27

Commission v Denmark (Case 302/86) [1989] ECR 4607 96

Commission v France (Case 7/71) (EURATOM case)
[1971] ECR 1003 55

Commission v Germany (Additives in Beer) (Case 325/82)
[1985] 2 CMLR 719 . . . . .97, 101

Commission v Germany, Re German Sausage (Case 274/87)
[1989] 2 CMLR 733 . . . . .96, 101

Commission v Ireland (Case 113/80) [1981] ECR 1625 109

Commission v Ireland (Case 206/84) [1987] 2 CMLR 197 94

Commission v Ireland (Case 249/81) [1982] ECR 4005 ....94, 106, 108

Commission v Italy (Case 39/72) [1973] ECR 101 30

Commission v UK (Case C-146/89) [1989] 3 CMLR 601 67

Commission v UK (Case 466/98) (2002) 192, 195

Commission v UK (Turkey case) (Case 40/82)
    [1982] ECR 2793 56

Commissioners of Customs and Excise v Samex ApS
    [1983] 3 CMLR 194 80

Confederazione Italiana Dirigenta di Azienda
    v EC Council (Case 297/86) [1988] ECR 3531 14

Consten and Grundig v Commission (Cases 56 and 58/64)
    [1964] CMLR 489 ....127, 128

Continental Can v Commission (Case 6/72) [1972] CMLR D11 ....31, 113, 124, 125,
                                                                127, 131, 135

Cornelis Kramer (Cases 3, 4 and 6/76) [1976] ECR 1279 ....193, 194, 196, 197

Costa v ENEL (Case 6/64) [1964] ECR 585 ....32, 35–37, 65, 75, 76

Council of the European Union v European Parliament
    (Case 34/86) [1986] 1 CMLR 138 6

D v Council (Case 122/99) [2001] ECR 1-4319 175

Da Costa en Schaake (Cases 28–30/62) [1963] ECR 31 89

Danfoss (Case 109/88) [1989] ECR 3199 ....179, 182

Defrenne v Sabena (No 2) (Case 43/75) [1976] ECR 455 ....32, 41, 49, 172, 173,
                                                            175–77, 179, 180, 186

Dekker v Stichting Vormingscentrum voor Jong
    Volwassenen (Case C-177/88)
    [1990] ECR I-3941; [1991] IRLR 27 174

Deuka v EVGF (Case 78/74) [1975] ECR 421 27

Deutsche Grammophon (Case 78/79) [1981] ECR 487 103

Dias (Case 343/90) [1992] ECR 1 83

Dillenkofer and Others v Germany
    (Cases T-178, 179, 188–90/94) [1996] ECR I-4845 ....47, 67

Duke v GEC Reliance Ltd [1988] AC 618 ....46, 49

Dyestuffs *See* ICI v EC Commission—

ERT (Case C-260/89) [1991] ECR 1 27

ERTA (Commission v Council) (Case 22/70) [1971] ECR 263 ....32, 75, 192–97, 199

Emmott v Minister for Social Welfare (Case C-208/90)
[1991] 3 CMLR 894 46
Enderby v Frenchay HA (Case 127/92) [1994] 1 CMLR 8 . . . . .176, 179–81
Extramet Industrie v Council [1991] ECR I-2051 63

Firma Foto-Frost v Hauptzollamt Lubeck-Ost (Case 314/85)
[1988] 3 CMLR 57 . . . . .77, 87, 88
Foglia v Novello (No 1) (Case 104/79) [1980] ECR 745 . . . . .81, 82
Foglia v Novello (No 2) (Case 244/80) [1982] 1 CMLR 585 .81, 82
Foster v British Gas plc (Case C-188/90) [1990] ECR 1 . . . . .46, 49
Fragd (Case 33/84) [1985] ECR 1605 37
France v UK (Re Fishing Net Mesh Sizes) (Case 141/78)
[1979] ECR 2923 54
Francovich v Italian State (Cases C-6/90) [1992] IRLR 84 . . . . .43, 46, 48, 51, 57,
64–67, 76, 119
Frontini (Case 183/73) [1974] 2 CMLR 372 37
Fruit and Vegetable (Cases 16 and 17/62) [1962] ECR 471 59

Garden Cottage Foods Ltd v Milk Marketing Board
[1984] AC 130 . . . . .115, 119
Garland v BREL (Case 12/81) [1982] ECR 359;
[1983] 2 AC 751 . . . . .50, 91, 173, 177, 186
Gencor Ltd v Commission (Case T-102/96)
[1999] ECR 1-1753 134
Grad v Finanzamt Traunstein (Case 9/70) [1970] ECR 825 . . . . .41, 42, 44, 45
Grant v South West Trains Ltd [1998] All ER (EC) 193 174
Gravier v City of Liège (Case 293/83) [1985] ECR 593 . . . . .154, 155

Haegeman v Belgium State (Case 181/73) [1974] ECR 449 . . . . .75, 190, 192
Henn and Darby v DPP [1981] AC 580 91
Hoechst (Case T-10/89) [1989] ECR 2859 122
Hoffman-La Roche v Centrafarm (Case 107/76)
[1977] ECR 957 126
Hoffman-La Roche v Centrafarm (Case 102/77)
[1978] ECR 1139 104–06
Hugin v Commission (Cash Register case)
(Case 22/78) [1979] ECR 1869 114

ICI v Colmer (Case 264/96) [1998] ECR 1-4695 84

ICI v Commission (Dyestuffs case)
(Cases 48, 49 and 51–57/69) [1972] CMLR 557 .20, 117, 127, 129

International Chemical Corp SpA v Amministrazione
delle Finanze dello Stato (Case 66/80) [1981] ECR 1191 . . . . .77, 87

International Fruit Co (Cases 21–24/72) [1972] ECR 1219 . . . . .42, 190, 192

Internationale Handelsgesellschaft mbH (Case 11/70)
[1970] ECR 1125 . . . . .26, 27, 35–37

Irish Creamery Milk Suppliers Association v Ireland
(Cases 36, 71/80) [1981] ECR 735 78

Isoglucose *See* Royal Scholten-Honig
v Intervention Board for Agriculture—

Japanese Ball-Bearing cases (Cases 113, 118–21/77) [1977] ECR 1185 60

Jégo-Quéré et Cie SA v Commission (Case T-177/01) [2002] 2 CMLR 44 63

Jenkins v Kingsgate (Clothing Productions) Ltd
(Case 96/80) [1981] ECR 911 173

Johnston v Chief Constable of the RUC
(Case 22/84) [1986] ECR 1651 . . . . .28, 174

Kalanke v Freie Hansestadt Bremen
(Case 450/93) [1995] ECR 1-3051 174

Kampelmann (1997) 49

Keck and Mithouard (Cases 267–68/91) [1993] ECR I-6097 101

Kempf v Staatssecretarisvan Justitie (Case 139/85)
[1986] ECR 1741; [1987] 1 CMLR 764 . . . . .140, 146

Kirklees MBC v Wickes Building Supplies Ltd
[1992] 3 All ER 717 66

Kolpinghuis Nijmegen (Case 80/86) [1989] 2 CMLR 18 42

Lawrie-Blum v Land Baden-Wurttemberg (Case 66/85)
[1987] 3 CMLR 389 . . . . .138, 142, 145, 147,
148, 155

Les Verts v Parliament (Case 249/83) [1989] 2 CMLR 845 70

Levin v Staatssecretaris van Justitie (Case 53/81)
[1982] ECR 1035 . . . . .139, 140, 142, 145, 146

Lister v Forth Dry Dock and Engineering Co Ltd
[1990] 1 AC 546 . . . . .42, 48, 51

Luisi v Ministero del Tesoro
(Cases 286/82 and 26/83) [1984] ECR 377 . . . . .154, 155

Macarthys Ltd v Wendy Smith
(Case 129/79) [1980] ECR 1275 ....50, 175, 177

Maize and Starch *See* Maizena GmbH v Council—

Maizena GmbH v Council (Maize and Starch cases)
(Case 139/79) [1980] ECR 3393 ....4, 88

Markus v Hauptzollamt Hamburg-Jonas
(Case 14/69) [1969] ECR 349 33

Marleasing SA v La Comercial Internacional de
Alimentacion SA (Case C-106/89)
[1992] CMLR 305; [1990] ECR 1 ....42, 47, 48, 50, 51

Marschall v Land Nordrhein Westfalen
(Case 409/95) [1997] ECR 1-6363 174

Marshall v Southampton and South West Hampshire
Area Health Authority (Case 152/84) [1986] ECR 723 ....42, 46, 48–50, 174, 184

Meijer v Department of Trade (Case 118/78)
[1979] ECR 1387 56

Meilicke (Case 83/91) [1992] ECR 1 83

National Panasonic (UK) v Commission (Case 136/79) [1980] ECR 2033 121

Nestlé SA and Perrier SA [1993] 4 CMLR M17 134

Netherlands State v Reed (Case 59/85)
[1986] ECR 1283; [1987] 2 CMLR 448 157

Newstead v Dept of Transport (Case 192/85)
[1988] 1 All ER 129 173

Nimz v Freie und Hansestadt Hamburg (Case 184/89)
[1992] 3 CMLR 699 ....179, 181

Oebel (Belgian Bakery case) (Case 155/80) [1981] ECR 1993 95

Ordre des Avocats v Klopp (Case 107/83) [1984] ECR 2971 160

P v S and Cornwall County Council [1996] 2 CMLR 247 174

Patented Feedingstuffs, Re [1989] 2 CMLR 902 91

Patrick v Ministre des Affaires Culturelles
(Case 11/77) [1977] ECR 1199 166

Pfizer Inc v Eurim-Pharm GmbH (Case 1/81)
[1981] ECR 2913 ....105, 106

Pharmacia & Upjohn SA v Paranova SA (Case 379/97) 104

Philip Morris Case (1987) *See* British-American Co and
Reynolds (RJ) Industries Inc v Commission
(Philip Morris Inc and Rembrandt Group intervening)—

Pickstone v Freemans plc [1989] 1 AC 66 ....48, 50, 51

Pioneer Hi-Fi Equipment [1980] 1 CMLR 457 122

Plaumann v Commission (Case 25/62) [1963] ECR 95 ....60, 61, 63, 67–69, 86

Politi v Italian Ministry of Finance (Case 43/71)
   [1971] 2 ECR 1039 30

Polypropylene (1986) OJ L230/1 115

Prais v Council (Case 130/75) [1976] ECR 1589 ....26, 175

Procureur du Roi v Dassonville (Case 8/74) [1974] ECR 837 ....93–96, 98, 99, 101

Procureur du Roi v Royer (Case 48/75) [1976] ECR 497 ....138, 139, 155

R v British Coal Corp ex p Vardy [1993] 1 CMLR 721 51

R v Henn and Darby (Case 34/79) [1981] AC 850 80

R v HM Treasury ex p BT (Case 392/93) [1996] IRLR 300 51

R v HM Treasury ex p Daily Mail & General Trust plc
   (Case 81/87) [1989] 1 All ER 328 80

R v Immigration Appeal Tribunal ex p Antonissen
   (Case 292/89) [1991] 2 CMLR 373 ....139, 142

R v Intervention Board for Agricultural Produce
   ex p ED and F Man (Sugar) Ltd (Case 181/84)
   [1985] 3 CMLR 759 ....86, 87

R v Pieck (Case 157/79) [1980] ECR 2171 80

R v Plymouth Justices ex p Rogers [1982] 3 CMLR 221 80

R v Secretary of State for the Home Office
   ex p Dannenberg [1984] 2 All ER 481 156

R v Secretary of State for Transport ex p Factortame Ltd
   (No 2) (Case C-213/89) [1991] 3 CMLR 769 ....39, 65, 76

R v Secretary of State for Transport ex p Factortame Ltd
   (No 3) (Case C-221/89) [1991] 3 WLR 288; [1996] ECR 1 ....39, 48, 51, 88

R v Secretary of State for Transport ex p Factortame Ltd
   (No 4) (Case C-48/93) [1999] 4 All ER 906 ....39, 52, 67

R v Secretary of State for Transport ex p Factortame Ltd
   (No 5) [1999] 3 WLR 1062 39

R v Tymen (Case 269/80) [1981] 2 CMLR 544 80

Ratti (Ministero Pubblico v Ratti) (Case 148/78) [1979] ECR 1629 ....41, 45, 46, 49

Rau v BALM (Berlin Butter case) (Cases 133–36/85)
   [1987] ECR 2289 87

Raulin (Case 357/89) [1992] ECR I-1027 140

Rewe-Zentral v Bundesmonopol Verwaltung für Branntwein
   (Cassis de Dijon) (Case 120/78) [1978] ECR 64 ....93, 94, 96–103, 106, 107

Rewe-Zentrale v Hauptzollamt Emmerich (Case 37/70)
[1971] ECR 23 83
Rewe-Zentralfinanz v Hauptzollamt Landau/Pfalz
(Case 45/75) [1976] ECR 181 119
Reyners v Belgian State (Case 2/74) [1974] ECR 631 ....164, 165, 167, 168
Rheinmuhlen (Cases 146 and 166/73) [1974] ECR 139 ....78, 79, 81
Rinner-Kuhn v FWW Spezial Gebeaudereiniging GmbH
(Case 171/88) [1989] ECR 2743 ....173, 176, 178
Riseria Luigi Geddo v Ente Nazionale Risi
(Case 2/73) [1974] ECR 865 ....94, 98
Roberts v Birds Eye Walls Ltd (Case C-132/92)
[1993] 3 CMLR 822; [1994] ICR 338 178
Roquette Frères SA v Council
(Case 138/79) [1980] ECR 3333 ....67, 69
Roquette Freres SA v Council (Case 26/74) [1976] ECR 677 4
Royal Scholten-Honig v Intervention Board for
Agriculture (Isoglucose case) (Case 103/77 and 145/77)
[1978] ECR 2037 ....58, 59, 69, 70
Rutili v Ministre de l'Intérieur (Case 36/75)
[1975] ECR 1219; [1976] 1 CMLR 140 ....45, 147, 149, 150, 156

Sabbatini v European Parliament
(Case 20/71) [1972] ECR 345 ....26, 175
Schneider Electric SA v Commission
(Cases T-310/01, T-77/02) [2002] 135
Schoenenberg (Case 88/77) [1978] ECR 473 56
Schoppenstedt (Case 5/71) [1971] ECR 975 ....61, 67, 70
Sebago Inc v GB Unic SA (173/98) 106
Segers (Case 79/85) [1986] ECR 2375 ....143, 162
Sgarlata v EC Commission (Case 40/64) [1965] ECR 215 85
Shell-Berre, Re [1964] CMLR 462 89
Silhouette International v Hartlauer Handelsgesellschaft
(Case 335/96) [1998] 2 CMLR 953 105
Simmenthal SpA v Commission (Case 92/78)
[1979] ECR 777 ....35, 36, 38, 48, 65
Skimmed Milk *See* Bela-Muhle Josef Bergman v Grows-Farm—
Sotgui v Deutsche Bundespost (Case 152/73)
[1974] ECR 153 ....146, 149
Stauder v City of Ulm (Case 29/69) [1969] ECR 419 ....27, 32

Sugar case *See* R v Intervention Board for Agricultural Produce
  ex p ED and F Man (Sugar) Ltd—
Sugar cases (Cases 40–48, 59, 54–56/73) [1975] ECR 1663 125
Sutton v Secretary of State for Social Security
  (Case 66/95) [1997] 2 CMLR 382 . . . . .52, 67

TWD Textilwerke Deggendorf GmbH v Germany
  (Case C-188/92) [1994] ECR 1 61
Telemarsicabruzzo SpA v Circostel
  (Case 320-322/90) [1993] ECR 1-393 84
Tetra Laval BV v Commission
  (Cases T-5/02, T-80/02) (2002) 123, 135
Thieffry (Case 71/76) [1977] ECR 765 166
Toepfer v EC Commission
  (Cases 106 and 107/63) [1965] ECR 1019 . . . . .59, 86
Transocean Marine Paint Association v Commission
  (Case 17/74) [1974] ECR 1063 28
Turkey case *See* Commission v UK—

Union de Pequeños Agricultores (Case 50/00P) (2002) 60–63
United Brands v Commission (Case 27/76) [1976] ECR 207 . . . . .113–15, 124–27, 130
URBSA v Bosman [1996] 1 CMLR 645 169

Van Binsbergen (Case 33/74) [1974] ECR 1229 . . . . .164, 167, 168
Van Duyn v Home Office (Case 41/74)
  [1975] 1 CMLR 1; [1974] ECR 1337 . . . . .43–45, 49, 156, 184
Van Gend en Loos (Case 26/62) [1963] ECR 1 . . . . .35–37, 40, 41, 43, 44, 47,
                                                                     56, 75, 89, 183
Verbond van Nederlandse Ondernemingen (VNO)
  (Case 51/76) [1977] ECR 113 42
von Colson (Case 14/83) [1984] ECR 1891 . . . . .42, 43, 47, 48, 50
von Harz *See* Bilka-Kaufhaus v Weber von Harz—

Walgrave and Koch v Ass Union Cycliste
  (Case 36/74) [1974] ECR 1405 . . . . .164, 168
Watson and Belman (Case 118/75) [1976] ECR 1185 155
Webb v EMO Air Cargo (UK) Ltd
  [1992] IRLR 116 51
Webb v EMO Air Cargo (UK) Ltd
  (Case 32/93) [1994] ECR 1-3305; [1994] 2 CMLR 729 (ECJ) 174

Williams v Dutch Secretary of State [1977] 1 CMLR 669 142
Wood Pulp *See* Ahlström and Others v Commission—
Worrington v Lloyds Bank Ltd (Case 69/80)
    [1981] ECR 767 186

Zino Davidoff SA v A&G Imports Ltd (No 1)
    [1999] 3 WLR 849 . . . . .105, 106
Zuckerfabrik Watenstedt (Case 6/68) [1968] ECR 409 . . . . .29, 60

TABLE OF LEGISLATION

UK legislation

European Communities Act 1972 ....36, 48, 49
s 2 36
s 2(4) 50
s 3 36
Obscene Publications Act 1959 ....36, 77
Rules of the Supreme Court—
Ord 114 81
Sex Discrimination Act 1975 ....51, 184
s 6(4) 50
Shops Act 1950—
s 47 66
Trade Union and Labour Relations Act 1992 51

European Directives

Directive 64/221 (Movement and residence of
foreign nationals) 45, 137, 152–54
Art 3 ....139, 150, 151
Art 3(1) 151, 156
Art 3(2) 151
Arts 6, 8 156
Directive 68/360 (Rights of entry into EU for workers and
their families) 137, 138, 142
Directive 70/50 (Free trade between Member States) 94, 95, 99
Art 2(1) 95
Art 3 ....95, 99
Directive 73/148 (Rights of entry and residence) 153
Directive 75/34 (Rights to remain after employment for the
self-employed and their families) 153
Directive 75/117 (Equal pay) 49, 171, 172, 173, 177, 178, 186
Art 1 180
Directive 76/207 (Equal treatment) 28, 42, 49–51, 171, 172, 174, 184–86
Art 1(2) 185
Art 2 174
Art 5(1) 185
Art 6 28
Directive 77/249 (Free movement of lawyers) 158, 159
Directive 77/338 (Sixth VAT Directive) 45
Directive 79/7 (Equal treatment in matters of social security) 46, 171, 186
Directive 80/987 (Protection of employees in cases of
insolvency of employers) 47, 64, 65

Directive 86/378 (Equal treatment for occupational
  pension schemes) 49, 171
Directive 86/613 (Equal treatment for self-employed) 49, 171
Directive 89/48 (Mutual recognition professional
  qualification) 143, 153, 158, 159
  Arts 1(a), 3 159
Directive 89/104 (Trade marks) 102
Directive 90/364 (Rights of persons of independent means) 144
Directive 90/365 (Retired persons) 144
Directive 90/366 (Rights to students undertaking a vocational
  course at a university in another Member State) 144, 157
Directive 91/533 (Employees) 49
Directive 93/96 (Students) 154, 157
Directive 94/45 (Water purity) 42
Directive 98/5 (Lawyers) 160
Directive 2000/43 (Equal treatment between persons
  irrespective of race or ethnic origin) 171, 172, 175
Directive 2000/78 (Framework Directive for equal
  treatment in employment and occupation) 171, 172, 175

European Regulations
Regulation 17/62 (Implementing the EC Treaty) 20, 118–20, 122, 123, 128
Regulation 769/68 (National sugar prices) 71
Regulation 1612/68 (Freedom of movement of workers
  within the Community) 137, 138, 145, 148
  Art 1 145
  Art 10(1) 139, 142
Regulation 1251/70 (Right to remain in EU State after employment) 137
Regulation 1408/71 (EC legislation on social security) 139
Regulation 1111/77 (Laying down common provisions
  for isoglucose) 69
Regulation 2173/85 (Establishing the economic interest groupings) 163
Regulation 4064/89 (Merger) 20, 127, 132, 135
  Art 4(1) 133
Regulation 1310/97 (Merger) 132–35
  Arts 1(3), 6(1), 8 133
  Art 14(1)(a), (2) 133

Treaties and Conventions

Act of Accession 1972—
Art 102 198

Charter of Fundamental Rights 62
    Art 47 62

EC Treaty 3–8, 13, 14, 16, 19, 23, 25–27, 29–32, 36–42,
                      45, 49, 53, 54, 56, 57, 75, 78, 83, 89, 106, 108–10, 113, 120,
                          140–44, 147, 149, 150, 154, 155, 157, 158, 160–62,
                                 165, 166, 174, 177, 183, 189, 190, 192,
                                        193, 196–98, 211, 212
    Pt 1 ....15, 194, 197
    Pt 2 190
    Pt 3 190
    Art 2 ....109, 148, 168, 174
    Art 3 ....109, 172
    Art 3(c) 169
    Art 3(f) 120, 123
    Art 5 211
    Art 7 ....26, 168
    Art 10 ....38, 47, 49, 65
    Art 11(2) 17
    Art 13 ....171, 172, 175
    Art 23 93
    Art 25 ....37, 40, 44, 89, 93
    Art 25(3) 68
    Art 28 ....66, 91, 93–103, 107–09
    Art 29 ....93, 94, 102, 103
    Art 30 ....56, 93, 96, 97, 100–03, 105, 107, 110, 206, 207
    Art 31 89
    Art 37(3) 71
    Arts 39–42 32
    Art 39 ....137, 138, 141, 142, 144–51, 153–55, 168, 184
    Art 40 30
    Arts 43–48 158
    Art 43 ....138, 141, 143, 144, 146, 153, 154, 161, 162, 165, 166
    Art 44 ....161, 163
    Art 45 ....165, 166
    Art 46 ....153, 155
    Art 47 158
    Art 48 ....143, 148, 161–63
    Arts 49–55 143

EC Treaty (Contd)—
Art 49 . . . . .138, 141, 144, 146, 153–55, 161, 162, 167, 168
Art 50 . . . . .153, 155, 161, 167, 168
Art 55 155
Art 71 . . . . .13, 197
Art 81 . . . . .20, 103, 111, 112, 115–23, 128–30, 132, 135
Arts 82–86 119
Art 82 . . . . .20, 31, 103, 111–17, 120, 122–24, 126,
127, 131, 132, 134, 135
Art 86 . . . . .20, 31, 125
Art 87 . . . . .108, 111, 120, 123
Art 88 . . . . .111, 120, 123
Art 90 . . . . .40, 83, 93
Arts 131–34 . . . . .189, 190, 193
Art 132 199
Art 133 . . . . .190, 191, 193, 195, 199
Art 136 32
Art 141 . . . . .26, 32, 41, 171–73, 175–86
Art 141(4) 174
Art 149 207
Art 169 . . . . .51, 54, 55
Arts 189–99 2
Arts 189, 197, 201 3
Arts 202–07 2
Arts 202–10 . . . . .14, 15
Art 205 . . . . .16, 203, 207
Art 208 19
Arts 211–19 18
Arts 211–14 2
Art 211 . . . . .18, 19, 54, 55, 202
Arts 220–45 2
Art 220 . . . . .7, 8, 25, 82
Art 222 8
Art 223 8
Art 225 12
Art 226 . . . . .9, 18, 19, 21, 38, 40, 49, 53–57, 66, 108, 109, 183, 206
Art 227 . . . . .9, 40, 49, 53, 54, 56, 57, 206
Art 228 . . . . .10, 19, 49, 53–56, 66
Art 229 122
Art 230 . . . . .9, 13, 24, 25, 29, 32, 53, 58–62, 68, 70, 71, 75,
84–88, 119, 120, 122, 123, 128, 130, 131, 194, 196, 211
Art 230(4) 61, 63, 64
Art 230(5) 62
Art 231 . . . . .60, 70, 85, 87
Art 232 53

EC Treaty (Contd)—

Art 234 ....9, 31, 37, 38, 41, 45, 53, 57, 61, 62, 65, 66, 70,
73–90, 95, 99, 100, 109, 148, 149, 151, 152, 165,
167, 168, 176, 177, 183, 185, 192, 194, 197
    Art 234(2) 76, 78, 88, 90
    Art 234(3) 76, 78, 82, 88–92
    Art 235 ....58, 62, 71
    Art 241 ....9, 53
    Art 243 ....9, 57
    Art 249 ....19, 20, 23, 24, 29, 30, 32, 38, 40–42, 44,
49, 58, 59, 75, 85, 120
    Art 253 ....29, 33
    Art 254 29
    Art 257 ....13, 14
    Art 263 13
    Art 266 91
    Art 272 6
    Art 281 ....189, 193, 194, 197, 198
    Art 288 ....25, 28, 58, 61, 62, 64, 70, 71, 120
    Art 293 ....161, 163
    Art 295 ....103, 129
    Art 300 ....189, 190, 195, 198
    Art 301 20
    Arts 302–04 ....189, 190
    Art 308 19
    Art 310 189–91
    Annex II 89
European Coal and Steel Community Treaty 1952 (ECSC) 1, 12
European Convention on the Protection of Human Rights
and Fundamental Freedoms 1951 ....27, 62
    Arts 6, 13 62

General Agreement on Tariffs and Trade 1948 (GATT) 20, 42, 192, 193
    Art XI 192

Laeken Declaration 2001 ....202, 204

Luxembourg Accords 1966 16

Merger Treaty 1965 11
    Art 10 18

North East Atlantic Fisheries Convention 197

Single European Act 1986 . . . . .1, 3, 5, 12, 16, 17, 70, 201, 204–08, 210, 212
    Preamble 27
    Art 6 4
    Art 7 . . . . .4, 17, 207
    Art 13 205
    Art 18 . . . . .201, 205, 206, 208
    Arts 19, 20 206
    Art 95 . . . . .201, 205–08

Treaty of Amsterdam 1997 . . . . .1, 5, 7, 18, 63, 88, 174, 175, 201, 202, 208, 212
    Art 251 5
Treaty of Nice 2000 . . . . .7, 13, 14, 17, 21, 64, 201–04, 212
    Art 225(3) 81
Treaty on European Union 1992 (Maastricht Treaty) 7, 17, 49, 55, 201, 208–12
    Arts 7, 8 210
    Arts 17–21 211
    Arts 49, 251, 264, 265 210
    Protocol 2 187
Treaty of Rome 1957 . . . . .1–4, 12, 128, 205, 208, 210
    Arts 2, 3 207
    Art 149 17
    Art 173 70

Yaounde Convention 43, 192

TABLE OF EQUIVALENCES

Treaty establishing the European Community (EC Treaty)

Previous numbering	New numbering
Art 2	Art 2
Art 3	Art 3
Art 3(c)	Art 3(c)
Art 3(f)	Art 3(f)
Art 3(b)	Art 5
Art 4	Art 7
Art 5	Art 10
Art 5(a)	Art 11
Art 6	Art 12
Art 6(a)	Art 13
Art 9	Art 23
Art 12	Art 25
Art 12(3)	Art 25(3)
Art 30	Art 28
Art 34	Art 29
Art 36	Art 30
Art 37	Art 31
Art 43(3)	Art 37(3)
Art 48	Art 39
Art 49	Art 40
Art 50	Art 41
Art 51	Art 42
Art 52	Art 43
Art 54	Art 44
Art 55	Art 45
Art 56	Art 46
Art 57	Art 47
Art 58	Art 48
Art 59	Art 49
Art 60	Art 50
Art 61	Art 51
Art 63	Art 52
Art 64	Art 53
Art 65	Art 54

Previous numbering	New numbering
Art 66	Art 55
Art 75	Art 71
Art 85	Art 81
Art 86	Art 82
Art 87	Art 83
Art 88	Art 84
Art 89	Art 85
Art 90	Art 86
Art 92	Art 87
Art 93	Art 88
Art 95	Art 90
Art 110	Art 131
Art 112	Art 132
Art 113	Art 133
Art 115	Art 134
Art 117	Art 136
Art 119	Art 141
Art 119(4)	Art 141(4)
Art 126	Art 149
Art 130	Art 169
Art 137	Art 189
Art 138	Art 190
Art 138(a)	Art 191
Art 138(b)	Art 192
Art 138(c)	Art 193
Art 138(d)	Art 194
Art 138(e)	Art 195
Art 139	Art 196
Art 140	Art 197
Art 141	Art 198
Art 142	Art 199
Art 144	Art 201
Art 145	Art 202
Art 146	Art 203
Art 147	Art 204
Art 148	Art 205

Previous numbering	New numbering
Art 150	Art 206
Art 151	Art 207
Art 152	Art 208
Art 153	Art 209
Art 154	Art 210
Art 155	Art 211
Art 156	Art 212
Art 157	Art 213
Art 158	Art 214
Art 159	Art 215
Art 160	Art 216
Art 161	Art 217
Art 162	Art 218
Art 163	Art 219
Art 164	Art 220
Art 165	Art 221
Art 166	Art 222
Art 167	Art 223
Art 168	Art 224
Art 168(a)	Art 225
Art 169	Art 226
Art 170	Art 227
Art 171	Art 228
Art 172	Art 229
Art 173	Art 230
Art 173(4)	Art 230(4)
Art 173(5)	Art 230(5)
Art 174	Art 231
Art 175	Art 232
Art 176	Art 233
Art 177	Art 234
Art 177(2)	Art 234(2)
Art 177(3)	Art 234(3)
Art 178	Art 235
Art 179	Art 236
Art 180	Art 237

Previous numbering	New numbering
Art 181	Art 238
Art 182	Art 239
Art 183	Art 240
Art 184	Art 241
Art 185	Art 242
Art 186	Art 243
Art 187	Art 244
Art 188	Art 245
Art 189	Art 249
Art 190	Art 253
Art 191	Art 254
Art 193	Art 257
Art 198(a)	Art 263
Art 198(d)	Art 266
Art 203	Art 272
Art 210	Art 281
Art 215	Art 288
Art 220	Art 293
Art 222	Art 295
Art 228	Art 300
Art 228(a)	Art 301
Art 229	Art 302
Art 230	Art 303
Art 231	Art 304
Art 235	Art 308
Art 238	Art 310

CHAPTER 1

COMMUNITY INSTITUTIONS

Introduction

It is very important to develop a good understanding of the functions, powers and relationships between the main institutions of the European Union. This requires knowledge of four key institutions, which have their origin in the first Community, the European Coal and Steel Community established in 1952. Although there have been some changes since then, the basic principles have remained the same.

You should try to get a feel for the need for such institutions. It is sometimes forgotten that the European Community was an innovative idea, in the sense that a supranational body was being created by the transfer of sovereignty from Member States to a Community which was to act on behalf of all its members. Therefore, it was important to ensure that the institutions established would provide a forum for an input by the Member States, a body to implement and police policies decided by the Community, a court to settle disputes and provide authoritative judgments and, finally, a body which would allow an input from a wider base of views from the Member States. Hence, the Treaty of Rome established the Council of Ministers, the European Commission, the European Court of Justice (ECJ) and the European Assembly, later to be called the European Parliament in the Single European Act.

The starting point for an understanding of the EU institutions is their origin, that is, the Treaty Articles. Although they need not be learned by heart, there are key points which must be grasped as you build up an understanding of their functions and relationships. Do not be confused by the fact that the numbering of the Articles has been affected by the Treaty of Amsterdam, where the opportunity was taken to re-order them. As some textbooks and old judgments still refer to the 'traditional' numbering, I have included a Table of Equivalences on p xxv to help you. This details old and new Treaty numbers.

One of the best ways to get an overview of the variety of institutions is to read material which is intended for the non-specialist reader. Some of the publications produced by the European Commission are very good and have the added advantage of being free. There is also a very good website (www.europa.eu.int). Once you have an overview, you should begin to build up a more detailed picture, which shows the more complex functions and relationships between the institutions. However, you should always be alert to practical examples of the friction or otherwise generated by these institutions and reported in the media. Such examples are invaluable in impressing the examiner but, more importantly, they should convince you that you are not dealing with a theoretical group of institutions, but 'a living community'.

Checklist

You need to have a good understanding of the functions, procedures and membership of the main Community institutions, plus an awareness of the less significant ones. You should also look at Chapter 12, where some of the proposed changes to the institutions are mentioned. In particular, you should concentrate on:

*   the European Parliament – Arts 189–99;
*   the Council of Ministers – Arts 202–07;
*   the European Commission – Arts 211–14;
*   the ECJ – Arts 220–45; and
*   the European Council, the Court of First Instance, the Economic and Social Committee, the Committee of Permanent Representatives, the Committee of the Regions and the Court of Auditors.

Question 1

'Although the European Parliament has limited powers, one cannot claim that the Community legislative process is devoid of democratic participation.'
Discuss.

Answer plan

This type of question has become very popular in recent years. This is largely due to developments which have affected the Parliament. The main points to cover in your answer are:

*   powers and composition of the European Parliament;
*   procedures of the Parliament; and
*   role of the Parliament in the legislative process.

Answer

Since 1979, the Members of the European Parliament have been directly elected by their constituents in the 15 Member States. Before that time, when the members were nominated by their respective governments, they had determined, as early as 1962, to call themselves a Parliament, even though the Treaty of Rome referred to them as an Assembly. Under Art 189, the European Parliament consists of 'representatives of the peoples of the States brought together in the Community'. It was not until the Single European Act 1986 that the Member States formally recognised the European Parliament by this name.

The European Parliament has certain characteristics similar to national parliaments, such as the UK Parliament at Westminster. There are a number of standing committees, which mirror the major policy areas of the Community. The committees carry out inquiries, hear evidence from experts and interested parties, including the Commission, and issue reports. In addition, parliamentary questions are an important element of control over the Commission. Under Art 197, the Commission must reply orally or in writing to questions put to it by MEPs. In fact, the Council and foreign ministers also take part in this process. It is common practice now for the President of the Council of Ministers to make a report to the Parliament at the end of his or her term as President.

There are two important powers associated with the European Parliament. The Treaty of Rome made the European Commission responsible to the European Parliament and is of little importance now. Once appointed by the Member States, the 20 Commissioners can only be removed by the European Parliament passing a censure motion by a two-thirds majority vote and an absolute majority of its Members. Such a motion, successfully passed, would force the resignation of the Commission. However, this power under Art 201 can only be used against the whole Commission and not against individual Commissioners. This power has never been exercised, although it has been threatened on a number of occasions. However, in order to avoid the motion of censure, the Commission did resign in March 1999, although its members remained in office until replaced by a new Commission in September of that year. With a view to making the institutions more democratic, the Treaty on European Union gave the European Parliament an important role in the process of appointing the President and Members of the Commission. This was achieved by the need for the Commission to be approved by Parliament in a vote of investiture.

Secondly, and perhaps the most important input that would be recognised as part of democratic participation, is the involvement of the European Parliament in making European laws, principally regulations and directives. There are many policy areas of the Treaty which give the Parliament the right to be consulted on proposed legislation. This is illustrated by the phrase, which is very familiar to any student of the Treaty, 'the Council, acting on a proposal from the Commission and after consulting the European Parliament, shall ...'. The normal procedure is that the proposal from the Commission is first considered by one of the Parliament's committees mentioned above, which will produce a report and a draft resolution. These then go to the full Parliament for debate before its opinion, including any suggested amendments, is sent to the Council. As a result of this opinion, the Commission may modify its proposal, but there is no obligation on either the Council or the Commission to respond to it. However, whatever weight is given to the European Parliament's view, its right to be consulted must be respected. Failure to follow this procedural requirement may lead to the measure being declared invalid.

This happened in the cases of *Roquette v Council* and *Maizena v Council*, both reported in 1980. An interesting discussion took place in these cases with regard to what extent this requirement gave power to the Parliament to block legislation. Is the requirement that the European Parliament should be asked for its opinion or must it actually give it? The Council argued that if the latter was true, then the Parliament could delay legislation indefinitely by the simple expedient of not giving an opinion. The ECJ interpreted the requirement under the Treaty to mean that the Parliament has to give its opinion. However, it left open the question of what would happen if the Parliament were to be deliberately obstructive and the Council wished to go ahead with the legislation. Such an impasse has not yet occurred.

It is understandable that in these circumstances, where their opinion carried limited importance to the Council, the European Parliament was often called 'a mere talking shop' by national politicians. With the direct elections of 1979, MEPs saw themselves as the true representatives of their constituents and increasingly called for an active part in the legislative process. This was given by Arts 6 and 7 of the Single European Act 1986, which amended the original Treaty. This required a co-operation procedure to be operative in some instances, but by no means all, where the Treaty required the Parliament to be consulted. The main difference is that in theory, the views of the European Parliament carry more importance, although in practice, this change may not be so significant. When the Council receives a proposal from the Commission, it adopts a 'common position', which is sent to the European Parliament. The Parliament now has three months in which to act. If Parliament rejects the common position, the Council can adopt the proposal only by unanimity. If Parliament wishes to amend the proposal, such amendments are sent back to the Commission for consideration. These amendments may be adopted, but there is no obligation on the Commission to do so. The proposal is then sent back to the Council along with any parliamentary amendments it had not accepted and the reasons for this refusal. The Council can accept the amended proposal by a qualified majority or it can amend it by adopting its own amendments or those proposed by the Parliament. This has to be done by a unanimous vote in the Council.

In practice, the co-operation procedure appears to grant the European Parliament very little extra power. It provides for a possible alliance between a Member State and the Parliament in the sense that the Council of Ministers would not have the unanimity to overrule amendments. But does this give more authority to the Member State or the European Parliament? Also, the requirement on the Commission under the co-operation procedure to consider the Parliament's amendments and to give reasons for not adopting them makes a legal requirement of something which was a matter of practice before. In fact, perhaps the most significant increase in the Parliament's powers brought about by the Single European Act is the requirement for its approval in relation to the admission of new members to the Community or the conclusion of association agreements with third countries. Under the Act, the European Parliament thus has a veto in such matters.

However, the big step forward in democratic involvement was the introduction of the co-decision procedure in the Treaty on European Union. Under this procedure, Parliament shares the decision making power equally with the Council. If Parliament decides to reject the proposal, it cannot be adopted by the Council. To avoid this deadlock, a conciliation committee is convened with a membership drawn from the European Parliament, the Council and the Commission. If agreement is still not reached, the European Parliament can reject the proposal definitively. The Treaty of Amsterdam 1998 simplified the procedure to make it more efficient in Art 251.

An aspect of democratic participation which has always been considered important in any parliament is the involvement of elected representatives in the setting of expenditure and income levels, that is, a budget. Although it is the President of the European Parliament alone who has the power to adopt the budget, the procedure for the Community budget is rather complex and has been varied on several occasions. The effect of these changes has been to transfer certain powers from the Council to the Parliament.

The European Parliament's right to make changes in the budget depends on the distinction between expenditure which is 'compulsory' and that which is 'non-compulsory'. Compulsory expenditure covers that expenditure which is committed under Treaty provisions or Community legislation. The main example is expenditure on the common agricultural policy. Parliament can only propose modifications to this category of expenditure, thus giving the Council the final say in such matters. However, non-compulsory expenditure, which includes all expenditure which is not the inevitable consequence of Community legislation, can be amended by the majority of MEPs voting in favour of such proposals. This expenditure includes the Community social policy, regional and industrial policies, and accounts for about 42% of the total Community budget. For this type of expenditure, it is the European Parliament which has final control. Therefore, although the Parliament does have some powers of approval as far as the budget is concerned, these are weak with regard to compulsory expenditure, which comprises the majority of the total budget.

However, in 1975, the European Parliament was given increased powers in relation to the Community budget by a conciliation procedure. The aim of these powers is to give the Parliament more effective participation in the budgetary process by seeking agreement between the Parliament and the Council of Ministers. If the Parliament refuses to pass the budget as presented to it by the Council, a number of important consequences follow. First, the budget cannot be implemented, which has implications for the expenditure level of the Community (limited to one-12th of the previous year's budget per month). Secondly, a 'conciliation committee', consisting of the Council and representatives of the European Parliament, is established to try to resolve the disagreement. The European Commission assists the work of the committee.

Ultimately, the Parliament may reject the budget outright under Art 272 of the EC Treaty by a two-thirds vote cast by a majority of its members. This has now happened on four occasions, in 1980 by the newly directly elected Parliament, eager to use its budgetary powers, and in 1982, 1986 and 1988. Although it may reject it, the Parliament cannot increase the total amount of the budget beyond the maximum rate of increase set by the Commission, unless the alteration is agreed by the Council. The disagreement is generally, therefore, centred on the distribution of the budget. Such disagreements sometimes erupt into the public domain and have been subject to proceedings before the ECJ, as in *EC Council v European Parliament* in 1986. In 1988, in an attempt to improve the budgetary procedure, an institutional agreement was entered into by the Council, Commission and the European Parliament. While recognising the varying competencies of the institutions in the budgetary field, it fixed new rules for co-operation between the institutions. However, the Council successfully obtained the annulment of the adoption of the budget by the European Parliament because the Parliament had exceeded its powers regarding compulsory expenditure (*Council of the European Union v European Parliament* (1995)).

The normal authority of a parliament is that the national government is dependent upon confidence and continued support to remain in office. There is no such relationship between the European Parliament and the main political decision making body in the Community, the Council of Ministers.

The ministers who form the Council are representing their national governments, who in turn must retain the support of their national parliaments. Therefore, any vote cast by a minister at Council meetings must be supported by their national parliament. Is this the main democratic control over European legislation? Are the national Members of Parliament, representing the same constituents as the MEPs, exercising democratic control? In theory, this could be possible, at least for major issues. However, it has one major drawback, in that the national parliaments rarely have the procedures or time necessary for clear debate of issues before they are discussed and agreed at the Council of Ministers. Although attempts are being made to ensure better information and debate in national parliaments of European issues, this is not happening at the moment. The only really genuine and consistent debate takes place in the European Parliament, but what authority does that have? As indicated above, it has some important powers, and there is pressure for these to be extended. Since the TEU, both the Treaty of Amsterdam and the Treaty of Nice have extended the area of EU policy subject to the co-decision procedure. It is likely that at the next important Inter-Governmental Conference (IGC) in 2004 the extension of the co-decision procedure will be on the agenda again.

Question 2

'The European Court of Justice is unlike any English court.'
Discuss.

Answer plan

This illustrates a common type of essay question on the ECJ. The task is to discuss the special features of the Court. This has a special impact for the UK because it is very different from the national courts, including the House of Lords.

The main points of the question are:

- function of the ECJ as defined by Art 220;
- personnel, term of office, function – judges and Advocates General;
- procedures and languages;
- form of judgments; and
- comparison with the English courts.

Answer

The ECJ is one of the main institutions of the European Community. It provides the independent judicial function necessary to ensure, as Art 220 states, 'that in the interpretation and application of this Treaty the law is observed'. The main influence on the characteristics of the ECJ was the French legal system, notably the highest administrative court in France, the Conseil d'Etat. However, this is not the only reason why the Court is different from any English court. Another important factor is that the Court was established to work not within a State, but within a community which brought together a number of States in a new relationship, which had implications for their own legal systems.

There are 15 judges on the ECJ, with each Member State providing one judge. Appointed for a term of six years, the judges elect their own President of the Court, who serves in that post for three years. Like all posts within the Court, it is possible for the period in office to be renewed. Although this fixed but renewable term of office is not found in English courts, the attributes the judges should have are the same. Article 223 specifies that they should be independent and qualified for the highest judicial office within their respective countries. However, an important difference is that, whereas English judges are selected from barristers and, to a lesser extent, solicitors, judges in some Member States are chosen from a much wider field, including academic lawyers. Thus, when the judges in the European Court deliberate, they are bringing together a variety of legal backgrounds which would not be found in an English court.

Perhaps a striking difference about the ECJ is the role given to Advocates General, a post derived from the French legal system and unknown in English law. There are nine Advocates General appointed to the Court. They have the same backgrounds as judges, the same term of office and, perhaps most importantly, the same status. Therefore, Advocates General should not be seen as inferior to judges, as the precedent within the Court for both depends upon the date of appointment and not the designated office. Advocates General are given a specific role under Art 222, which states that 'it should be the duty of the Advocate General, acting with complete impartiality and independence, to make, in open court, reasoned submissions on cases brought before the ECJ, in order to assist the Court in the performance of' its tasks. Unlike in senior English courts, where a full judgment is given, including dissenting views, only one judgment is given by the ECJ. All the judges must agree to the one judgment, which is why they appear so terse and lacking in any real discussion of the law. They do not contain the *obiter dicta* or the *ratio decidendi* found in the common law tradition.

Hence, the importance of the Advocate General is that he hears and reads all the evidence as a judge would do, but he gives his opinion to the Court as to what the judgment should be before the judges themselves reach their decision. In his opinion, the Advocate General can range over the case law of the Court or, if appropriate, the jurisprudence of the Member States. In this way, some insight is given as to the direction European Community law may take in the future. Obviously, the judges do not have to follow the Advocate General's opinion, but if they do not it can be just as illuminating as when they do!

The workload of the ECJ has increased tremendously since the Court was established in 1957. To help the Court deal with cases, the 15 judges sit in chambers of up to five judges, but always with an odd number, so that there can be a clear decision in the case. In 1989, the Court of First Instance was set up to assist the ECJ by taking a specific jurisdiction with the safeguard of appeal to the ECJ itself. This is not unusual, as all Member States have a hierarchy or structure for their courts. The ECJ itself has a general jurisdiction with regard to Community law, only fettered by the types of action specified in the Treaty. There are a number of direct actions available which include judicial review (Art 230), actions against a Member State for failure to fulfil an obligation (Arts 226 and 227) and illegality (Art 241). It is also possible to obtain interim measures under Art 243, such as interlocutory injunctions.

In addition, there is the special procedure for preliminary references under Art 234. Under this procedure, courts in the Member States can ask the ECJ questions regarding the interpretation of the Treaty or validity and interpretation of Community acts. This does not amount to an appeal relationship, but is the recognition of a 'co-operation' between the national courts and the ECJ. The nearest procedure to this in English law is appeal by case stated in criminal cases, but this is insignificant compared to the preliminary reference procedure. With regard to the doctrine of precedent so familiar to common law systems, such as in the UK, there is no such rigid adherence in the ECJ. There is, however, the Community law general principle of certainty and therefore it is unlikely that the ECJ would depart from its previous decisions without good reason.

As indicated above, the greatest influence on the ECJ has been the French judicial system. Perhaps it is to be expected, therefore, that although cases may be brought in any of the 12 official languages recognised by the Court, the working language of the Court is French. Whenever a case is brought to the ECJ, whether as a direct action which is heard in its entirety only by the Court or a request for a preliminary reference from a Member State under Art 234, it is processed by the Court Registry to ensure that the progress of the case can be recorded. This is especially important with preliminary references, where the whole procedure is dominated by the 'file' of written documentation sent by the national court. The procedure is that on receipt by the Registrar, the President of the Court will assign the case to one of the six chambers and nominate one of the judges to act as *rapporteur*. The First Advocate General will, at the same time, designate the Advocate General for the case.

The role of the judge *rapporteur* is that, although all the papers will go to every judge hearing the case, only he will have studied them closely in order to produce a preliminary report. This report, together with any views expressed by the Advocate General, will help the Court decide what the relevant issues are. It may be decided that the case should be heard by the full Court, as normally happens with cases between the Member States or Community institutions. These early stages, covering the written proceedings and the preparatory inquiry, are held in private. Where oral proceedings follow, as with direct actions, these are held in open court in Luxembourg. The next stage is for the Advocate General to deliver his opinion to the Court. Some time after this, the Court will deliver its judgment. If it is a preliminary reference, the answers given by the Court to the questions raised by the national court will be sent back to that court so that it can complete its hearing. If it is a direct action the Court will deliver its judgment, which may take the form of a declaration, as with Art 228. However, if the judgment needs to be enforced, for example against a company, the Court itself has no mechanism for enforcing its judgments. Any enforcement has to be left to the appropriate judicial machinery of the Member State.

Note

See Chapter 4 on Direct Actions and Chapter 5 on Indirect Action before the ECJ and the Court of First Instance.

Question 3

Briefly describe the role of at least two of the following:

- the Committee of Permanent Representatives;
- the Court of First Instance;
- the Economic and Social Committee.

Answer plan

This question follows the tradition, mentioned above, of essay questions on the institutions. However, instead of asking a narrower question on only one institution, this question gives you the opportunity to exercise some choice. However, it must be remembered that this type of question is not as easy as it looks with regard to obtaining marks!

Answer

(a) The Committee of Permanent Representatives (COREPER)

The Council of Ministers is the main political power within the Community, bringing together the government ministers of the 15 Member States. However, such ministers are busy individuals with many demands upon their time. They are members of their national parliaments and governments. They do not have the time to spend in long debate on routine Community matters. To assist them, COREPER, an acronym from the name of the Committee in French, was established first under the Council's Rules of Procedure but then formally under the Merger Treaty 1965. The Committee of Permanent Representatives is composed of individuals of ambassador rank who are accredited to the European Community. Their main task is to carry out work preparatory to Council meetings and other work delegated to them by the Council.

The Committee works very closely with the Commission, as it seeks to represent the views of its governments in the discussion of Commission proposals. In order to carry out this task effectively, it is very important that there is very good liaison between members of COREPER and the appropriate national government departments. Thus, in discussing draft Community legislation, national viewpoints can be aired. This is not just a one way transmission of information, in that the views of the representatives of other governments can be channelled back. In this way, disagreements can usually be ironed out before the proposal comes before the Council to make its decision.

When the Council of Ministers meets to discuss Commission proposals, there are two agendas, A and B. Items on the A agenda are those upon which provisional agreement has been reached in the course of the preparatory COREPER meetings. This allows the Council to concentrate on the items on the B agenda, where there is still disagreement and where political compromise is needed.

As the activity of the Community has increased, so the workload on COREPER has led to it being divided into two. COREPER 1 is composed of deputy Permanent Representatives, who generally discuss matters of a more technical nature, and COREPER 2 is composed of the Ambassadors, who discuss politically important matters.

(b) The Court of First Instance (CFI)

This court was established under the Single European Act (SEA) 1986 and came into operation in 1989. The ECJ, which had been established by the Treaty of Rome, had experienced increasing difficulties in coping with the workload, as the number of Member States had increased and the policy area had expanded. The solution finally accepted by the Council of Ministers was to 'attach' the CFI to the ECJ and to give it a limited jurisdiction with a possible appeal to the ECJ itself. As the CFI has been very successful in its operations, the scope of its jurisdiction has been widened.

Although it is quite common for judicial structures in the Member States to form a hierarchy of courts, the SEA uses the word 'attach' quite deliberately. The CFI is not a separate institution. It shares not only the building in Luxembourg with the ECJ, but also other facilities, such as the library. It appoints its own Registrar, but other administrative services are shared.

The CFI is based on Art 225. There are 15 judges appointed to the court, one from each Member State. Although there are no Advocates General specifically appointed to the CFI, the need for such a role to be fulfilled is recognised. Where an Advocate General is required in a particular case, one of the judges will be requested to carry out this role. This will not happen in every case before the CFI. The court may sit in chambers of three or five judges in order to hear cases brought before it.

Like the judges appointed to the ECJ, those appointed to the CFI have a six year term of office, which is renewable. Unlike their colleagues, the criteria for selection as a judge in the CFI are not so high as in the ECJ. In the ECJ, prospective judges must possess the ability for appointment to high judicial office. Article 225 states that for the CFI, judges are to be chosen 'from persons whose independence is beyond doubt and who possess the ability required for appointment to judicial office'.

As already indicated, the ECJ's workload increased dramatically in the 1980s, and concern was expressed about the effect this was having in the time it was taking it to deal with cases. The resultant jurisdiction of the CFI indicates that one of the problems encountered by the ECJ was those cases which required a long examination of questions of fact. These are very time consuming and involve sifting through a great deal of evidence. Originally, there were three categories of case which came before the CFI. These were: staff cases, where employees of the Community have a dispute with regard to their employment; cases brought under the European Coal and Steel Community Treaty, concerned with production and prices; and, most importantly, competition cases. In 1994, this jurisdiction was extended to include any action brought by any natural or legal persons against an act of a

Community institution. If these cases also contain a claim for damages, the CFI can hear that claim as part of the action. However, the CFI itself now has a 30 month wait for cases to be heard. This is unsatisfactory for the individual concerned. Therefore, the Treaty of Nice seeks to reduce some aspects of the CFI's workload, for example by setting up specialist chambers to deal with staff cases. However, it also adds others to relieve the pressure on the ECJ, such as giving the CFI some requests for preliminary rulings.

Appeals from the CFI are to the ECJ and have to be brought within two months. The appeal will only be heard on points of law and not of fact. Some writers believe that large companies involved in competition cases will always seek to appeal to the ECJ and therefore the reduction on the ECJ's workload envisaged by establishing the CFI will not materialise. It is something which only experience will tell, but the time consuming factual aspects of the case will not be something which can be raised on appeal and will not therefore take up the time of the ECJ. The three grounds of appeal mirror the grounds of annulment under Art 230, namely, lack of competence, breach of procedure or infringement of Community law by the CFI.

(c) The Economic and Social Committee (ECOSOC)

The Committee is established under the EC Treaty, but it is not an institution of the Community. It is in fact an advisory committee appointed under Arts 257 and 263. It consists of representatives of the various sections of economic and social life of the Community. It provides a sounding board for informed and general opinion of matters relating to the policies of the Community and this helps the Council and Commission as they develop European legislation. Although the opinions of the Committee are not binding, they do appear to have influence. The Commission has a very good working relationship with the Economic and Social Committee. This is perhaps reflected by the fact that generally, the Committee supports the proposals put forward by the Commission. The relationship with the Council has not been so well developed, although attempts have been made in recent years to improve this. Since 1987, it has become a regular practice for the person holding the office of President of the Council to address the Committee on matters discussed at the European Council. This has spread to ministers from the Member State holding the presidency to address meetings of the Committee.

Although advisory, the Commission or Council consults the Committee when it considers it appropriate, in addition to those instances where it is obligatory to do so under some Articles of the Treaty. An example of this is Art 71, which deals with international transport within the Community and the common rules established to implement the policy.

There is a total of 220 members of the Economic and Social Committee. These are allocated to the different Member States to reflect their size, with the large countries such as France, Italy, Germany and the UK having 24 each, down to six for Luxembourg. The Committee reflects three particular groups of people: the Employers' Group, which is made up of representatives of employers' organisations and chambers of commerce; the Workers' Group, which represents trade unions, and a group of 'Other Interests', which includes small businesses, family, environmental and similar representatives. Within these groups can be found the representatives of the various categories of economic and social activity specified in Art 257. It is impossible within the limited number of members from each country for all these interest groups within that country to be represented. This is recognised by the obligation placed on the Council to ensure that the total Committee at Community level reflects the requirement of Art 257 as stated in the case of *Confederazione Italiana Dirigenta di Azienda v EC Council* in 1988. In order to achieve this, each Member State submits a list of potential members amounting to twice its actual allotted members. The Council appoints the members on the basis of unanimity. Once appointed, the members of the Economic and Social Committee act in their personal capacity, and not as representatives following instruction from their Member State or interest group. In preparation for enlargement of the EU, the Treaty of Nice has set a ceiling of 350 members to the Committee.

Question 4

Critically review the tasks and powers of the Council of Ministers. What procedures does it have in order to carry out its tasks under the Treaty?

Answer plan

This question allows you to draw upon other parts of the syllabus to look critically at the work of the Council of Ministers. The main points to cover are:

- Arts 202–10 – Treaty source for the Council;
- membership and procedure of the Council;
- relationship of the Council of Ministers with the European Council;
- support given by COREPER;
- the voting procedures of the Council; and
- the co-operation and co-decision procedures and the European Parliament.

Answer

The task of the Council is to ensure that the Community's objectives set out in Pt 1 of the Treaty are attained. These objectives are generally specified in economic terms with a commitment to improving the standard of living and closer relations between the Member States. In order to achieve this, the Council is given authority under the Treaty to play a very important part in the legislative process of the Community. The Council of Ministers is specified in Arts 202–10. This is the main political institution of the EU. Its membership is made up of one representative of each Member State, so there are 15 members. Although the main representative is the foreign minister of each member, the actual minister varies according to the main business of the meeting. Thus, if the Common Agricultural Policy is being discussed, it will be the agricultural ministers who will attend, and so on.

The Presidency of the Council is held in rotation by each Member State for a period of six months. The minister representing the Member State holding the Presidency takes the chair of meetings of the Council and has an important role with regard to setting the agenda and progressing Community business. This causes problems for the small Council secretariat as the focus of the political element of the EU moves around Europe. It has also been criticised on the grounds that the period is too short for individual ministers to acquire expertise in the role. The formal reference to the role of the Presidency in the Treaties and the Council's Rules of Procedure are extremely brief. The Presidency's basic duty is simply to get results. Each Presidency usually begins with the holder making a statement to the European Parliament with regard to what they hope to achieve during their six months in office. The Presidency of the Council of Ministers coincides with the Presidency of the European Council where the procedural framework is less rigid, but the need for good conduct and organisation of business is even more pressing in view of the potential importance of the results.

The sheer burden of business now coming before the Council of Ministers causes problems. This was affected by two developments in the 1980s. The Community had basically achieved the objectives it had originally set itself and was operating in a less economically favourable time. This had led to discussions in the Council becoming more narrowly national in character, with the members of the Council negotiating more strongly within an inter-governmental forum. Secondly, the Council's position as the main seat of political authority was eroded by the establishment of the European Council. When the European Council, composed of the Heads of Government, was first introduced in 1974, it was to provide political initiatives to deal with policy deadlock. However, it now seems to deal with many of the major decisions facing the Community. It was formally recognised in the Single European Act 1986.

However, is it realistic to expect government ministers to play a significant role in the Council of Ministers to develop policy at Community level as against making decisions to adopt such policies or legislation? For example, any British minister who may be involved in a meeting of the Council of Ministers is in charge of a government department, and takes part in debates and answers questions in the House of Commons or, in exceptional cases, the House of Lords. As an MP, there are also constituency problems and interests to deal with. How much time is there for EU matters? Obviously, there has to be some time, because this is part of his job, but a great deal of the work of the Council of Ministers is undertaken by the Committee of Permanent Representatives (COREPER). This group of diplomats represent the views or interests of their particular government. They liaise with the various government ministries and bring these views to the discussions which take place in Brussels. The idea is that when the Council of Ministers meets, much of the preliminary discussion has taken place and the ministers can concentrate on those issues which may require a political compromise or are politically sensitive.

Recently, the main discussion and action involving the Council of Ministers has centred on its voting procedures. In Art 205, it was envisaged that the Council would move, after the transitional period, to majority voting, except for those specific matters identified by the Treaty as requiring unanimity. This was not to be a simple majority, but generally a qualified one on the basis of Art 205. This Article gives each Member State a number of votes depending roughly upon the size of its population, ranging from 10 for the largest Member States to two votes for the smallest country, Luxembourg. On any issue before the Council, it requires a combination of the larger and smaller Member States to accumulate the necessary votes to adopt the measure. This seeks to ensure that no interest group in the Council can dominate the voting and encourages a compromise in the sense that the measure must be acceptable to a range of Member States. The necessary voting majority is 62 votes in favour of the measure. The intention of the Treaty was hindered by the events of 1966 that led to the Luxembourg Accord or Compromise, which was instituted to obtain the co-operation of the French Government in the working of the EU. This recognition of a 'veto', in the sense that unanimity was required on particular issues not specified as requiring unanimity under the Treaty, slowed down the actions of the Council, in that it could not proceed faster than its slowest participating government. Governments who joined in the 1970s and 1980s assumed that they did so with a power of veto on issues they considered important to them, although they were politically shocked on occasions when they tried to exercise it. It was not until the Single European Act 1986 that attempts were made to speed up the decision making process of the Council of Ministers to meet the target of completing the Internal Market by 1 January 1993. Although academic debate still continues on whether the veto still exists, it is important to recognise the political nature of the Council. If the President of the Council is aware of the political implications of calling for a vote where a minority of the Council have strong objections, it is likely that such a vote will be postponed for further discussion. Under Art 11(2), the matter can be referred to the European Council.

The Inter-Governmental Conference (IGC) at the end of 2000 in Nice was dominated by the implications for voting in the Council of Ministers of the planned enlargement of the EU to 27 members. Under the Nice Treaty, the larger Member States such as the UK will have 29 votes, down to Malta with just three votes. The number of votes needed for adoption of a measure has been raised to 258 votes. However, the Nice Treaty also introduced the idea of a 'dual majority' in the voting procedure. In addition to these votes where a qualified majority is needed, a Member State may require that the qualified majority represents at least 62% of the total population of the Union. This arrangement maintains the balance between the large and smaller Member States, whilst respecting the democratic rights of the majority.

The Treaty now recognises that the Council of Ministers no longer has the final say on legislation and concluding treaties or agreements with third countries. Also the Council can only act on the basis of a proposal from the European Commission. Article 7 of the Single European Act 1986 replaced the original Art 149 of the Treaty of Rome and introduced the co-operation procedure, which gives the European Parliament greater involvement in the legislative process on certain issues. If the Council wishes to ignore Parliament's amendments to its common position, it must do so by unanimity. Likewise, if it wishes to amend the proposals from the Commission it must do so unanimously. The Treaty on European Union extended the involvement of the European Parliament so that it shares power equally with the Council on some matters, to the extent that the Parliament can prevent the adoption of the proposal. As the European Parliament exercises more authority in the legislative process, it has to be at a reduction of that held by the Council. However, as the powers of the Community institutions are being reviewed in the context of enlargement, the Council of Ministers remains the main political power within the Community, although the scope of the co-decision procedure was extended in the Treaty of Nice.

Note

See Chapter 12 on the possible impact of suggested reforms on the relationship between the Council and the European Parliament.

Question 5

Critically assess the powers and functions of the European Commission.

Answer plan

This question allows you to draw upon the other areas of your European law syllabus to illustrate the powers and functions of the European Commission. The main points to cover are:

- Art 211 and the general duties of the Commission;
- the appointment and organisation of the European Commission;
- the role of the Commission and Community legislation;
- the Commission's role in external relations;
- the enforcement powers of the Commission under Art 226; and
- the powers of the Commission with regard to competition policy.

Answer

The European Commission is sometimes thought of as a kind of European civil service, which it is not. Civil servants are merely expected to carry out the wishes of their political masters. It is obvious from studying the work of the Commission that its role goes much further than this. There are 20 Commissioners, with two each from the big four Member States plus Spain, and one each from the remaining Member States. Articles 211–19 deal with the European Commission. Generally, Commissioners have held political office in their Member State, but, once appointed, they are to act completely independently as required by Art 10 of the Merger Treaty. They are not to be 'mandated' by their Member State or to be seen favouring one Member State or organisation. This may not be welcomed by the government of the Member State which nominated them, as Mrs Thatcher's accusation that Lord Cockfield had 'gone native' illustrates. They are sometimes referred to as the 'true Europeans', in that they are to act in the best interests of the Community as a whole. They are appointed by common accord by the governments of the Member States and approved by the European Parliament for a term of five years, which is renewable. The term of office of the Commission has now been synchronised with the European Parliament elections. They can only be removed as a group by the European Parliament. One Commissioner is appointed to head the Commission as its President. The Treaty of Amsterdam strengthened the position of the European Parliament by requiring its approval to the appointment of the President of the Commission. Each Commissioner is allocated a portfolio or area of responsibility from the 20 Directorates General covering all Community policy.

The functions of the European Commission are found in Art 211, and indicate the key role envisaged for it by the Treaty. The important functions, initiator of Community policy and executive arm of the Community, are clearly stated. Although the main political power of the Community rests with the Council of Ministers, the Council is dependent upon receiving a proposal from the Commission before it can act. These proposals cover the full range of Community policy specified in the Treaty and the general power under Art 308. In exceptional cases, the Council, and now the European Parliament, can request proposals under Art 208 but, even here, a proposal must come from the Commission. The introduction of the co-operation and co-decision procedures, whereby the European Parliament's legislative role in certain policy areas has been increased, requires the involvement of the Commission. If the European Parliament wishes to amend the Council's common position, such amendments are first considered by the European Commission, which can either adopt them or give reasons for its refusal to the Council.

Once the Community acts have been passed, such as those mentioned in Art 249, it is for the Commission to ensure that they are applied. Some observers refer to this as the policing role of the Commission, but it goes further than this. The Commission is acting in an executive role, implementing the agreed policy of the Community. In order to ensure that Member States implement the Community act and generally fulfil their obligations under the Treaty, the Commission is granted a power under Art 226. This Article gives authority to the Commission to deliver a reasoned opinion to those Member States which it feels are failing to fulfil an obligation. If the Member State is unable to satisfy the Commission that it is not failing to do so, the Commission can bring the matter before the ECJ. If the Court agrees with the Commission's view, it can make a declaration under Art 228, requiring the Member State to comply with its judgment and, if appropriate, imposing a fine. This is a very powerful weapon, which has led to the Commission being called 'the guardian of the Treaties'. The Commission has complete discretion as to whether to bring an action under Art 226, but this has to be seen within the context of its overall duty under Art 211 to ensure that the Treaty and the associated measures taken are applied.

As the Commission is seen as the body representing the Community interest, it perhaps follows that it should be given a special role in the Community's external relations. The Community is a large economic trading area, and as such belongs to a number of international organisations, such as GATT. In addition, the Community is party to bilateral and multilateral agreements with countries or trading blocs. Under Art 301, such international agreements are to be negotiated by the Commission, although they are concluded by the Council of Ministers after consulting the European Parliament.

It is perhaps in the important area of competition policy where the wide powers of the Commission can be observed. The competition policy of the Community is founded upon Arts 81, 82 and 86, covering both the private sector and the activities of governments of Member States. The authority of the Commission with regard to the private sector is not restricted to those undertakings which are based in the European Community, but includes all those who are involved in an economic activity within the Community. This was a lesson learnt by ICI before the UK became a member of the Community in the *Dyestuffs* case in 1972. As indicated above, the Commission is involved in the Community acts specified in Art 249. In the specific area of competition policy, this results in decisions being taken, which are binding upon those to whom they are addressed. Thus the Commission, exercising its powers under Regulation 17/62, can investigate restrictive practices or abuses of a dominant position affecting the Community and, if the competition policy has been breached, they can impose very large fines. Many of the undertakings involved in such cases complain that the Commission's powers are excessive, in that it is 'prosecutor, judge and jury'. However, there is the possibility of appeal to the Court of First Instance. The Commission's role with regard to mergers was also increased by the Merger Regulation (4064/89). Under this regulation, the Commission must approve such mergers between undertakings with a worldwide turnover of more than 2,500 m euros, where at least two of the firms have a combined turnover of more than 100 m euros in the European Community. Actions by governments of Member States, which may affect undertakings by providing subsidies or other unfair treatment, are also within the powers of enforcement by the Commission.

It can be seen that the powers and functions of the European Commission are very wide. Without the European Commission, the European Community could never have been constructed and developed to the extent it has. The Commission has also taken a very pro-Community stance, supported by the ECJ. As the influence of the European Parliament has increased, so the Commission has worked closely with it in recognition of its democratic role within the Community. With the introduction of the European Council, the role of the Commission was recognised with the invitation to the President of the Commission to join their meetings. However, there have been calls for reform of the Commission. Although it should operate on a collegiate basis, the increased number of Commissioners and the policies of the Community make this difficult. It has been agreed in the light of enlargement that the number of Commissioners should be reduced, with only one from each Member State. This smaller body should be able to work more efficiently and provide meaningful portfolios to all Commissioners. From 2005, this will in fact be the case. But in the preparation for the enlargement of the EU to 25 Member States, the Nice Treaty accepted that when this number of members is achieved, the European Commission should not be equal to one Commissioner from each State. Instead there will be a rotation system based on the principle of equality, with the Council appointing the Commissioners by unanimity. The policy areas of the Community have not been reduced, but it has been accepted that the principle of subsidiarity should apply. Under this principle, decisions should be taken at the lowest level possible. Thus more decisions would be taken at national or local level. This should reduce some of the workload of the Commission.

Note

You should look at Chapter 4 on Direct Actions, where Art 226 actions are dealt with in more detail, and Chapter 7 on Competition Policy.

CHAPTER 2

SOURCES OF LAW

Introduction

As you are no doubt aware by now, the European Union is based upon treaties which, under international law, have a special significance. They form the basis not only of the institutions, but also the powers which can be exercised by those institutions and the procedures under which they must operate. Therefore, it is no wonder that the starting point for any discussion of the legal basis of the European Community are the treaties upon which it is founded. The treaties are considered to be the primary source of Community law. The basis of any other legal action must be founded on a treaty provision.

Although it is perhaps an over-simplification to use this analogy, if you think of the treaty as an enabling Act, then what is required is the equivalent of delegated legislation to provide the structure and detail necessary to produce an effective measure upon which individuals can base their actions and which the legal system can enforce. Hence we come to what are generally called secondary sources of Community law. These are listed in Art 249 as regulations, directives and decisions. Although recommendations and opinions are mentioned, these are not legally binding. This Article provides the key definitions of these Community administrative acts which are so important to the study of European law.

As every student of a common law system is aware, the judiciary, in their deliberation and judgments on the law, create rules or principles which are followed in subsequent cases. Although the European legal system does not have such a rigid adherence to precedent as found in the common law, the judges in the European Court of Justice (ECJ) have provided an additional secondary source of law to add to the administrative acts found in Art 249. Examples of this will be found in specific questions throughout the later chapters of this book, but a few points can be made now to show the impact of this source of law. As will be discussed in Chapter 3, there is a clear acceptance within the Community that the ECJ provides definitive and authoritative judgments on points of European Community law which are followed by the courts of the Member States.

Checklist

You need to have a good understanding of the role of the EC Treaty as an authority for Community acts or judgments of the ECJ. When you are tracing the authority of a particular Community act, you will generally go back to a Treaty Article. In addition, you should cover the following points:

• primary and secondary sources of Community law;

• administrative acts defined in Art 249;

• general principles of Community law; and

• methods of interpretation used in Community law.

Question 6

Critically review the development of general principles of law as part of the law of the European Community.

Answer plan

Generally, questions covering only general principles of Community law are essay questions, similar to this one. However, you must be prepared to deal with this topic within problem questions, where a particular general principle may be the ground which will allow a remedy to be granted to one of the parties. The most common question where these occur asks you to deal with an action for judicial review under Art 230. You should look at Chapter 4 to see how the topic of general principles can be integrated into a problem question drawing upon a number of topics in the syllabus.

With regard to this question, the main points for discussion are:

• the role of general principles within a legal system;

• authority for the development of general principles within the EC legal system; and

• specific examples of Community general principles, including the most important ones.

Answer

General principles of law are found in all legal systems, including the common law system. Within the common law system of England, they are seen as a device to hide judge made law, whereby a judge seeks to show that his ruling was derived from a principle of sufficient generality so as to command common assent. In this way, a firm legal base could be provided for the judgment. Within the legal systems of the Member States, the development of general principles has taken place over a number of years and has been cloaked in historical respectability or authority. However, the European Community was facing the possible development of general principles in a modern era and therefore had to be more conscious of what it was undertaking. The ECJ has developed a doctrine that rules of Community law may be derived from general principles of law in addition to treaties and Community legislation.

The ECJ has pointed to three Articles of the EC Treaty to provide some justification for general principles as a source of law. These are:

(a) Art 220, which states that 'The Court of Justice shall ensure that in the interpretation of the Treaty the law is observed'. In view of the word 'law' being used, it is considered that it must refer to something over and above the Treaty itself, and it is not unreasonable for this Article to oblige the judges of the Court to take general principles into account;

(b) Art 230 deals with judicial review and specifies the grounds upon which an annulment can be based. The first paragraph of the Article includes the words 'infringement of this Treaty, or of any rule of law relating to its application ...'. The phrase 'any rule of law' must refer to something other than the Treaty itself. This has been used by the ECJ as a basis for the principle that a Community act may be quashed for the infringement of a general principle of law; and

(c) Art 288 is concerned with non-contractual liability (tort), and expressly provides that the liability of the Community is based on the 'general principles common to the laws of the Member States'.

Given this authority from the Treaty, three points should be noted before going on to specific general principles:

(a) the Court is prepared to apply principles of law, even if they are not found in the legal system of every Member State;

(b) whatever the factual origin of the principle, it is applied by the ECJ as a principle of Community law and not of national law. This is very important, as can be noted by the development of the general principle of protection of fundamental rights given below;

(c) there is little doubt that the ECJ would have applied general principles of law even if none of these Treaty provisions existed, because of the function of such general principles.

Proportionality

This principle is derived from German law, where it underlies certain provisions of the German Constitution. 'A public authority may not impose obligations on a citizen except to the extent to which they are strictly necessary in the public interest to attain the purpose of the measure' (*Internationale Handelsgesellschaft* (1970)).

Thus, if the burdens imposed are clearly out of proportion to the object in view, the measure will be annulled. Proportionality is important in economic law and therefore has a wide application within the EU. It frequently involves imposing taxes, levies, duties, etc, in the hope of achieving economic advantages. The ECJ will not interfere unless there is a very clear and obvious infringement of the principle.

An example is the *Skimmed Milk Powder* case (*Bela-Muhle Josef Bergman v Grows Farm* (1977)), where the Council had sought to reduce a surplus of skimmed milk powder in the Community by forcing animal feed producers to incorporate it in their product in place of soya, which was the normal protein element used. The drawback to the producers was that the skimmed milk was three times more expensive than the soya. The ECJ held that the regulation embodying the scheme was invalid, partly because it was discriminatory and partly because it offended against the principle of proportionality. The effect of making animal feed producers use skimmed milk was to increase the price of animal feed and thus harm all livestock breeders. The imposition of the obligation to purchase skimmed milk powder was not necessary in order to diminish the surplus. On the other hand, the benefits of the policy were felt only by dairy farmers. Therefore, the policy worked in a discriminatory fashion between different categories of farmers.

Non-discrimination or equality

Specific reference to this principle can be found in the Treaty, notably in the original Art 7, which dealt with discrimination on the grounds of nationality, and Art 141 which deals with equal pay. However, the ECJ has gone beyond these provisions in holding that there is a general principle of non-discrimination in Community law. This does not mean that Community institutions must treat everybody alike, but that there must be no arbitrary distinctions between different groups within the Community. For an example concerning a business, see the *Skimmed Milk Powder* case, above. The case of *Sabbatini v European Parliament* (1972) illustrates how the principle applies to discrimination between the sexes. The Court went further in the case of *Prais v Council* (1976), where it held that the principle also covered discrimination on the basis of religion.

Protection of legitimate expectations

According to this principle, derived from German law, Community measures must not, in the absence of an overriding matter of public interest, violate the legitimate expectations of those concerned. Thus, a business, holding a reasonable expectation which it has acted upon in the normal cause of business and having suffered a loss, may seek to have the Community measure annulled. The ECJ sometimes seeks to avoid annulment by adopting a strained interpretation of the measure concerned.

In *Deuka v EVGF* (1975), the German intervention agency (EVGF) was the national authority concerned with the payment of premiums to processors who made wheat unfit for human consumption and only suitable for animal feed. In order to qualify for a premium, Deuka had to obtain the prior agreement of EVGF and to carry out the process under their supervision. A European Commission regulation increased the premium payable as from 1 June 1970, that is, during a crop year. Deuka processed a quantity of wheat which had been purchased before 1 June, and thus claimed they were entitled to the increased premium. This was refused. Following legal proceedings in the German courts, a reference was made to the ECJ. The regulation was not declared invalid, but the Court stated that, in view of the principle of legal certainty, it should be interpreted so that the increase was payable, even if processing took place after 1 June, provided that the wheat was purchased and the relevant authority approved before 1 June. Therefore, this interpretation gave full protection to the legitimate expectations of the processors (see also *Commission v Council* (1973), which is concerned with salary payments to Community staff).

Fundamental rights

It was not until the case of *Stauder v City of Ulm* (1969) that the ECJ recognised this general principle. The refusal to do so earlier had created pressure between the Court and some of the Member States, notably Germany and Italy, where such rights had been enshrined into their respective constitutions. The matter was resolved when an administrative judge in Stuttgart asked the ECJ whether a particular requirement was compatible with the general principles of Community law. The result was that the ECJ expressly included the protection of 'fundamental human rights enshrined in the general principles of Community law and protected by the Court'. In the later case of *Internationale Handelsgesellschaft* (1970), the Court stated that 'fundamental rights form an integral part of the general principles of the law, the observance of which it ensures; [and] in safeguarding those rights, the Court is bound to draw inspiration from constitutional traditions common to the Member States ...'. The European Convention on Human Rights was recognised in the Preamble to the Single European Act 1986 and the ECJ has accorded a special significance to the Convention (*ERT* case (1989)). At the IGC held in December 2000 in Nice, it was decided not to include the Charter of Fundamental Rights into the Treaty. Although a joint proclamation by the Council, Parliament and the

Commission was made in support of the Charter, there is legal uncertainty as to its status.

Procedural rights

These rights have been developed to fill the gaps where EC legislation does not provide specific safeguards for a person's rights. Examples include:

(a) *the right to a hearing* – this is drawn from the tradition of English law and was first used in *Transocean Marine Paint Association v Commission* (1974), where Advocate General Warner submitted that there was a general rule that a person whose interests are perceptibly affected by a decision taken by a public authority must be given the opportunity to make his views known. As the Commission had failed to do so in this competition case, its decision was annulled;

(b) *the right to due process* – in the case of *Johnston v Chief Constable of the Royal Ulster Constabulary* (1986), Mrs Johnston claimed that she had been subject to sex discrimination by her employer, contrary to Directive 76/207. A certificate issued by the Secretary of State sought to provide conclusive evidence that the derogation from Community obligations was on the grounds of national security. The Court held that such a provision was contrary to the 'requirement of judicial control stipulated by [Art 6 which] reflects a general principle of law which underlies the constitutional traditions common to the Member States'.

The advantages of general principles are the same for the Community legal system as for Member States. They help to fill the gaps which always arise when it is not possible to have a written text to cover every legal eventuality. They constitute the unwritten law of the Community. Also within the Community, the characteristic role of general principles as limiting the power of the administration to take measures affecting the citizen has been continued.

General principles of law are relevant in the context of EC law in a number of ways:

(a) they may be invoked as an aid to interpretation in the sense that 'the measure should not conflict with general principles';

(b) general principles may be invoked by both Member States and individuals in order to challenge Community acts;

(c) general principles may also be invoked as a means of challenging action by a Member State, where the action is performed in the context of a right or obligation arising from Community law; and

(d) general principles may be invoked to support claims for damages against the Community (Art 288).

Question 7

Explain the nature and legal effect of regulations, directives and decisions made by the Council of Ministers and the Commission of the European Community.

Answer plan

Most questions on sources of law are essay questions like this one. However, you must remember that a good understanding of these topics can be invaluable when answering problem questions, which come up in later chapters. The best example is that of cases brought under Art 230, where the ability to discuss what is meant by a regulation is very important.

This question is looking for a clear understanding of the definitions in Art 249 and the legal effect of a regulation, a directive and a decision.

Answer

The forms of EC legislation or administrative acts are listed in Art 249. This provides the basic definitions for a regulation, directive and decision. Article 249 does not give the authority to issue such legislative measures, as they have to be authorised by specific Articles of the Treaty. However, where the Council or the Commission, in order to carry out their tasks, do need to issue a legally binding act, it is to Art 249 that attention must be given.

Under Art 249, the definition of a regulation is that it shall have general application and be binding in its entirety and directly applicable in all Member States. It does not mean that a regulation necessarily has to apply to all Member States. It could be applicable in only one Member State. However, as long as it retains its character of being applicable to an abstract group of persons it will still be a regulation. This is important if an individual is seeking to challenge the validity of a regulation by using the Art 230 procedure, as was discussed in the *Zuckerfabrik Watenstedt* case (1968).

Under Art 253, it is a requirement that certain formalities are completed in order for a valid regulation to be made. The reasons upon which the regulation is based must be given and any proposals or opinions which were required by the Treaty to be obtained must be referred to. The next Article, Art 254, requires that regulations are published in the Official Journal of the Community. The Council's Rules of Procedure for regulations requires them to be numbered, dated and signed. Regulations also carry a formula describing their legal effects, that is, 'this Regulation is binding in its entirety and directly applicable in all Member States'.

This formula raises two points about the effects of regulations. The first is whether national legislation is required by the Member State to implement the regulation. The view of the ECJ is that regulations have a mandatory effect and have the force of law in the Member States without the need for transformation or confirmation by their legislatures. The Court went further in the 1972 case of *EC Commission v Italy*, when it stated that 'all methods of implementation are contrary to the Treaty which would have the result of creating an obstacle to the direct effect of Community regulations and jeopardising their simultaneous and uniform application in the whole of the Community'. Although there are exceptional cases where such national legislation is required, in such cases, the national law must not disguise its Community character by altering the wording of the regulation or its date for coming into force.

The second point concerns the meaning of 'directly applicable in all Member States'. 'Directly applicable' means that the regulation does not require a national measure to become binding upon the citizens and also that national authorities and national measures cannot prevent its application. There is often confusion between 'direct applicability' and the term 'direct effect', especially as the ECJ itself seems to use the terms interchangeably. The Treaty and other sources of Community law can have direct effect, but only regulations are directly applicable. In *Politi v Italian Ministry of Finance* (1971), the ECJ held that, under Art 249, 'Regulations shall have general application and shall be directly applicable in Member States ... Therefore by reason of their nature and their function in the system of the sources of Community law, regulations have direct effect and are as such capable of creating individual rights which national courts must protect'. Therefore, not only may individuals rely on specific provisions as against other individuals and Member States, they may invoke the general objective and purpose of regulations as against national legal provisions. Thus, in *Amsterdam Bulb BV v Producktschap voor Siergewassen* (1977), it was stated that 'the moment that the Community adopts regulations under Art 40 of the Treaty establishing a common organisation of the market in a specific sector, the Member States are under a duty not to take any measure which might create exemptions from them or affect them adversely'.

Question 8

Critically review the methods of interpretation used by the European Court of Justice (ECJ).

Answer plan

This question is seeking an answer which shows knowledge and understanding of how the ECJ goes about the process of interpreting Community law.

The main points raised by this question are:

- purpose of methods of interpretation;
- influences on the ECJ; and
- methods used by the ECJ – teleological, contextual, literal, historical.

Answer

With regard to EC law, the ECJ is the final arbiter. There are no appeals against judgments it gives. Under the preliminary ruling procedure of Art 234, the ECJ can be requested to provide a definitive interpretation of the Treaty or of a Community act. This can be extended under other Articles of the Treaty to include other sources of law which are legally binding in the European Community. In order to carry out its tasks, the ECJ has developed a number of tools of interpretation. The European Court 'tool box' is not unlike the English methods of literal, golden, mischief, etc, but with the very important difference that it has been developed in the context of influence of domestic law (mainly France and Germany) and international law. However, like English judges, the judges of the ECJ very rarely use one method of interpretation in a particular case. They use a variety of rules of interpretation and then decide, as part of the judicial art, which is the most appropriate in the circumstances. Given the authority of the ECJ, this gives the judges a great deal of influence over the character and effectiveness of Community law.

Whatever method or approach to interpretation the Court may utilise, it must be remembered that they are operating in a legal system which has a strong linguistic dimension. There are 11 official languages, so all the Community texts written in the languages of the Member States are recognised as having equal validity. The main approaches to interpretation are characterised by the teleological approach, which is increasingly favoured by the ECJ. The teleological approach requires the judge to look to the purpose or object of the text before him. As Lord Denning observed in *Bulmer v Bollinger* in 1974: '... the [EC] Treaty is quite unlike any of the enactments to which we have become accustomed ... It lays down general principles. It expresses its aims and purposes ... But it lacks precision.' Faced with a body of law couched in such terms, the ECJ uses the teleological approach. In the Art 82 competition case of *Continental Can*, the ECJ referred to the 'spirit, general scheme and wording of Art 86, as well as to the system and objectives of the Treaty'. In the *Colditz* case, certain social security regulations were before the Court, which declared that 'the solution to this question ... can only emerge from the interpretation of those regulations in the light of the objectives of [Arts 39–42] of the Treaty'.

The contextual approach involves the Court placing the provision, whether from a treaty or a Community act, within its context and interpreting it in relation to other provisions of Community law. Given the lack of precision in many Community provisions, it is no wonder that frequent reference is made to the 'framework of Community law', as in *Costa v ENEL*, or 'one must have regard to the whole scheme of the Treaty no less than to its specific provisions', in the *ERTA* case. Contextual interpretation is also used for Community legislation.

In the important case of *Defrenne*, the ECJ was considering whether the Equal Pay Article, now Art 141, had direct effect. It brought together a teleological approach when looking at the socio-economic purpose of the Article, but within a particular context (or contextual approach), in that Art 141 has a close relationship with Art 136 (Art 117 at the time of the case), which concerned the need to promote improved working conditions and an improved standard of living for workers.

Although not stated in the judgments of the Court, writings of retired members of the ECJ indicate that they favour the teleological and context approaches to interpretation because they reflect the way that the Community is changing as it seeks to fulfil its aims and objectives in the future.

The literal interpretation is an approach which every court takes when faced with the question 'what does this mean?'. The ECJ is no exception, but whereas the national judge may feel that his task is then at an end, the ECJ may decide that the plain meaning of the words should not be followed, but preference should be given to allow for the aims and objectives of the treaties to be achieved. In other words, the teleological or contextual approaches are given priority. In the *ERTA* case, the Commission sought to have the Council decision to co-ordinate the Member States' negotiations under the European Road Transport Agreement annulled. The Council argued that the action under Art 230 (then Art 173) was not valid, in that the Community acts mentioned were those found in Art 249 (then Art 189), namely, regulations, directives or decisions. Despite the clear wording of Art 249, the ECJ held that the purpose of Art 230 was to subject to judicial review all those measures which had legal effect. They declared: 'It would be inconsistent with this objective to interpret the conditions under which the action is admissible so restrictively as to limit the availability of this procedure merely to the categories of measures referred to by Art 189 [now Art 249].' In *Stauder v City of Ulm*, the ECJ had to consider the different wording of a Commission decision permitting the sale of cheap butter to those in receipt of welfare benefits. Stauder was a German national who, under German law implementing the decision, was required to give his name when purchasing the butter, something which he claimed was contrary to his fundamental rights. The Dutch text followed the German text, but the Court referred to the French and Italian texts, which only stipulated that a coupon referring to the person concerned needed to be presented. The Court adopted this more liberal version of the decision, which would enable its objectives to be achieved without any breach of fundamental rights.

Historical interpretation is associated with the attempt to ascertain the subjective intention of the author of the text before the Court. It is not used very often, because of the lack of documentation available to help the Court. The negotiations surrounding the original treaties are shrouded by secrecy and thus the *travaux preparatoires* are not available. However, the Official Journal publishes all legislative proposals by the Commission as well as formal opinions of the European Parliament. In addition, the legislative acts of the Community are required, under Art 253, to state in their Preamble the reasons on which they are based and to refer to any proposals or opinions which were required by the act. These Preambles give some assistance to the Court, as they did in *Markus v Hauptzollamt Hamburg-Jonas* (1969).

CHAPTER 3

EC LAW AND NATIONAL LAW

Introduction

One of the central principles established by the European Court of Justice (ECJ) is that of the supremacy of Community law over national law. Having gained acceptance for this, the Court went on to establish the principle or doctrine of direct effect, which gives rights to individuals which can be enforced in the courts of the Member States. Both of these developments were signalled in the early cases of *Van Gend en Loos* and *Costa v ENEL*.

However, it is also important to note that the Court has built upon these principles in other topics, such as preliminary references, which are dealt with in Chapter 5. Generally, the specific questions on this topic are essay types, but aspects of the principles associated with the relationship of Community law and national law also arise in questions on other topics which can be in both essay and problem format.

Checklist

You should understand the principle of supremacy of Community law and direct effect developed in the following cases: *Van Gend en Loos, Costa, Simmenthal SpA (No 2)* and *Internationale*. In addition, the following specific points should be covered:

- the principle of direct effect in relation to direct applicability;
- the direct effect of treaty provisions, regulations, directives and decisions;
- the test for direct effect; and
- vertical and horizontal direct effect.

Question 9

Critically discuss the development of the principle of supremacy of EC law.

Answer plan

This essay question requires a discussion of the supremacy of Community law over national law and how it has come about. The main points for this question are:

- the Treaty basis used to justify supremacy of Community law, notably Art 10;
- the foundations of the Community referred to in *Van Gend en Loos, Costa, Internationale* and *Simmenthal*;
- how Community law is incorporated into national law;
- the reaction of the Member States to this development.

Answer

When the EC was established, it required a transfer of sovereignty for certain specific areas of policy from the Member State to the Community. This meant that some legal matters that had been the sole prerogative of a Member State were no longer within its control. This inevitably led to a situation of conflict between national and EC law. Yet if the Community was to fulfil its aims, it was necessary that such conflicts were speedily resolved, with a minimum of uncertainty. However, this question raised constitutional problems of varying magnitude for all Member States.

The primary source of Community law, the Treaties, contain no specific mention of any priorities in the relationship between national and EU law. However, in the view of the ECJ, the legal basis on which the Community rests necessarily presupposes the supremacy or primacy of Community law. Under international law, the question is resolved by the constitutional rules of the State concerned. Principally, it will depend on the means by which international law is incorporated into the domestic law of that Member State. There are two approaches to this incorporation, in that the legal systems of States are generally either monist or dualist in their approach to international law. In monist States, such as France, all law is treated equally, in the sense that national courts can apply international treaties, as long as the appropriate constitutional procedures have been followed. In cases of conflict with national law, monist countries usually recognise the supremacy of treaty provisions. However, in dualist States, such as the UK, international law and national law are considered to be fundamentally different. As such, international treaties can never be applied by national courts, but only domestic legislation brought about by the international treaty. Thus, the EC Treaty has to be specifically incorporated into domestic law. In the UK, this was achieved by the European Communities Act 1972, specifically ss 2 and 3. However, whatever the method of incorporation used by the Member State, this does not in itself settle the question of priorities.

The ECJ has placed great importance upon the uniformity of application of Community law in the Member States, and the desire to see that the

Community was not weakened by diversity in interpretation or application. Therefore, it is understandable that the Court would develop its own constitutional rules to ensure that where there was a conflict between EU and national law, it would be EU law which prevailed. It was in the case of *Van Gend en Loos* that the ECJ took its first tentative steps in this process. The case was an Art 234 (then Art 177) preliminary reference from the Dutch courts on whether Art 25 (then Art 12) of the Treaty had direct effect. The Court took the opportunity of declaring that 'the Community constitutes a new legal order in international law, for whose benefit the States have limited their sovereign rights, albeit within limited fields'. In *Costa v ENEL*, the Court went further when asked a specific question by the Italian court on the priority of EU law and national law. With the transfer of sovereignty mentioned in *Van Gend* 'comes ... a clear limitation of their sovereign rights upon which a subsequent unilateral law, incompatible with the aims of the Community, cannot prevail'. Thus, by establishing a European Community, now the EU, with real powers, the Member States created a body of law which applies to their nationals as well as to themselves.

In the important case of *Internationale Handelsgesellschaft mbH*, the Court was concerned with a conflict between an EC regulation and provisions of the German Constitution protecting fundamental rights. Under German law, the Constitution was superior to a statute. As a country with a mitigated dualist legal system, it was necessary for the EC Treaty to be incorporated into the national legal system and the vehicle used to do this was a statute. Thus, given that there was no provision in the Constitution to allow it to be overridden by EC law, the plaintiff claimed that the regulation should be nullified. Which should prevail: the regulation or the Constitution? The ECJ took a very strong view and insisted that the legality of a Community act cannot be nullified by national law. The German Constitutional Court was concerned about the lack of protection for fundamental rights within the Community. Until this changed, the fundamental rights provision of the German Constitution would take priority. This would not mean that they would rule on the validity of a Community act, but rather they would conclude that such a measure could not be applied in Germany. This did not happen in the *Internationale* case or in any subsequent German case, but it does indicate a possible conflict in particular circumstances. A similar conclusion occurred in the *Frontini* case, only here it was the Italian Constitution's protection of fundamental rights which was involved. The Constitutional Courts in both Germany and Italy were not happy with the hard line taken by the ECJ. The important difference is that the Italian Constitutional Court has repeated the possibility of declaring that a Community measure may not apply in Italy. This was in the *Fragd* case in 1990.

Thus, as far as the ECJ is concerned, all EU law, regardless of whether it is a Treaty provision, a Community act or an agreement with a third country, must take priority over all conflicting domestic law. This applies whether the national law is enacted prior or subsequent to Community law. In the absence of any specific Treaty provision, how can this be justified? It in fact reflects the approach of the Court, which is pragmatic and pro-Community based on the purpose, the general aims and the spirit of the Treaty. In its view, Member States apply to join the Community and must therefore take the necessary measures to comply with EU law. The Community was established with its own institutions which have powers under Art 249, with no qualification or reservation, to make laws binding upon all Member States. Regulations are specifically said in Art 249 to have 'binding force' and to be directly applicable in all Member States. To the Court, this shows a clear indication of the supremacy of the legislative provisions conferred on the Community. If a State could unilaterally nullify its effects by means of domestic legislation, overruling Community law, Community legislation would be quite meaningless.

The ECJ has repeatedly used Art 10 to emphasise the fundamental obligation upon Member States to implement Community legislation, so that it receives uniform application throughout the Community. Under Art 10, Member States are required to abstain from any measure that could jeopardise the attainment of the objectives of the Treaty. Where Member States fail to fulfil their obligations the Treaty, Art 226 gives authority to the Commission to instigate enforcement procedures. The Community would not survive if States were free to act unilaterally in breach of such obligation. If the aims of the Community are to be achieved, there must be uniformity of application of Community law throughout all the Member States. This will not occur unless all States accord priority to EU law. In fact, all new members of the Union must accept the principle of *acquis communautaire*, which requires them to accept not only the Treaties, but the whole body of Community law.

A final case provides guidance to national judges faced with a case that shows a conflict between a national law and EU law. In *Simmenthal SpA (No 2)*, an Italian judge was faced with a conflict between a Council regulation on the common organisation of the market in beef and veal and the Italian veterinary and public health laws. Under Italian law, domestic legislation contrary to EC regulations may be held unconstitutional, but only by the Constitutional Court and not by the ordinary courts. Should the Italian judge of first instance disregard inconsistent national legislation without waiting for its repeal or a declaration from the Constitutional Court making it invalid? The instructions given in answer to the Art 234 (then Art 177) reference were that a national court was under a duty to give full effect to

Community law, even if there was a conflicting provision of national law, and without waiting for a higher court to rule on the matter. This is similar to the *Factortame* case in the House of Lords, where it was accepted that directly effective Community law must prevail over any inconsistent subsequent domestic legislation. Any incompatible national law is automatically inapplicable, because, unless Community law is given priority over conflicting national law at once, from the moment of its coming into force, there can be no uniformity of application throughout the Community.

Within a short space of time, the courts of the Member States, despite their different constitutional rules and traditions, have adapted to the principle of supremacy of EU law. This is perhaps due in part to the persuasive judgments of the ECJ and the attitudes of the courts of the Member States. They have accepted that Community law, stemming as it does from the Treaty, has an independent source. It cannot be challenged by judicial process on the basis of any national provisions, however framed, without being deprived of its character as Community law and, more importantly, without the legal basis of the Community itself being called into question. The supremacy of Community law stems from the Treaties and not from the national constitutions. The special and original nature of Community law requires that its supremacy over national law is acknowledged. The ECJ recognised the importance of this and, as Lord Bridge stated in the House of Lords' judgment in *Factortame (No 2)*, 'If the supremacy within the European Community over the national law of the Member States was not always inherent in the EC Treaty, it was certainly well established in the jurisprudence of the Court of Justice'. The decision of the House of Lords was subsequently confirmed in *R v Secretary of State for Employment ex p EOC* (1994), when it was stated that in judicial review proceedings in UK courts, an Act of Parliament can be declared incompatible with EU law.

Question 10

Critically examine the development of the doctrine of direct effect.

Answer plan

This is an important topic and it is very likely that in any question where advice is required on enforcing a Community right, it will be appropriate to discuss the topic of direct effect. This question is an essay question, but it is not uncommon for problem questions to be asked on this topic. The main points that should be discussed in this essay are:

- what is meant by direct effect;
- the difference between direct effect and direct applicability;
- the test for direct effect;
- the direct effect of Articles of the Treaty, regulations, directives and decisions; and
- the difference between vertical and horizontal direct effect.

Answer

When a State joins the European Union, all Community law becomes part of its own legal system or, to use the international law phrase, 'directly applicable'. However, the ECJ has also developed a principle of direct effect whereby a provision of Community law may confer rights upon an individual which are required to be directly applied by national courts at the suit of individual litigants, without the need for domestic implementing legislation. Not all EU law is directly effective. This will depend upon the construction of a particular provision, its language and purpose, although there is often confusion, because of the phrase in Art 249 which describes regulations as directly applicable. This does not mean that only regulations are capable of direct effect. Many categories of EU law are capable of direct effect as long as they satisfy the test established by the ECJ. This began with the case of *Van Gend en Loos* (1963), which concerned a preliminary reference made by a Dutch court about Art 25 obliging Member States to refrain from setting new customs duties. The view of the Dutch Government and other Member States was that this was a matter which did not allow an individual to bring an action enforcing rights, but should rather be left to an enforcement action under Art 226 or 227.

The ECJ set out the basic requirements for direct effect to be identified when it said in *Van Gend*: 'Art 25 [formerly Art 12] sets out a clear and unconditional prohibition, which is not a duty to act, but a duty not to act. This duty is imposed without any power in the Member States to subordinate its application to a positive act of internal law. The prohibition is perfectly suited by its nature to produce direct effects in the legal relations between the Member States and their citizens.' However, the Court has not restricted direct effect to prohibitions. In *Alfons Lutticke's* case, which concerned Art 90, it was established by the ECJ that a positive obligation to repeal or amend discriminatory provisions was directly effective.

Subsequent to this case, many Articles of the Treaty have been declared to have direct effect, thus giving the citizen the ability to claim and enforce a right under the Treaty which the government of the Member State concerned has failed to provide. A good example of this development is *Defrenne v Sabena (No 2)*. This case involved a claim made by Madame Defrenne for equal pay with male stewards. She based her claim upon Art 141 (then Art 119). Whereas Van Gend was seeking to enforce a right against the Dutch State, Madame Defrenne was seeking to enforce a right against her employer, Sabena Airlines. This was an important point, because before it was thought that direct effect was limited to relationships with State bodies, that is, vertical effect. The judgment in *Defrenne* said that the direct effect of Art 141 extends to all agreements which are intended to regulate paid labour collectively, as well as to contracts between individuals. Thus, many Treaty provisions have now been successfully invoked vertically and horizontally. The fact of their being addressed to States has been no bar to their horizontal effect.

It was more surprising for Member States when the ECJ took a similar line with directives. Under Art 249, 'a directive is binding, as to the result to be achieved, upon each Member State to which it is addressed, but shall leave to the national authorities the choice of form and methods'. They are not described as 'directly applicable', as are regulations. This, the Member States argued, was an indication that they should not produce direct effects. In addition, they required further action by the Member State and thus could not meet the test for direct effect indicated in *Van Gend*. However, in *Grad*, the ECJ ruled that a directive and a decision could be directly effective. The directive, in this case on VAT, specified a limit for its implementation, as is common with all directives. These directives, addressed to Member States, impose an obligation to achieve the required result. As the ECJ said in *Becker*, another case involving VAT, 'wherever the provisions of a directive appear ... to be unconditional and sufficiently precise, those provisions may, in the absence of implementing measures adopted within the prescribed period, be relied upon as against any national provision which is incompatible with the directive or in so far as the provisions define rights which individuals are able to assert against the State'.

If the time limit given for the implementation of the directive has not expired, it cannot have direct effect, as was stated in *Ratti*. Ratti was an Italian who ran a firm selling both solvents and varnishes in Italy. Two directives had been adopted covering the packaging and labelling of these products. Ratti complied with these directives, but they had not been implemented in Italy, with the result that he was prosecuted for failure to comply with the provisions of the Italian law. At the relevant time, the deadline for the implementation of one of the directives had expired, but that for the second had not. On an Art 234 reference, the ECJ held that the directive for which the time for implementation had expired was directly effective, but the other was not. This gave Ratti a defence to the charges relating to the packaging and labelling of the solvents, but not for those concerning the varnishes. It must be remembered that in all cases when an individual is seeking to enforce direct effect, the test must be satisfied.

Even if the Member State has introduced the required legislative act, it may be that what they have done is defective. In this type of situation, the directive may still be directly effective, as was held in the *Verbond van Nederlandse Ondernemingen* (*VNO*) case. However, unlike Articles of the Treaty, directives cannot have horizontal effect. They cannot have direct effect as against another individual or company. This type of horizontal direct effect is felt to be contrary to the principles of equality. This was stated in *Marshall v Southampton and South West Hampshire AHA* (1986), where Marshall was said to be employed by a 'public' body in the form of the Health Authority and thus able to enforce the direct effect of the Equal Treatment Directive 76/207. However, the ECJ in *von Colson* put an obligation on the courts of Member States to 'take all appropriate measures to ensure fulfilment of a directive'. Under the *von Colson* principle, the courts of Member States should interpret national law so as to ensure that the objectives of the directive are achieved. In *Lister v Forth Dry Docks* (1990), the House of Lords took this line by interpreting the UK domestic regulation on safeguarding employees whose employer's business was transferred on the basis that it had been introduced for the purpose of complying with an EC directive. This has obviously greatly extended the possibility for an individual to obtain the benefits of the direct effect of a directive, even though the State (or any emanation of the State) is not the defendant to the action. In the *Marleasing* case, the ECJ took the *von Colson* principle a further step when it held that the principle could be applied, even if the necessary national legislation had not been introduced to comply with the directive.

As in other circumstances where the ECJ has developed the scope of its interpretation, there is one important limitation to the *von Colson* principle. This is in relation to criminal proceedings, as in *Kolpinghuis Nijmegen*, where the Dutch authorities sought to prosecute Kolpinghuis for breach of a Water Purity directive which had not been implemented in The Netherlands. The ECJ held that, when interpreting national law to comply with Community law, regard must be had to the general principles of the Community, notably that of legal certainty and non-retroactivity (see *Arcaro* (1997)).

In addition to regulations and directives, the other source of law specified in Art 249 is decisions, which are legally binding on the person to whom they are addressed. The Court stated in the *Grad* case that these can have direct effect. With regard to international agreements, the ECJ has not taken a consistent approach. Some, like the GATT Treaty in *International Fruit Co*, were held not to be directly effective, whereas others were, such as the

Yaounde Convention, under the ACP policy of the EU, in *Bresciani*. It would appear that each agreement must be considered by the ECJ on its own merits.

The test for direct effect requires three criteria to be passed by the provision concerned. The provision must be sufficiently clear and precise; it must be unconditional; and it must leave no room for the exercise of discretion in implementation by the Member State or Community institution. Each criterion is given a broad interpretation by the ECJ, so that some provisions which are not particularly clear or precise have been found to produce direct effects. The interpretation skills of the ECJ can always be used to clarify the meaning of the provision. It is also important to note that, if the provision should not yet have been implemented by the Member State, it will not have direct effect. Obviously, you cannot enforce an obligation until the time has expired for that obligation to have been fulfilled. However, the development of the doctrine of direct effect has been an important one for the Community, but more importantly for the individual.

Question 11

'Directives are addressed to the governments of Member States and therefore cannot give rights to individuals of Member States.'

Discuss.

Answer plan

Although there are general questions on direct effect, like the previous question, a topic which has dominated in the last few years is the direct effect of directives. Problem questions are generally not asked specifically on this topic, but it does lend itself to being included in particular situations, for example, where an individual is seeking to enforce a right based upon a directive which has not been incorporated in national law. However, it is essay questions, like this one, which allow for a discussion of the diverse points arising from the development of the principle of direct effect as applied to directives. The specific areas which need to be discussed are:

* the doctrine of direct effect generally, based on *Van Gend en Loos*;
* the application of direct effect to directives (*Van Duyn v Home Office*);
* the response to the direct effect of directives (*Cohn-Bendit* case);
* the *von Colson* principle; and
* developments in State liability (*Francovich v Italian State*).

Answer

It is true that directives are clearly defined in Art 249 as being addressed to the governments of Member States, but the Article also adds that they are binding as to the result to be achieved. There is an obligation on the Member State to fulfil this requirement, even though they have discretion as to how this is achieved. Thus, directives are a source of European Community law and are part of the new legal order which developed with the establishment of the Community. As the ECJ stated in the important case of *Van Gend en Loos*, this new legal order is for the benefit not only of the Member States themselves, but also their nationals or citizens. The Court went on to say that, in this way, obligations and rights would be conferred on individuals. How does this apply to directives? Presumably, there is no problem if the government of the Member State receiving the directive fulfils it by selecting an appropriate domestic mechanism, such as an Act of Parliament or Statutory Instrument, to implement it. In this way, any rights associated with the directive will become available to the individual and recognised and enforced by the national courts. However, what if the government of the Member State fails to implement the directive, or does so in such a way as to deprive the individual of some of the rights associated with the directive? It is in this context that this statement has been made, and will now be discussed.

The principle of direct effect was established by the ECJ in the case of *Van Gend en Loos*, which concerned Art 25 (then Art 12). The judgment stated that, if certain criteria were satisfied, the provisions in question would give rise to rights or obligations on which individuals may rely before their national courts, that is, they would be directly effective. The criteria are that the provision must be clear and unambiguous, it must be unconditional and it must take effect without further action by the EU or Member State. Could this principle apply to directives? There are obvious questions to be asked because, by definition, directives do require further action, in that Member States have the choice as to the form and methods to be used to implement the directive. The Court did not find this a hindrance.

In the case of *Van Duyn v Home Office* (1974), the ECJ held that provisions of directives could be directly effective on their own. Before this case, questions about directives were always linked with Articles of the Treaty or decisions, so no clear principle could be established. In the *Grad* case, involving a decision and the directive introducing the VAT system, the Court held that, although regulations under Art 249 (then Art 189) were directly applicable, it did not follow that other categories of administrative acts could not have similar effects. They added that this was particularly the case where the Community had imposed an obligation on Member States to act in a certain way, as *l'effet utile* of such a measure would be weakened if they did not fulfil that obligation. It would mean that the nationals of that State would not be able to invoke it before the courts, and the national courts would not be able to consider it as part of Community law.

In *Van Duyn*, the Court had to consider in an Art 234 (then Art 177) reference whether a private individual could invoke an Article of a Council directive dealing with the personal conduct of an individual and the derogation allowed to a Member State on the grounds of public policy – specifically, whether the UK Government could refuse leave to enter the UK to a Dutch Scientologist because of the UK Government's policy towards the Church of Scientology. The Court repeated its judgment in *Grad*, only making the specific reference to directives instead of a decision, as it had done in that case. Thus, Van Duyn could ask the national courts to enforce the individual rights given to her by the directive.

This judgment did not go without criticism, notably by the French *Conseil d'Etat* in the *Cohn-Bendit* case (1979). Cohn-Bendit wished to challenge a decision taken by the French Minister for the Interior expelling him from French territory on the grounds of Directive 64/221. An Article in this directive requires the person against whom such measures are ordered to be informed of the reasons, for example, public security, public policy, etc. In the *Rutili* case of 1975, this Article had been declared by the ECJ to be directly effective. However, even though the minister had decided not to oppose Cohn-Bendit's entry into France and thus remove the substance of the case, the *Conseil d'Etat* went on to give judgment. They had not made an Art 234 (then Art 177) reference, but gave their clear view that directives cannot be invoked by the nationals of Member States, that is, they cannot have direct effect when challenging an administrative decision of the State. This was completely contrary to the case law of the ECJ.

The judgment in *Cohn-Bendit* prompted the European Court to clarify its ruling on the possibility of individuals involving the provisions of directives. It considered that if a Member State had not adopted the implementing measures required by a directive in the prescribed periods, that State should not be able to rely upon its own failure to deprive individuals of seeking to enforce rights before the national courts. This was clearly stated in *Ratti*. However, direct effect as applied to directives was to have some limitations. Unlike Articles of the Treaty and, to a certain extent, regulations, directives were to be limited to vertical direct effect and not encompass horizontal direct effect. If it was the government which had not fulfilled its obligations arising from the directive, it should be against the government that rights arising from the directive should be enforced. In *Becker* (1982), a German credit broker successfully claimed the benefit of a provision of the sixth VAT Directive against the German VAT authorities. However, it was also made clear in this judgment that there was no question of a directive being involved to impose obligations on individuals, or to have an incidence on mutual relations between individuals, that is, horizontal direct effect. The contrast between the UK cases of *Marshall* (who was employed by an area health authority) or *Foster* (who was employed by a pre-privatisation British Gas corporation) on the one hand, with *Duke* (employed by GEC Reliance Ltd, a public company) on the other, clearly shows how a right can be enforced by some, but not by others, under the principle of direct effect of directives. It would appear, therefore, that unless the individual is able to show that there is some relationship with the State, the quotation forming this question is correct.

It is also correct in that every directive involves a timescale for implementation. This period, normally two years, is to give the government of the Member State time to formulate and pass the appropriate domestic measure. Until this period has elapsed, the directive cannot, as was confirmed in *Ratti*, have direct effect.

In *Emmott v Minister for Social Welfare* (1991), Mrs Emmott brought an action against the Irish Minister for Social Welfare on the basis that she received less benefit than a man would have done in equivalent circumstances. Under a directive issued in 1979, all discrimination on the grounds of sex in matters of social security are prohibited. The directive should have been implemented by 1984, but was not implemented in Ireland until 1988. Mrs Emmott brought her action in 1987, when another case before the ECJ had led to it, declaring that the directive had direct effect. The vertical relationship between herself and the Irish Government satisfied the case law of the Court. The Irish Government, however, claimed that her action was statute-barred, because it had not been brought within the three months required by Irish law for judicial review. Could this national procedural requirement be used to deny Mrs Emmott a remedy? The Court held that directives had a particular nature, imposing an obligation on Member States to adopt, within the framework of their national legal systems, all the measures necessary to ensure that the directive is fully effective. Thus, Community law precludes the competent national authorities from relying on national procedural rules relating to time limits to stop an action by one of its citizens seeking to enforce a right that that Member State has failed to transpose into its domestic legal system. The time limit does not run until the date when the national implementing legislation is correctly adopted.

In *Francovich v Italian State*, the ECJ extended the impact of the law regarding directives by stating that 'Community law lays down a principle according to which a Member State is liable to make good damage to individuals caused by a breach of Community law for which it is responsible'. Mr Francovich was owed 6 m lire by his insolvent employers.

However, because he was unable to enforce a judgment against them, he brought an action against the Italian Government for compensation. Under a Council directive aimed at protecting employees in the event of the insolvency of their employers, Member States were required to ensure that payment of employees' outstanding claims arising from the employment relationship and relating to pay was guaranteed. Unfortunately, the Italian Government had not set up any Italian system to act as a guarantor in these circumstances, hence his claim against them. The ECJ held that, subject to three conditions, damages are available against the State for failure to implement EC directives. The conditions specified are that the result required by the directive includes the conferring of rights for the benefit of individuals, the content of those rights is identifiable by reference to the directive and, lastly, there exists a causal link between the breach of the State's obligations and the damage suffered by the person affected.

The ECJ has further developed this idea of indirect effect in its judgments in *Brasserie du Pêcheur* (1996) and *Dillenkofer* (1996). It is clear now that failure by a Member State to take any measure and transpose it as required into national law will constitute a serious breach of Community law *per se*. It will give rise to a right to damages for those individuals who suffer injury and there is a causal link between the breach of the State's obligation and the loss and damage suffered.

The ECJ has continued to evolve its principles with regard to providing the individual with the possibility of enforcing a right derived from a directive. In the *von Colson* and *Harz* cases in 1984, the Court developed an approach to interpretation based on Art 10 (then Art 5), which requires Member States to take all appropriate measures to ensure fulfilment of their Community obligations. Under this principle, the national courts should interpret national legislation so as to ensure that the objectives of the directive are achieved. This assists those litigants who are unable to satisfy the test for direct effect, or who are bringing an action against a private employer, rather than the State or an emanation of the State. This method of interpretation has maximised the impact of directives for individuals. As a further development of the *von Colson* principle, the Court held, in the *Marleasing* case (1990), that the principle could be applied even if the necessary national legislation had not been introduced to comply with the directive.

The development of the ECJ's approach to directives conferring rights upon individuals has continued throughout the last 20 years. It has been a true reflection of the comments made by the Court in *Van Gend en Loos* and subsequent cases that, when establishing the European Community, the Member States were creating a new legal order which has given rights to the citizens of the Member States and which must be recognised by their courts.

In some circumstances, the Court has applied the principle of direct effect to achieve this and in others it has extended its approach to interpretation. It is clear that although directives are addressed to the governments of Member States, they do confer rights on those who live within the Community.

Question 12

Do the decisions of the English courts assist an individual seeking to enforce a Community right?

Answer plan

This essay question provides an opportunity to trace through English judgments the approach taken to direct effect of directives and the interpretation of domestic legislation. You should cover the following points:

- direct effect of directives – the *Marshall* case (1986);
- vertical and horizontal effect of directives;
- European Communities Act 1972;
- the *von Colson* case (1984);
- the *Marleasing* case (1992);
- *Pickstone v Freemans plc* (1989);
- *Lister v Forth Dry Dock and Engineering Co Ltd* (1990);
- *Francovich* (1990); and
- the *Brasserie du Pêcheur* and *Factortame* cases (1996).

Answer

When a Member State joins the Community, it undertakes to fulfil all the obligations arising from the Treaties and other binding sources of Community law. This is achieved by accepting that Community law overrides any conflicting national law (*Simmenthal* (1978)). However, there were problems for the individual who tried to enforce a right arising from Community law not recognised in the national courts, for example, if the conditions associated with identifying direct effect, such as the measure being precise and unconditional, were not satisfied. More importantly, he or she may not be able to use direct effect to enforce the right against another private individual (*Marshall* (1986)). In circumstances where the government was at fault, the European Commission could bring an action before the ECJ under Art 226 for failing to fulfil a Community obligation. It would also be open to the government of another Member State to use Art 227. However, both Articles lead to the same remedy under Art 228. This is mainly declaratory, although under the Treaty on European Union (TEU) 1992, the Court can impose a fine, but this provides no redress for the individuals affected by the Member State's action.

Articles of the Treaty and regulations have been held by the ECJ to have direct effect in both vertical and horizontal terms (see *Defrenne (No 2)* (1976)). Thus, in such circumstances, the individual can enforce the right against the government or another individual. However, the other main source of Community law, directives, was in a much weaker position, even though such measures are important in creating rights under Community law. The ECJ has sought to redress this imbalance by making directives come within the principle of direct effect. In the *Van Duyn* case (1975), the ECJ relied on the binding effect attributed to a directive under Art 249 (then Art 189), coupled with the civil law doctrine that a legal measure must be presumed to have an *effet utile*, or useful effect. Furthermore, the Court thought it was inequitable to allow a Member State to rely on its own failure to implement a directive as a defence (*Ratti* (1979)). This view was strengthened by Art 10, which requires a Member State to take all appropriate measures to ensure fulfilment of the obligations arising out of the Treaty or resulting from action taken by the institutions of the Community. In this way, it became impossible for the Member State to evade an obligation imposed by a directive.

However, the Court limited the impact of this extension of the principle of direct effect to directives by limiting it to vertical relationships. Thus, the individual who was employed by the State or an emanation of the State (see *Marshall* (1986) and *Foster v British Gas* (1990)) could enforce a right arising from Community law in a national court and obtain the appropriate remedy. Those who could not prove such a relationship with the government were unable to do either, as was confirmed in the case of *Kampelmann* (1997) involving the Employee Directive 91/533. *Duke v GEC Reliance* (1988) provides a good example of the division that vertical and horizontal application of direct effect of directives brought about. Unlike Mrs Marshall or Mrs Foster, Mrs Duke was unable to enforce her rights under the Equality Directives.

There is a potential conflict between the doctrine of parliamentary sovereignty in UK law and the principle that Community law takes priority over inconsistent national laws. The European Communities Act 1972 attempts to deal with this problem by making all provisions of Community law which are directly effective part of English law. Lord Denning, in

Macarthys Ltd v Smith (1979), suggested that English courts would give effect to a directly effective provision of Community law, notwithstanding any subsequent enactment by Parliament, unless Parliament had made it clear that it intended to override any inconsistent provisions of Community law. Lord Diplock, in *Garland v BREL* (1982), stated that the words of a statute passed after the adoption of a Community measure dealing with the same subject were to be interpreted, if they were reasonably capable of bearing such a meaning, as being intended to carry out the UK's obligations under the Community measure and not as being inconsistent with it.

Mrs Duke in 1988 maintained that the Equal Treatment Directive, as interpreted in *Marshall*, required Member States to prohibit discrimination in relation to retirement ages and that s 6(4) of the Sex Discrimination Act 1975 had to be interpreted in a way consistent with that requirement. Lord Templeman, giving the main judgment in the House of Lords, rejected this argument. He held that, although the Equal Treatment Directive had been adopted subsequent to the 1975 Act, s 2(4) of the European Communities Act 1972 did not require the courts to give it priority over the 1975 Act in Mrs Duke's case, because the directive was not directly effective as between her and her former employers. Section 2(4) only required the court to construe an Act of Parliament in accordance with directly effective provisions of Community law. This judgment has been criticised as taking too narrow a view of the European Communities Act. However, in *Pickstone*, Lord Templeman made the point in his judgment that the Sex Discrimination Act had not been passed to give effect to the directive. But, in *Pickstone,* the 1983 Regulations had been introduced to meet the obligations of the directive and the rulings of the Court against the UK Government.

The division between vertical and horizontal direct effect of directives was circumvented to a certain extent by the judgment in the *von Colson* case (1984). This required national courts to construe national law to give effect to the provisions of a directive. In this way, the provisions entered into domestic law and could be relied upon before national courts. The provisions of the directive become an aid to construction of the national law and in this way are enforced by the national court. The *Marleasing* judgment (1992) extended this principle by requiring a national court to construe national law in the light of the wording and purpose of any relevant Community directive, whether the national law originated before or after the adoption of the directive.

This approach has been taken up by the UK courts. In *Pickstone v Freemans plc* (1989), the House of Lords said that English courts must adopt this interpretation, even if to do so would involve departing from the normal canons of construction. This could amount to reading certain words into the relevant national legislation in order to achieve a result compatible with

Community law. The Court of Appeal encountered difficulties in the appeal by Mrs Webb against her dismissal by her employer when she became pregnant (*Webb v EMO Air Cargo (UK) Ltd* (1992)). The national legislation that the Court of Appeal had to interpret was the Sex Discrimination Act 1975. Judgments of the ECJ on the Equal Treatment Directive appeared to indicate that dismissal on the grounds of pregnancy was automatically contrary to the directive. However, the Court of Appeal held that the Sex Discrimination Act did not automatically forbid the dismissal of a woman on the grounds of pregnancy and to give it that meaning would be to distort, rather than construe, English law. On the subsequent appeal to the House of Lords, it was indicated that national law had to be open to an interpretation consistent with the directive if the duty of construction were to apply. Following a further reference to the ECJ, it was stated that Mrs Webb's dismissal could not be justified on the grounds of pregnancy (1994).

The House of Lords cited *Pickstone* with approval in *Lister v Forth Dry Dock and Engineering Co Ltd* (1990), where a claim had been made against a private party. The judgment suggests that, where legislation has been introduced specifically in order to complement an EC directive, UK courts must interpret domestic law to comply with the directive. In some circumstances, this may require supplying the necessary words by implication, in order to achieve a result compatible with EC law. In the *Lister* case, no reference was made to the fact that the directive in question was not directly effective.

However, there is some inconsistency in approach. The judgment in *R v British Coal Corp ex p Vardy* (1993) indicated a reluctance to apply the *Marleasing* principle. In this case, Glidewell J found it impossible to follow the House of Lords' approach in *Lister* since the wording of the statute, the Trade Union and Labour Relations Act 1992, was clearly at odds with the directive. In such circumstances, the wording of the statute approved by Parliament was to be followed. An action by the European Commission under Art 169 would have seemed until recently to be the only possibility. However, the ECJ has developed a remedy by stating that it is a principle of Community law that the Member States are obliged to make good any loss and damage caused to individuals by breaches of Community law for which they were held responsible (*Francovich* (1990)). In the *Brasserie du Pêcheur* and *Factortame* cases (1996), the ECJ held that, provided the conditions for State liability were satisfied, the principle could and did apply to all Community law as a whole, whether or not directly effective. Therefore, if there is not a manifestly serious breach by the Member State, they are not required to compensate for any loss suffered (*R v HM Treasury ex p BT* (1996)). Where there is liability, it is up to the national court to assess the amount of damages, provided that the domestic law does not treat breaches of EU law less favourably than similar domestic claims (*Sutton v Secretary of State for Social Security* (1997)). In *Levez v Jennings*, the UK rule that damages for sex discrimination should not go back further than two years was considered. Although the rule itself was not criticised, the ECJ indicated that there may be circumstances where its application would be incompatible with the principles of EU law, for example, where there had been deceit by the employer. In the House of Lords' judgment in *Factortame 4* (1999), the UK's breach of its Community obligations was sufficiently serious to entitle the Spanish owners of the vessels to substantial damages.

CHAPTER 4

JUDICIAL REMEDIES AND REVIEW (1): DIRECT ACTIONS

Introduction

As part of its jurisdiction, the ECJ can hear cases brought before it by individuals, Community institutions or governments of Member States. These actions must be brought under specific Articles of the Treaty and are heard solely by the Court, hence the term direct actions as compared with indirect actions or preliminary references made under Art 234. These are covered in the next chapter. This area of Community law lends itself to both problem and essay questions, as the 'popular' areas are suitable for both question formats.

Checklist

You should have a general knowledge of how the European Court operates. In particular, you must be familiar with the following areas:

- enforcement actions brought by the European Commission under Art 226, including both the formal and informal stages of the procedure;
- enforcement actions brought by Member States under Art 227;
- the remedy available by Art 228 to actions under Arts 226 and 227;
- the action for annulment under Art 230, especially the question of *locus standi* and grounds for annulment;
- the possible action under Art 232 and its relationship with Art 230;
- the remedies provided for under Arts 230 and 232; and
- the plea of illegality – Art 241.

Question 13

What enforcement actions are available against a Member State in breach of its obligations? Are such actions effective?

Answer plan

This is typical of questions set on this topic. It should be noted that it is in two parts, both of which must be answered in the essay that follows if good marks are to be gained. It is not sufficient merely to describe the possible actions, as some evaluation must also be included. The main points to be raised are:

- direct actions under Arts 226 and 227;
- the remedies available under Art 228;
- the role of the Commission under Art 226; and
- possible action available in a Member State.

Answer

The EC Treaty allows two types of direct enforcement actions under Arts 226 and 227. The most usual action taken against a Member State is by the European Commission under Art 226. Although Member States have a possible action under Art 227, which allows them to take another Member State before the ECJ, as in *France v UK (Re Fishing Net Mesh Sizes)* (1978), this is rarely used. It is therefore Art 226 which is the predominant enforcement action used against Member States that are in breach of their obligations, although it is possible for action to be taken in the national courts of the Member State in certain circumstances.

It is appropriate that Art 226 should give the Commission power to bring an action against a Member State in breach of its obligations, as it has a duty to make sure that Community law is applied. This duty is found in Art 211, which lays down the general duties of the Commission. The instigation of the Art 226 procedure may be due to an act or omission, such as national legislation contrary to Community law or a failure to implement Community law. Therefore, a Member State's failure under the Treaty can be sufficient grounds, as can an action contrary to Community law. However, the procedure under Art 226 is lengthy and does not provide a speedy process for getting the breach rectified. Whether it is a failure of a positive or negative act, the consequence of a successful action under Art 226 is for a declaration by the Court under Art 228 requiring the Member State to take action to fulfil its obligations and the possible imposition of a fine.

The first stage of the Art 169 procedure is often described as the administrative stage. The ECJ has stated that the purpose of this stage is to allow the Member State either to comply with its obligations under Community law or to put forward an effective defence to the complaints made by the Commission. Initially acting on a complaint, perhaps from a trade association, MEP or another government, the Director General responsible for that sector of Community policy will write to the Member State concerned. These informal communications with the Member State will attempt to ascertain the facts and if possible reach a settlement. They are conducted with discretion, so as to avoid any embarrassment that might result for the Member State. The Commission, having fully investigated the possible breach, will consider whether there is sufficient evidence to justify the commencement of formal proceedings. If the Commission has taken the view that a Member State is in breach of its obligations, the Commission will write to the Member State under its powers in Art 169, indicating the breach and inviting the Member State's observations. The Member State then responds to this letter with its own view, which is generally that they are not in breach of this particular obligation. If a settlement acceptable to the Commission is not possible, this administrative stage of Art 226 will end with the Commission issuing a Reasoned Opinion. This Opinion is very important, as it provides the Member State with a final opportunity to remedy its failure and to this end informs them of what, in the Commission's view, needs to be done to accomplish this. If the Commission decides to go on to the judicial stage of the Art 226 procedure, the Opinion defines the matters which the Court will be requested to adjudicate on.

It could be argued that the matter could end before the judicial stage, especially as the number of contraventions of Community law is large. To take all the matters further under the procedure would require a large staff. There is also the fact that many Member State governments resent the initiation of the formal enforcement procedure. Does the Commission have to take the matter further? Some writers argue that the Commission has a discretion as to whether it takes further action. However, this ignores the duty given to the Commission under Art 211 to ensure that Community law is applied. This duty requires the Commission to take the most appropriate action in the circumstances to ensure compliance with Community law. In the EURATOM case of *Commission v France* (1971), Advocate General Roemer indicated that, in some circumstances, the Commission might be justified in not initiating the enforcement procedure. These included situations where an amicable settlement may be achieved if formal proceedings were delayed, or where a major domestic political crisis could be aggravated if proceedings were commenced concerning matters of secondary importance.

An attempt is made to reach a satisfactory settlement without resorting to litigation and in the great majority of cases this has proved possible. If this is not possible, an action by the Commission can be brought before the European Court. The aim of the action is to obtain a declaration that the Member State has failed to fulfil its obligation. The Member State will be bound under Art 228 to take the necessary measures to comply with the judgment. At one time, the only sanction available to the Commission was to institute a further action against the Member State if it did not comply. The Maastricht Treaty made an important amendment to Art 228 in relation to an action brought under Art 226. This now allows the Court to impose a lump sum or penalty payment on any Member State failing to fulfil its obligations, based upon a sum specified by the Commission when it brings the matter before the Court. The basic penalty is fixed at 5,000 euros per day multiplied by factors reflecting the gravity and duration of the non-compliance.

A common form of infringement by Member States has been the adoption of measures that restrict the free movement of goods within the Community, contrary to Art 228. Such measures are against one of the fundamental principles of the Community and are often disguised under legitimate derogations allowed by Art 30. Action taken by the Commission in these circumstances is seeking effective rather than purely formal compliance with the Treaty obligations, that is, with the spirit rather than just with the letter. For example, in the *Turkey* case (1982), the UK Government had imposed a ban on the importation of poultry not vaccinated against Newcastle disease. Although ostensibly to protect animal health, which is possible under Art 30, its effect was to protect the British poultry industry against imports, notably from France. Although the Court held that such restrictions were contrary to the UK's obligations under the Treaty, the measure did give the British poultry industry some limited protection before the UK Government complied with the Art 228 (then Art 171) order. There are many such examples involving all Member States where, perhaps for domestic political reasons, national measures have been adopted, only to be repealed when judgment has been given by the Court against them. In this sense the Art 226 action is ultimately effective, but it does take time.

The action available to a Member State under Art 227 is very similar to that used by the Commission under Art 226. However, the Member State must inform the Commission, which is given three months to investigate the matter and deliver a Reasoned Opinion. Here, the Commission is acting more as an umpire and conciliator than an accuser. After the Reasoned Opinion has been given by the Commission, or if three months have elapsed without its doing so, the complainant Member State can bring the matter before the Court. The burden of proof is on the complainant Member State, with the Commission intervening in support of one side or the other. This procedure is very unpopular with the Member States, who generally leave such enforcement actions to the Commission, unless there is a strong political or other reason for them to do otherwise.

In the early years, the Commission did not pursue defaulting Member States with vigour. However, in 1977, the Jenkins Commission decided that, in future, more rigorous use would be made of the Art 226 procedure. Nevertheless the volume of work places a heavy burden upon the staff of the Commission, which now encourages complainants to seek remedies in the national courts where appropriate. In the landmark case of *Van Gend en Loos* (1963), the Court had recognised that individuals should be able to protect their rights themselves in addition to relying on the Commission. This has become much easier with the development of the principle of direct effect. For example, in *Schoenenberg* (1978) and *Meijer* (1979), individuals were able to claim that national legislation was contrary to obligations imposed by the

Treaty in the Member State concerned. This was achieved by the courts concerned using the preliminary reference procedure provided by Art 234 (then Art 177). This happened at the same time as the Commission was taking action against the Member State under the Art 226 (then Art 169) procedure. However, while the Art 226 procedure has its value in bringing the Member State into line for the future, action in the national courts coupled with an Art 234 reference does concentrate the mind of the Member State involved! The developments of the law relating to the award of damages has given new emphasis to the possibility of using the national courts for enforcement purposes. In *Francovich v Italian State*, the European Court stated that 'Community law lays down a principle according to which a Member State is liable to make good damage to individuals caused by a breach of Community law for which it is responsible'.

It can be seen that, although the Treaty only specifies enforcement action under Arts 226 and 227, these are not the only possibilities. Action under Art 226 by the Commission does achieve the desired result, but its main drawback is the time it takes to achieve this, although it is possible to obtain interim measures under Art 243 where proceedings are being taken under Art 226 against a Member State. For example, both the UK Government, in relation to a temporary subsidy to pig farmers, and the Irish Government, over its fisheries conservation measures, were brought before the Court in 1977 and appropriate orders were made to stop their infringements immediately. However, the most effective actions are those indirect actions brought in the courts of the Member State concerned.

Question 14

NOALC plc is one of six manufacturers in the EC of a new type of wine substitute made from parsnips. Doddy Drinks was so impressed with the product that it installed new machinery at a cost of £1.2 m into its factory to handle the product range it intended to introduce under licence from NOALC plc.

Last month, the Council was concerned that there would be adverse effects on the Community's grape industry and associated wine producers. A regulation was therefore adopted, imposing a limit on the production of the wine from parsnips. An appendix to the regulation mentioned the six manufacturers by name and fixed their output quota at low levels.

The result is that NOALC cannot supply Doddy Drinks in the quantities required to make their planned range economically viable. Given that a great deal of money will be lost if this regulation is applied, NOALC seeks your advice.

Answer plan

This problem question is the kind of practical scenario question often set on this topic. It requires you to advise NOALC, not merely describe all you know about the subject! This topic is often found difficult by students, but one way of solving this is to break the problem down into a number of small questions, pose them and then answer them as if you were advising someone in front of you. The main points to be raised for NOALC are:

- the procedure under Art 230, including the time limit;
- is the measure a 'true' regulation – what is a 'true' regulation?;
- the Court's interpretation of 'direct and individual concern';
- possible action in the national courts if *locus standi* for Art 230 is not accepted by the European Court; and
- possible action for damages under Arts 235 and 288.

Answer

If the regulation is applied, NOALC will make a substantial loss on its investment. NOALC should therefore consider the possibility of challenging the regulation under Art 230. If the challenge is successful, the remedy provided by this action will be annulment of the regulation, thus allowing NOALC to proceed with its business plan. There may also be the possibility of a claim for damages against the Council under Arts 235 and 288. However, it is very rare that a successful action can be brought under Art 230 by non-privileged applicants like NOALC. Careful consideration must be given, therefore, to the wording of Art 230 and the interpretation given by the ECJ.

Under Art 230, any legal person may bring an action against a decision addressed to that person or against a decision which, although in the form of a regulation or a decision addressed to another person, is of direct and individual concern to the former. Thus, if NOALC wish to challenge a regulation they are not barred from doing so, provided they can show that it is not a true regulation but a 'bundle of decisions'. When approaching this question, the ECJ is not restricted by the title of the Community measure. Merely because it is called a regulation is not conclusive. In *Calpak* (1980), it was pointed out that this is to prevent Community institutions choosing to issue a decision in the form of a regulation so as to deny the opportunity to an individual to challenge the measure. In *Royal Scholten-Honig v Intervention Board for Agriculture*, the ECJ said: 'In examining this question (re Regulation) the Court cannot restrict itself to considering the official title of the measure, but must first take into account its object and context.' A starting point is the definitions given to various Community measures in Art 249, where regulations are described as the main legislative instrument of the Community.

A regulation under Art 249 should apply to objectively determined situations and produce legal effects with regard to categories of persons regarded generally and in the abstract. It should have a 'normative' character. As long as the regulation maintains these objective characteristics, it will still be considered a regulation, even though the number or even identity of the persons to whom it applies can be ascertained. The Court insisted in *Royal Scholten-Honig* that an individual cannot challenge a true regulation.

It is not always easy to state clearly that a particular Community measure is a true regulation but, in the *Fruit and Vegetable* case (1962), the Court said: 'A measure which is applicable to objectively determined situations and which involves immediate legal consequences in all Member States for persons viewed in a general and abstract manner cannot be considered as constituting a decision, unless it can be proved that it is of individual concern to certain persons within the meaning of Art 230.' There have been relatively few cases where the applicants have satisfied the Court on this point. One which may support NOALC is *CAM SA v Commission* (1975), where a fixed number of traders were held to be individually concerned because of a factual situation which differentiated them from all other persons and distinguished them individually. Here there was a fixed and known number of cereal traders, because the regulation affected those who had already applied for export licences. This factual situation differentiated them from all other persons and distinguished them individually from others affected by the regulation. Thus the action was admissible, since he was individually concerned because the applicant was one of a fixed and identifiable category.

NOALC may only challenge a regulation if the 'regulation' is really a decision. Decisions are characterised by the limited number of persons to whom they are addressed. In order to determine whether or not a measure constitutes a decision, one must inquire whether that measure concerns specific persons. In NOALC's case, the number of producers is limited and in fact they are named in an appendix to the regulation. They can be said to be directly concerned, in that the regulation leaves the Member State no discretion in implementation, but are they individually concerned as is required by Art 230? A person can only claim to be individually concerned if the decision being challenged affects them by reason of certain attributes which are peculiar to them, or by reason of circumstances in which they are differentiated from all other persons, and by virtue of these factors distinguishes them individually, just as in the case of the person addressed. It will not be sufficient for NOALC to prove that its business interests will be adversely affected. In the cases where it has been successfully pleaded, such as the *Toepfer* case (1965), the decision being challenged referred to a fixed list of importers which could not be amended. In NOALC's case, there is not this fixed list, although the companies are named in the regulation. Could it be argued that anyone could enter this business activity, as it was with *Plaumann* clementines? In *Zuckerfabrik Watenstedt* (1968), a producer of raw beet sugar asked for an Article of a regulation to be declared void with no success. The Court said that a regulation does not lose its characteristics as a regulation simply because it may be possible to identify the persons to which it applies, as long as it fulfils the objectivity of a regulation mentioned above.

However, in the *Japanese Ball Bearing* cases, four major Japanese producers of ball bearings were held entitled to challenge a regulation. Although the measure was of general application, some of the Articles specifically referred to the applicants. Even a 'true' regulation can be of individual concern to some individuals if it is referable expressly to their particular situation, either alone or as a member of a known or closed class: for example, the Japanese manufacturers.

The fact that NOALC is listed makes them, arguably, directly and individually concerned, as there is a close and specific relationship between NOALC and the measure being challenged. However, the ECJ has not always been consistent on this point. The Court has laid more emphasis on the requirement of individual concern. If the Court can be satisfied on this, the requirement of direct concern is often assumed.

Despite statements by the Court in *Plaumann* that the provision of Art 230 (then Art 173) should not be interpreted strictly, it has adopted a very restrictive approach towards individuals seeking to challenge acts other than decisions addressed to them. The ECJ in *Union de Pequeños Agricultores* (2002) reaffirmed its case law on the conditions for access of individuals to an action under Art 230. NOALC must fulfil all the criteria if the action is to be admissible. As they cannot challenge a regulation, they must prove that it is a decision which is of direct and individual concern to them.

All this advice has centred on the question of *locus standi*, as this is the major hurdle for any applicant in NOALC's situation. It must be remembered that the proceedings under Art 230 must be instituted within two months from the date of publication of the regulation. Having obtained the Court's agreement that the action is admissible, NOALC has to prove one of the grounds for annulment specified in Art 230. There are four such grounds, covering lack of competence, infringement of an essential procedural requirement, infringement of the Treaties or of any rule of law relating to their application and finally, misuse of powers. It is not clear from the problem which particular grounds NOALC may plead, but the most general one is infringement of the Treaties or of any rule of law relating to their application. If successful, the remedy under Art 231 is for the regulation to be declared void or *erga omnes*.

It is possible to challenge the validity of a regulation in the national courts of a Member State. However, if a company knew that they had a right under Art 230 and failed to take up that right, the ECJ may refuse to give a preliminary reference on validity (*TWD Textilwerke Deggendorf GmbH v Germany* (1994)). Assuming that this is not the situation for NOALC, they would have to be a party to an action in a Member State and the court hearing the case would have to make a reference under Art 234 concerning the validity of the regulation. As NOALC is likely to suffer financially because of the regulation, they may bring an action for damages for 'normative injustice' where the regulation constitutes a sufficiently flagrant breach of a superior rule of law protecting individuals under Art 288. In the *Schoppenstedt* case (1971), the Court held that the plaintiff company could sue the Council for damages on the basis of an allegedly illegal regulation even though as a 'natural or legal person' they would have no *locus standi* to seek its annulment under Art 230 (then Art 173(2)). The advantage of an action under Art 288 is that it is not restricted to the short time limit which applies to challenges under Art 230. The disadvantage is that the Court has adopted a very restrictive approach towards Community liability in tort.

Question 15

Critically review the ability of an individual to challenge the validity of a Community act under Art 230(4) EC.

Answer plan

This essay question reflects the discussion that is taking place with regard to the remedies provided by the Community Courts for individuals. Although the national courts can make a request for a preliminary ruling under Art 234, the restrictive tests used by the ECJ have raised criticisms from academics and practitioners. This developing area of EU law gives rise to many discussion questions and it is important to deal with the basic principles but then go on to discuss the issues.

The main points to be raised are:

- the procedure under Art 230;
- the ECJ's interpretation of 'direct and individual concern';
- the *Plaumann* test;
- the challenges to the case law of the ECJ on Art 230.

Answer

The case law of the ECJ acknowledges the principle that an individual who considers himself wronged by a Community measure must have access to a remedy and be able to obtain complete judicial protection. There are a number of ways in which this can be achieved, including an action for annulment under Art 234. There is also a possible action for damages under Arts 235 and 288 or an action before a national court where the question of validity can be raised.

However, there is an argument that proceedings before the courts of a Member State may not provide effective judicial protection for individual applicants because such courts cannot declare Community acts invalid. Where an applicant can raise the question of validity before a national court, that court may make a request for a preliminary ruling from the ECJ. Advocate General Jacobs in *Union de Pequeños Agricultores* argued that this strictly limited competence of national courts does not provide the individual with the rights identified in the European Convention on Human Rights and the Charter of Fundamental Rights. Article 6 of the European Convention requires a fair trial and Art 13 refers to an 'effective remedy'. More recently, the Charter of Fundamental Rights, although not legally binding, states in Art 47 that 'everyone whose rights and freedoms guaranteed by the law of the Union are violated has the right to an effective remedy before a tribunal'.

Also, under Art 234 the right to make a request for a preliminary ruling is with the court and not the parties to an action. Therefore, the national court may, using its discretion, refuse to make a request for a ruling and delay may occur if the individual appeals that decision through his national legal system. If no implementing legislation is required of the national authorities of a Member State, there may be no basis for an action before the national courts. Even if there is such legislation, Advocate General Jacobs stated in his Opinion in *Union de Pequeños Agricultores* (2002) that it is wrong to expect someone to 'breach the law in order to gain access to justice'. Such actions are both expensive and time consuming for the individual who wishes to challenge a Community act.

On the other hand, there is the advantage under an Art 230 challenge that the institution that adopted the measure in dispute is a party to the proceedings from the beginning. However, the difficulty arises in the question of *locus standi*, or the right to bring the action before the Court. If the individual wishes to challenge a decision addressed to themselves there is no problem, other than meeting the time requirements under Art 230(5). Given the substance of most Community measures that may be challenged, it is desirable for reasons of legal certainty that this happens as soon as possible. Where the decision is addressed to another, or where the challenge is against a decision disguised as a regulation, the individual must show that the measure is of direct and individual concern to them.

This has been very restrictively interpreted by the ECJ, and it was in this context that the remarks of Advocate General Jacobs arose in *Union de Pequeños Agricultores*. The Union de Pequeños Agricultores, a trade association that represents and acts in the interests of small Spanish agricultural businesses, wished to have annulled a regulation that set up a common organisation in olive oil. As the regulation in question had the normative characteristics associated with a regulation, it could not be challenged by the Union under Art 230(4). This follows the case law identifying that the general rule to be applied is that if a decision is not of individual concern to an undertaking, that undertaking cannot challenge it even though it may be adversely affected by it (*Plaumann v Commission* (1962)). If that condition is not satisfied, then a natural or legal person does not have, under any circumstances, the standing to bring a challenge before the Community Courts (*CNPAAP v Council* (1996)). Is there a compelling reason to read into Art 230(4) a requirement that individual applicants must be differentiated from all others, in the same way as an addressee? In Jacobs' opinion, the key factor is whether an individual is likely to be adversely affected by the measure. Such an interpretation would improve judicial protection and greatly simplify the application of Art 230(4), but it was rejected by the ECJ.

In *Jégo-Quéré et Cie SA v Commission* (2002), the Court of First Instance had to consider whether the plaintiff could challenge a regulation concerned with the size of fishing nets used off the Irish coast. The regulation established emergency measures to protect fish stocks and as such it would be hard to show it to be of individual concern under the case law of the ECJ. However, taking up the points made by Advocate General Jacobs in *Union de Pequeños Agricultores*, the CFI said that the interpretation of Art 230(4) should be reconsidered in the context of the EC establishing a complete system of legal remedies and procedures so that the Community Courts could review the legality of measures adopted by the institutions.

However, the ECJ has rejected these requests to reconsider the way that Art 230(4) is applied. The ECJ has taken the view that general measures in the form of regulations may be challenged by individual applicants in such cases as *Extramet* (1991). The Court has also recognised that a factual situation may arise which differentiates the applicant from other persons and may be regarded as individually concerned, as in *Codorniu* (1994), but the Court will not go further. In the discussions leading up to the Treaty of Amsterdam, the Court itself raised the issue of whether Art 230(4) is sufficient to guarantee effective protection against infringements of fundamental rights arising from the legislative activity of the institutions.

In this context, though, the view of the ECJ is that it is for the Member States to establish a system of legal remedies and procedures, which ensure respect for the right to effective judicial remedy. For the ECJ itself to adopt the views of the Advocate General in the case would go beyond the jurisdiction conferred by the Treaty on the Community Courts. However, the ideas in the courts of the Member States on increasing the ability of an individual to bring an action for judicial review have not been mirrored by the ECJ when applying Art 230(4). Under the Treaty of Nice, it will be the Court of First Instance that will generally hear actions for annulment, subject to the possibility of appeal to the European Court of Justice, and that may maintain the pressure for reform.

Question 16

Critically discuss the development of State liability in damages in the national courts for violation of Community law.

Answer plan

This essay question is looking at the availability of damages in actions before a national court. This is in contrast to Art 288, which is more restricted. The main thrust of any answer is the *Francovich* case (1992), and the implications of the case in future proceedings before national courts. The ECJ has developed the principles of State liability since this case and this development needs to be analysed.

Answer

The ECJ recognised, in the *Francovich* case (1992), that individuals may have a right to damages in the national courts against the national authorities where they have suffered loss as a result of the non-implementation of a directive by a Member State. The *Francovich* case involved Directive 80/987, which provided for the approximation of the laws of the Member States relating to the protection of employees in the event of the insolvency of their employer. The Italian Government had not implemented the directive, with the result that, when Francovich's employer became insolvent, the employees had substantial arrears of salary.

Consequently, the parties brought an action against the Italian State for failing to fulfil the obligations incumbent on it under Directive 80/987. The European Court, responding to an Art 234 reference, developed its analysis of direct effect of directives from *Costa v ENEL* (1964) to deal with the question of damages. It identified three criteria which would have to be satisfied. The Court began by restating the criteria for the application of direct effect. These are that the provision must be clear and unambiguous, it must be unconditional and, finally, its operation must not be dependent on further action being taken by Community or national institutions. In applying these criteria to the facts of the *Francovich* case, the provisions of the directive were insufficiently precise and were not unconditional, and so did not have direct effect. Thus, Francovich and the other employees involved could not rely on the directive as against the Italian Government in order to recover their lost wages.

In the *Francovich* case, the ECJ considered the question of the circumstances in which a Member State could be held liable in damages for its violation of Community law. Until this case, the approach taken by the Court had been to state that it was left to national law to determine in which courts an action could be brought and what procedural rules should govern the action. On this basis, the general rule was that Community rights were to be treated no less favourably than analogous domestic law rights. In this way, it was assumed that domestic law would fully protect Community rights by providing a remedy obtainable in national courts. The Court stated that the effectiveness of Community law could be called into question, and the protection of rights would be weakened, if individuals could not obtain compensation when Community rights were undermined by violation of Community law.

The Court emphasised the principle that national courts are obliged to give full effect to Community law to protect rights which individuals derive from Community law (*Simmenthal* (1978), *Factortame* (1991)). It also referred to the obligation imposed on a Member State by Art 10 (then Art 5) to take all appropriate measures to ensure fulfilment of Community law. Arising from these considerations, the Court stated that, as a general principle, Member States are obliged to make good damage caused to individuals by a violation of Community law for which they are responsible. In those cases where there has been a failure to implement a directive, three conditions are required to be satisfied. These are that the contents of the directive were intended to confer rights on individuals, that the contents of the rights can be identified from the provisions of the directive and, lastly, that there was a causal link between the damage suffered by the individual and the State's breach of its obligations. It was for national law to determine the courts dealing with such claims and the procedures to apply.

In his Opinion, Advocate General Mischo had given weight to the fact that the European Commission had already taken action against the Italian State under Art 226 (then Art 169) for its failure to implement the directive. This had resulted in a declaration by the Court against Italy under Art 228 (then Art 171). However, the Court did not make this point in its judgment. The ECJ held that all the conditions necessary to give a right of action in damages for non-implementation of the directive were present and, therefore, Francovich and the other applicants had a right to compensation from the Italian State.

Directives only have vertical direct effect and can be enforced only against the State. In the *Francovich* case, the applicants could not rely upon the principle of direct effect as against the State, as the State was not the body responsible for protecting the substantive right to payment of unpaid wages. However, if the directive had been implemented, the Member State would have designated a body responsible for respecting the substantive right. Italy had failed to implement the directive, and the Court recognised a right of action based on the responsibility of the Member State for damage caused by its failure to give effect to substantive Community rights in its legislative capacity.

Although *Francovich* involved the non-implementation of a directive, a broad interpretation of the Court's judgment could be that there is a general right to compensation where an individual has suffered loss as a result of a breach of Community law. Thus, the right to damages in the future might be understood as extending more broadly than the facts of *Francovich* would suggest. For example, in *Kirklees MBC v Wickes Building Supplies Ltd* (1992), the House of Lords held on the basis of *Francovich* that if the ECJ considered s 47 of the Shops Act 1950 to be invalid as being in conflict with Art 28 (then Art 30), the UK might be obliged to make good the loss caused to the individuals by the breach.

In *Bourgoin SA v Minister of Agriculture, Fisheries and Food* (1986), the Court of Appeal was dealing with a situation where a public authority had exercised its public law powers in a way that contravened Community law. The minister had imposed a ban on the import of turkeys contrary to Art 28 (then Art 30), which was directly effective. The Court of Appeal had held that the appropriate remedy was a public law remedy, obtainable by way of judicial review. Only if the public body had been guilty of misfeasance in a public office would the public body be liable in damages. This is difficult to prove and would result in damages not being available. In *Kirklees*, the House of Lords doubted whether, in the light of *Francovich*, the *Bourgoin* case was correctly decided and considered that the UK might be potentially liable in damages for a breach of Art 28 (then Art 30).

Francovich clearly represents a further development in Community law on remedies. Further references were made to the ECJ under Art 234 (then Art

177), in order to obtain clarification of the implications for individuals who have suffered loss through a breach of Community law. The ECJ subsequently elaborated on the *Francovich* criteria in *Brasserie du Pêcheur* and *Factortame (No 3)* (1996), where the Court developed the prerequisites for the application of the principle of State liability. The Court held that, provided the conditions for State liability were satisfied, the principle applied to all Community law as a whole, whether or not it was directly effective. In *Dillenkofer* (1996), there had been a total failure to implement a directive and the question of discretion was raised. The ECJ held that the Member State had manifestly and gravely disregarded the limits on its discretion, which gave rise to an individual right to a claim for damages provided the stated preconditions were satisfied. The Court took the view that difficulty in implementation of a directive was no defence.

In *Sutton v Secretary of State for Social Security* (1997), the ECJ stated that it is up to the national court to assess the amount of damages, provided that the domestic law does not treat breaches of EU law less favourably than similar domestic claims. In *Factortame (No 4)* (1999), the Court of Appeal held that the breaches of Community law identified in *Commission of the EC v UK* (1989) were sufficiently serious to give rise to liability for any damage that might subsequently be shown to have been caused to individuals. As a result of this judgment, it is likely that Spanish trawler owners will receive in excess of £80 m in damages. It would seem that State liability as a principle can be seen as an effective mechanism for safeguarding the rights of individuals who can meet the three criteria.

Question 17

Analyse TWO of the following cases which came before the ECJ and explain their importance in the development of Community law:

(a) *Plaumann* – Case 25/62;

(b) *Roquette Frères v Council* – Case 138/79;

(c) *Schoppenstedt* – Case 5/71.

Answer plan

When approaching a question like this, the temptation is to produce too descriptive an answer. The facts are important, but are only one element of the answer. You should deal with the following:

- the facts, the legal points raised and the decision of the Court;
- what kind of case was it? A preliminary reference or a direct action? What Article of the Treaty was it based upon?; and
- the cases chosen for this type of question have usually played their part in developing or reinforcing European Court judgments – what part has this case played?

Answer

(a) Plaumann v Commission – Case 25/62

This was an action by one of 30 German importers of clementines against a refusal by the Commission to grant a request by the Federal Republic of Germany for permission to suspend the customs duties on the import of fresh clementines from non-EC countries. The refusal by the Commission had been made in a decision under the now repealed Art 25(3). The implication for Plaumann was that it had to pay a customs duty of 13%, whereas the German Government had asked the Commission to reduce it to a 10% duty.

The main importance of this case concerned whether Plaumann could challenge this decision by the Commission. It was open to the German Government to challenge the decision because it was addressed to them. But could Plaumann as a 'private individual' bring the matter before the ECJ? An action for annulment can be brought under Art 230, but as far as individuals are concerned this Article has been restrictively interpreted by the Court. It is possible to challenge a decision addressed to oneself, but if it is addressed to another the applicant must show that it is of direct and individual concern to them.

The Commission contested the case by claiming that it was inadmissible under Art 230 (then Art 173(2)) because the decision addressed to the government of a Member State was of a special nature and therefore not susceptible to challenge by private persons. It also said that Plaumann was not directly and individually concerned. Thus, the argument before the Court concentrated on this issue of inadmissibility.

The Court accepted that Art 230 (then Art 173(2)) does allow an individual to bring an action against decisions addressed to another person if they are of direct and individual concern, but the Article neither defines nor limits the scope of these words. The words should be given their natural meaning and the broadest interpretation. As the provision provides a right for interested parties to bring an action, it must not be interpreted restrictively. Therefore, the Commission's argument was not considered to be well founded.

On the question of 'direct and individual' concern, the Court decided to look at whether the applicant was individually concerned, because if the answer is negative it will be unnecessary to inquire whether he is directly concerned. On this question of 'individually concerned', the decision must affect them by reason of certain attributes which are peculiar to them, or there must be certain circumstances which differentiate them from all other persons. As a result of these factors, the applicant is distinguished individually, just as if they were the person to whom the decision was addressed.

In the *Plaumann* case, the decision affects Plaumann as an importer of clementines, a commercial activity which may be practised by any person. Thus, he is not distinguished sufficiently to show individual concern. Therefore, the Court declared the action for annulment to be inadmissible on the second point put forward by the Commission. This case was followed by a number decided on a similar basis, to the detriment of the applicants – for example, *Spijker Kwasten BV v Commission*, which involved a six month import ban on Chinese brushes where Spijker was the sole importer into The Netherlands.

(b) Roquette Frères v Council – Case 138/79

This case arose in the wake of a successful challenge to Regulation 1111/77 in the *Isoglucose* case of *Royal Scholten-Honig* in 1978. The result was that the regulation was declared to be invalid on the ground of discrimination. The regulation had sought to control the sugar market. Isoglucose is a direct substitute for liquid sugar, of which there was a surplus. As this surplus had to be exported at a loss, it was felt that the isoglucose manufacturers should contribute to export costs by paying a levy. As the regulation imposing the levy was invalid, no such levy was being collected. Therefore, a new regulation was needed which imposed a levy, but did not discriminate between the producers. Under the Common Agricultural Policy, such a regulation required that the Parliament should be consulted before being adopted by the Council.

The problem was a matter of time. The new regulation was needed to come into force at the same time as the sugar scheme, namely July 1979. By March 1979, the Commission had drafted the regulation, which was based on the one which applied to sugar. Therefore, the new regulation did not discriminate between the two products. However, the regulation contained an annex which gave precise methods of calculation.

The draft regulation came before the Parliament in April, but no final decision was made. June 1979 was the first time that direct elections were to be made to the European Parliament. The old Parliament 'died' before it could give its opinion, although the specialist Agricultural Committee was in the process of reconsidering the regulation. The regulation was urgently needed, but there was no Parliament. In the recitals to any regulation the words 'having regard to the opinion of the European Parliament ...' are usually included. This regulation said that the Parliament had been consulted, but had not delivered its opinion! The Council believed that the judgment of the Court in the *Isoglucose* case had to be implemented before too long and that the regulation be adopted before the beginning of the sugar year on 1 July 1979.

Who could challenge the regulation? At that time, the Parliament was considered not to have *locus standi* under the then Art 173, although, following *Les Verts v Parliament* (1983), this would not be the situation today. Therefore, the only possibility was for an individual to bring an action for annulment under Art 230 (then Art 173(2)). However, no individual can challenge a true regulation. There was something special about this regulation, in that it contained the annex which applied the scheme set up by the regulation to particular firms. Therefore, as far as these firms were concerned, the measure affected them 'like a decision'. Such firms could also count on the Parliament intervening in the action on their support, as they are entitled to do under the Court Statute.

The Council challenged the firms' action under Art 230 (then Art 173), but the Commission observed that if the action was declared inadmissible, there would surely be a reference on the matter under Art 234 from a court of a Member State. The Court agreed that the action was admissible. The ground under Art 230 (then Art 173(1)) which was successfully pleaded was the breach of an essential procedural requirement, in that the Parliament had not been consulted. This raised the question as to what amounted to consultation? As the Parliament had received the draft regulation, was this sufficient? The Court found that it was not, as Parliament was allowed, under the Treaty, to play an actual part in the legislative process. This reflects the fundamental democratic principle of the Community.

Having found that the regulation was faulty, the Court had to declare it void under Art 231 (then Art 174). This case provides a good example of a decision which, although in the form of a regulation, is of direct and individual concern under Art 230. The importance of the case goes further in its effects on the balance of power of the Community institutions. Since the case, the Single European Act 1986 has introduced the co-operation procedure for certain policy areas, but this case shows that the Court recognised the importance of the democratic principle and the role it gives to the European Parliament.

(c) Schoppenstedt – Case 5/71

The undertaking Aktien-Zuckerfabrik Schoppenstedt brought an action in 1971 on the basis of Art 288 (then Art 215(2)), claiming damages from the

Council caused by Regulation 769/68. This regulation laid down the measures needed to offset the difference between national sugar prices. The European Court is given jurisdiction in disputes relating to compensation for damage by Art 235. However, this jurisdiction is linked to Art 288, which states that, in the case of non-contractual liability, the Community shall make good any damage caused by its institutions. The case is to be judged in accordance with the general principles common to the laws of the Member States.

The Council contested the admissibility of the application on the grounds that the applicant was claiming compensation for the removal of the legal effects arising from the contested regulation and not for any wrongful act or omission. Secondly, if the action was recognised as admissible it would undermine Art 230 (then Art 173), under which individuals are not entitled to bring applications for the annulment of regulations.

On the substance of the case, the Court said that the non-contractual liability of the Community presupposes at the very least the unlawful nature of the act alleged to be the cause of the damage. No non-contractual liability will arise involving measures of economic policy unless a sufficiently flagrant violation of a superior rule of law for the protection of the individual has occurred. Having set this principle, the Court had to decide whether such a violation had actually occurred in this case.

Analysing this sentence, 'a superior rule of law for the protection of individuals' includes any general principle of Community law. This would include such examples as equality or proportionality. The requirement that there should be a 'sufficiently flagrant' or serious violation has been narrowly construed by the Court. In the case of *Bayerische HNL Vermehrungsbetriebe GmbH v Council and Commission* (1978), the Court stated that no liability would be incurred by the Community institutions unless the institution concerned had manifestly and gravely disregarded the limits on the exercise of its power. In subsequent cases, the Court's view has been that the breach must be both serious and inexcusable.

The applicants contended that by adopting different criteria for the right of compensation of sugar producers, the regulation infringes Art 37(3). However, the Court rejected this argument, as the prices must be governed by market forces. Therefore, the applicant's action failed on the substance, because the condition mentioned above was not satisfied. The impact of the case has been the test set by the Court in actions under Art 288 in the field of legislative economic policy. Cases which have followed have been regularly rejected.

CHAPTER 5

JUDICIAL REMEDIES AND REVIEW (2): INDIRECT ACTION – PRELIMINARY REFERENCES

Introduction

This type of action has proved very important for the development of Community law. It has been used by the European Court of Justice (ECJ) as a vehicle for establishing many of the fundamental principles covered in other chapters of this book. It is very important, therefore, to have a good understanding of this topic, which can arise in both problem and essay questions.

Checklist

You should have a general knowledge of the reasons for such a procedure being incorporated into the Treaty and, in particular, you must be familiar with the following areas:

- the matters for referral under Art 234;
- the difference between interpretation and validity questions;
- what is a court or tribunal within the Article;
- the difference between courts which have a discretion and those which have an obligation to refer;
- the impact of the *CILFIT* case;
- the guidelines and procedures used in English courts; and
- the impact of a reference on the parties and subsequent cases.

Question 18

What are the objectives of the system of preliminary references? Has the ECJ extended the use of Art 234 beyond these objectives?

Answer plan

This type of essay question allows you to use your knowledge of areas of Community law to illustrate how the ECJ has extended the role of Art 234 within the Community. The following points should be covered:

- objectives of the Art 234 procedure (formerly Art 177; new numbering should generally be referred to, as in this answer);
- the relationship between the ECJ and national courts under the procedure;
- the role of policy in the ECJ;
- the extension of the scope of Art 234;
- the development of direct effect;
- the development of *acte clair* in the context of Art 234.

Answer

In the early stages of the European Community, the ECJ made it clear that a new legal order had been established. It was recognised by the authors of the Treaties establishing the Community that a court was necessary to ensure that there was a uniform interpretation and application of Community law throughout the Member States. It would undermine the new Community if the effect of its law varied from one Member State to another, especially in the economically sensitive areas associated with the European Economic Treaty. It was necessary to give ultimate authority to one court, whose jurisdiction extended over the whole Community. This was the ECJ. However, the relationship between the ECJ and the national courts was not to be on a hierarchical appellate basis associated with national court structures. It was important that the relationship should be seen to be based on co-operation, with the shared objective that all courts wished to apply the law, whether it be of national or Community origin. It was the ECJ which was granted the power to give definitive judgments on the validity and interpretation of Community law.

Thus, from the beginning, there were seen to be two clear differences between the procedure under Art 234 and the action of appellate courts. It is the parties to an action who normally decide whether to appeal or not. Secondly, when a case goes to appeal in a national context, it is normally the appeal court which decides the case and it may either uphold, amend or overturn the decision of the lower court. Neither of these apply to the Art 234 procedures. It is the national court which decides whether a reference should be made, and only specific issues are referred to the ECJ in the form of questions. Once the ECJ has answered these, they are sent back to the national court for a final decision. This suggests that national courts are not subordinate to the ECJ, but co-equal.

Given this need for uniformity in the Community, Art 234 specifies the initial boundaries of the role of preliminary references. Under Art 234, the Treaty specifies that references can be made requesting: (a) interpretation of the Treaty; (b) the validity and interpretation of acts of the institutions of the Community; and (c) in appropriate cases, the interpretation of the statutes of bodies established by the act of the European Council. It is (a) and (b) where the important developments have been made in Community law by the use of Art 234 references. In the early cases of *Van Gend en Loos* (1963) and *Costa v ENEL* (1964), the ECJ took the opportunity to stress the relationship between national law and Community law and the legal implications of the transfer of sovereignty when Member States established the Community. Both of these very important cases were brought before the Court via Art 234 references from their national courts. However, perhaps the best example of how the Court has used Art 234 to develop Community law is direct effect. Having established the supremacy of Community law over national law, the ECJ introduced the concept of direct effect. This was the result of the Court's view that a new legal order had been established with the Community and that this gave rights to individuals which their national courts had to uphold. Subject to three requirements being satisfied, this meant that an individual could claim a right under the Treaty, administrative act or other act treated as *sui generis* by the Court. This very important development was not expressly mentioned in the Treaty, the primary source of Community law. It was implied by the ECJ under its powers of interpretation and within its role in explaining what Community law was. Thus, it was possible to identify three issues which could be referred for a ruling under Art 234, namely, interpretation, validity and direct effect.

As a policy decision, the Court has developed the principle of direct effect of Treaty Articles, regulations and directives. However, this is not the only example of how the ECJ has extended the jurisdiction of Art 234. As mentioned above, the Court has extended 'acts' of the institutions to include not only those specified in Art 249, but also those acts which are *sui generis*. In the *ERTA* case (1971), the Court held that such acts of the Council could be an act for the purposes of judicial review under Art 230 (then Art 173) and thus likely to fall within Art 234 procedures. This was taken further in the *Haegeman* case (1974), where the Court held that the Association Agreement between the Community and Greece was covered by Art 234 (then Art 177(1)(b)). As agreements between the Community and non-Member States are normally concluded by the Council, this was sufficient grounds for the Court to regard such agreements as Community acts. It could be argued that, as the agreement was concluded by means of a Council decision, this was correct. However, it was not the decision which was interpreted by the Court, but the agreement itself. Obviously, the non-Member State was not bound by the Court's interpretation, but Member States were. As international agreements between the Community and non-Member States are part of Community law and binding on Member States, it is clearly important that uniform interpretations should be given to the agreement throughout the Community. The agreement had to be brought within Art 234 if it was to be interpreted by the Court. Thus, the Court said that the agreement constituted an act of a Community institution in so far as it concerned the Community. Even if the agreement between the Community and a non-Member State is a mixed agreement in that there is a shared authority between the Community and Member States, this does not seem to have affected the ECJ's view of its jurisdiction to interpret the agreement. This approach is another example of the Court's policy-orientated interpretation which has extended Art 234.

There are other examples of the impact of Art 234 references on Community law as its scope has been broadened by the ECJ. It is seen by the Court as the best way of moving Community law forward within the teleological interpretation of the Court. The flow of cases on the direct effect of directives is perhaps a clear example of this, culminating in the *Francovich* judgment (1992). However, the constitutional impact of references on Member States should not be ignored. In the UK, the *Factortame* case challenged long standing constitutional principles. However, if the objectives of the preliminary references system are to ensure uniformity and not to allow disparities due to legal traditions, it would appear that the ECJ is seeking to fulfil them. As the scope of Community action has increased, it is to be expected that the matters coming within Art 234 references will also increase. How else can the ECJ provide the interpretation and validity necessary for uniform application throughout the Community? If the ECJ did not provide these, there would be no focus for the Member States and a danger of various interpretations undermining the Community itself.

Another objective of Art 234 was to distinguish between those courts which had a discretion to refer under Art 234(2) and those which had an obligation to refer under Art 234(3). Courts under the latter paragraph are those against whose decisions there is no judicial remedy under national law. This does not automatically mean the highest court in the judicial structure of a Member State, but the highest court hearing that particular case (*Costa v ENEL*). In the UK, some judges, such as Lord Denning, consider that only the House of Lords comes within the category of Art 234(3).

However, whatever the arguments on this point, the ECJ has taken a policy decision to limit the obligation of such courts to refer. The *CILFIT* case (1982) is the most important development in this respect, where the ECJ held that final courts are in the same position as other national courts in deciding whether they need to refer a question of Community law before giving judgment.

If, for example, the ECJ had already given an authoritative interpretation under Art 234, there is no purpose in a further reference, although it could be made. However, the Court went further, to say that the correct application of Community law may be so obvious as to leave no scope for any reasonable doubt as to the manner in which the question is raised, thus enabling the Art 234 court to refrain from making a reference. This echoes the principle of *acte clair*, so familiar to the French legal system. The ECJ may have felt that the national legal systems were now so well schooled in the principles of Community law that this development could take place. It may be that they felt that this was a reasonable way of reducing the workload of the Court or to further the co-operation on which the relationship with national courts is based. However, to ensure that national courts did not remove this obligation as a matter of course, the Court indicated the special characteristics of Community law which had to be considered, for example, the linguistic nature of the Court's jurisdiction, the special terminology and the contextual approach of the ECJ. Only if the national court could satisfy itself on these matters could the obligation to refer be removed.

Given that the preliminary procedure was designed to deal with the danger of divergences in the interpretation of Community law in Member States (*International Chemical Corp* (1981)), it can be seen that the ECJ has extended the interpretation of Art 234 itself. This is in three respects, namely, the scope of Community law covered, direct effect and the mandatory nature of Art 234. However, there have been limitations on this development, as can be seen in the *Firma Foto-Frost* case (1988), where the ECJ reiterated that national courts could not declare a Community act invalid, but had to make a reference under Art 234.

Question 19

Christine is a secretary with Welch's Import Agency. On a recent visit to Amsterdam, Christine collected a number of boxes at the request of her employer and brought them back with her to England in her car. At Dover, she was stopped by customs officials and her car was searched for drugs. Although no drugs were found, the boxes belonging to her employer were opened and found to contain pornographic films and magazines, much to the embarrassment of Christine. She was subsequently charged with a criminal offence under the Obscene Publications Act 1959.

At the Crown Court hearing, Christine's counsel stated that the case raised a question of European law and requested that a reference be made to the ECJ. The judge said that he would make no reference, as the law was clear in his eyes and he did not wish to delay the case.

Can the judge refuse this request? What guidelines have been developed to assist English judges when deciding whether to make a reference?

Answer plan

This problem question on Art 234 requires the application of basic principles, including:

- the procedure under Art 234;
- the difference between Art 234(2) and 234(3);
- implications of *acte clair* and *CILFIT*;
- English guidelines produced by senior judges;
- the *Rheinmuhlen* case.

Answer

Christine's counsel has asked about a possible reference by the Crown Court judge to the ECJ. Under Art 234, it is possible for any court or tribunal to request a preliminary ruling from the ECJ on a matter of Community law in order for the national court to give a judgment in the case before it. This request can be on a question of interpretation of the Treaty, interpretation or validity of acts of the Community institutions or whether the principle of direct effect applies. The purpose is to provide the means for a definitive statement from the Court that will ensure that Community law is applied uniformly across all Member States. Thus, the Crown Court comes within the category of court which Art 234 was designed for. However, within Art 234, there are two categories of court. Under Art 234(2), courts or tribunals have a discretion in that they may make a reference.

Article 234(3) indicates that those courts or tribunals in Member States against whose decision there is no judicial remedy under national law have an obligation to make a reference. This obligation has been qualified by the case law of the ECJ, such as the *CILFIT* case. As Christine's case is being heard before the Crown Court, Art 234(2) clearly applies. However, in either instance, it is the court or tribunal which decides and not the parties to the action. Therefore, the judge hearing Christine's case can refuse the request for a preliminary ruling under Art 234 to the European Court of Justice.

Given the importance of the decision to make a reference to the Court, a number of guidelines would appear to be desirable to assist a judge hearing a particular case to decide whether to exercise discretion to make a reference or not. The European Court itself has refrained from producing guidelines as to the circumstances in which this step should be taken, but it has indicated that it is essential for the national court to 'define the legal context' (*Irish Creamery* case (1981)). However, national judges have attempted to fulfil this need. The first judge to do so in the UK was Lord Denning, in the first case to come before the Court of Appeal involving Community law. This case was *Bulmer v Bollinger* (1974), an action over the use of the term 'champagne' when describing an alcoholic drink called BabyCham. In this case, Denning indicated what he considered to be important factors. Perhaps the most important was that the point of Community law must be conclusive, in the sense that the case must turn on the point of Community law involved. In other words, if Community law was 'x', then the plaintiff would succeed, but if, on the contrary, it was 'y', then the defendant would defeat the action. It may be that, after hearing the evidence, the case could be settled on national law, thus making the reference unnecessary. The other factors he specified were associated with the time it took to get a ruling from the European Court, which required a stay of the English proceedings, which may have unfortunate results for the parties. Obviously, there was the expense of obtaining the ruling and the danger of overloading the European Court with too many references. He also felt that the wishes of the parties should be taken into account. Clearly, Christine wants a reference made, but this is not conclusive.

These guidelines have been criticised, in that they may fetter the English judge, contrary to the principle that national law cannot constrain the judge in the exercise of his discretion. This principle was stated by the ECJ in the German case of *Rheinmuhlen* (1974). In this case, the Court held that the power of a lower court to make a reference cannot be abrogated by any rule of national law. It also reiterated the importance of the Art 234 procedure by stating that it is essential for the preservation of the Community character of law and ensuring that the law is the same in all Member States. However, the Court did recognise in *Rheinmuhlen* that, although the widest discretion was given to national courts regarding when to refer, Art 234 does not preclude a decision to refer from remaining subject to the normal national law remedies. Thus, it would still be possible to appeal in these circumstances through the national court structure. Although in subsequent English cases, judges have been influenced by the words of Denning in *Bulmer v Bollinger*, they have repeated that they are only guidelines and do not fetter the discretion of the judge. However, one important point made by Lord Denning and repeated by subsequent English judges and the European Court itself is that it is important to ascertain the facts first, before the discretion to make a reference is considered.

In some civil cases, the facts may be agreed by the parties but, in criminal cases, such as Christine's, it is normally only after the case has been argued that conclusions can be drawn on the facts of the case. This is apparent in the context of deciding whether the point of Community law is conclusive. It may be that the case can be settled on the basis of national law. However, more importantly, it has a crucial role in framing the questions to be put to the ECJ in the request for a preliminary ruling.

MacPherson J, in *R v HM Treasury ex p Daily Mail and General Trust plc* (1987), provided a useful list of factors which consolidate those of previous English judges. His last point, that he did not find the point raised free from doubt, brings the wording of Art 234 back into focus. The judge hearing Christine's case has a discretion to make a reference if he considers it necessary to enable him to give judgment. Although Christine's counsel has stated that a question of European law has been raised by the case, the judge clearly feels that he has the answer. This may be gleaned from the case law of the Court itself on the point raised, which was recognised in the *CILFIT* case (1981). However, English judges have been warned by Lord Diplock in *R v Henn and Darby* (1981) that just because the meaning of the English text seems plain, it does not mean that no question of interpretation arises. Where this is necessary, the ECJ, as Bingham J pointed out in *Commissioners of Customs and Excise v Samex ApS* (1983), is far better equipped than national courts to resolve issues of Community law. Later, as Sir Thomas Bingham MR, he confirmed this view and added that if there was any real doubt a court should make a reference (the *Stock Exchange* case (1993)).

It may be different for Christine if the hearing is before magistrates and thus without a jury to decide on questions of fact. In such courts, once questions of facts have been decided, it may be appropriate for the magistrates to make an Art 234 reference if the guilt of the defendant turns on the interpretation or validity of Community law. This was followed in *R v Pieck* (1980), where the incompatibility of English law with Community law led to the defendant having the prosecution against him dropped. However, in *R v Plymouth JJ ex p Rogers* (1982), the Divisional Court dismissed the argument of the prosecution that no court or tribunal could refer questions to the Court of Justice unless all the facts had been admitted or found, because this would mean that, in criminal cases, there would not be an opportunity to request a ruling on the basis of no case to answer unless all the facts had been settled. On the other hand, it was better to call all the evidence so that there was no question of the defendant being acquitted on the facts, thus saving the expense and delay of a reference. A case before a judge and jury in a Crown Court highlights the problem of delay associated with making a preliminary reference. Lord Diplock stated in *Henn and Darby v DPP* (1981) that it can seldom be a proper exercise of a judge's discretion to hold up the proceedings for over nine months. The delay caused by a reference being made now would probably be at least double this length of time. The better course, he suggested, was to decide the case at first instance and allow an appeal against conviction through the hierarchy of national courts. This approach was subsequently adopted by the judge in *R v Tymen* (1981).

It would appear that the judge hearing Christine's case has complete discretion, but is there any appeal available to her? As mentioned above, the European Court recognised in the *Rheinmuhlen* case that Art 234 references are subject to the normal appeal processes. If a reference had been made under the Crown Court equivalent of the High Court procedure in RSC Ord 114, there would be a two week period before the reference was sent to the ECJ to allow for an appeal by one of the parties. However, in Christine's case, it is the decision not to make a reference that she is unhappy with. In these circumstances, the judge's refusal is interlocutory and leave to appeal is necessary either from the judge or from the Court of Appeal.

Question 20

If the system of preliminary rulings is based on partnership, should the ECJ ever refuse a request by a national court for such a ruling?

Answer plan

This essay question is looking for a well planned essay that develops the following points:

- purpose of Art 234;
- the *Foglia* cases;
- guidance provided by the ECJ;
- changing relationship with the national courts.

The objective of the preliminary ruling procedure is to provide uniformity across the whole Community, so that Community law is applied in the same way in all Member States. Under Art 234, the Court of Justice is under a duty to supply all courts in the Community with the information on interpretation of Community law that is necessary to enable them to settle genuine disputes which are brought before them (*Foglia v Novello (No 1)* (1980)). Under Art 225(3) of the Nice Treaty, the Court of First Instance will gain jurisdiction to hear requests for a preliminary ruling. Before the Nice amendment, only the European Court of Justice had jurisdiction under Art 234. However, despite this change, the relationship between the national courts and the European Union courts is, in theory, one of partnership in respect of Art 234. There is no hierarchy but a commitment to provide a definitive answer to questions from national courts where the latter need information in order to arrive at the appropriate application of EU law.

The procedure is available to any court or tribunal of any Member State. What constitutes such a court has been given a wide interpretation by the ECJ. It is not necessary that the body is recognised as a court by national law, neither must it be called a court. For the ECJ, the important question is whether the body concerned is performing a judicial function. The characteristic of such a function is the power to give binding determinations of the legal rights and obligations of individuals. The ECJ has used the mechanism of preliminary rulings to develop fundamental principles of Community law, such as supremacy and direct effect. However, Art 234 has also been used to facilitate a dialogue between the national courts and the ECJ on issues where national law and Community law seem to be in conflict.

The preliminary ruling procedure recognised the different functions of the national courts and the Community Court. It envisaged this relationship to be of equals as both were seen to be on a horizontal base. If the national court chose to ask a question it entered into a bilateral dialogue with the ECJ. The answers from the ECJ were sent back to that court, even though the answers were public and therefore available to everyone. The courts had different functions but a shared objective of applying the law. This is explicit in Art 220 EC but is mirrored in the national courts. Even though many now describe the relationship as more vertical as the importance of both Community law and the ECJ has increased, the Community Court still relies upon national courts to enforce Community law.

There has also been the wider recognition of the *acte clair* concept, so that even those national courts who were thought to be obliged to make a reference (Art 234(3)) need no longer do so (*CILFIT*). Although Advocate General Caporti in that case proposed that the concept should not be adopted, the Court rejected that opinion. However, some commentators have suggested that they indicated restrictions or considerations so as to limit its use, the fact remains that *CILFIT* led to a much more relaxed, yet responsible, approach by those national courts. There are some commentators who say that the development was just pragmatic; too many requests for a preliminary ruling. This may have been a factor but the development complemented the increasing role of the national courts in enforcing Community rights with the principle of direct effect or applying Community rules on competition.

In *Foglia (No 2)* the ECJ made clear that it would be the ultimate decider of the scope of its own jurisdiction. It would not answer hypothetical questions. If necessary it would have to examine the circumstances of the reference in order to determine whether the court's jurisdiction had been properly provoked. In the *Foglia v Novello* cases in 1980 and 1982, the Court held that the reference was an abuse of Art 234 as the case had been artificially constructed as a vehicle for obtaining clarification of Community law. There was, in the opinion of the Court, an absence of any real legal dispute between the parties. Novello, a French resident, had ordered some wine from Foglia, an Italian wine grower. The contract provided that Novello would not be liable for any French or Italian taxes which were contrary to the free movement of goods between the two countries. When a charge was subsequently levied by French customs, Novello claimed it was unlawful under Art 90 (formerly Art 95 EC). The ECJ said that both parties agreed that the French law was incompatible with Community law and the legal action had been a device to obtain a ruling that the French legislation was invalid. The Court went on to say that such arrangements obliging such rulings would jeopardise the system of legal remedies available to protect private individuals against tax provisions which were contrary to the Treaty. A subsequent second reference by the Italian judge was an attempt to clarify the role of Art 234 and the relationship between the national courts and the ECJ. However, the ECJ adhered to its earlier decision not to answer the question arising from the customs duty levied by the French law. It held that the Art 234 procedure was not to be used to give abstract advisory opinions, but to contribute to the actual decisions of the cases. The ECJ believes that, like any court, it must be in a position to make an assessment to ensure that it has jurisdiction to hear the case. Normally the Court will rely on the assessment made by national courts but in exceptional cases it reserves the right to make its own (*Dias* (1992)).

The original division of the functions between national courts and the ECJ may have been separate, but it was equal – with the former deciding whether to refer, while the latter gives the ruling on the questions placed before it. *Foglia* represented a reshaping of that conception as the ECJ would now assert some control over the suitability of the reference. The ECJ refrained from reviewing the relevance even in cases like *Rewe-Zentrale v Hauptzollamt Emmerich* (1971) where the national court making the reference admitted that the questions raised were not relevant to the litigation. The questions were answered by the ECJ because the litigation was a test case for similar forthcoming cases. There have been a number of cases where the ECJ has made use of the *Foglia* principle, such as with the hypothetical nature of the questions. However, a practical problem is the fine line between hypothetical cases and test cases.

A second reason why the ECJ may not wish to give a ruling is that the questions raised are not relevant, as in the *Meilicke* case (1992). The third category where the ECJ may refuse a reference is where the questions are not articulated clearly enough for the Court to give any meaningful legal response, as in *AGS Assedic Pas-de-Calais v Dumon & Froment* (1995). Although the ECJ may tease out the real question the national court is asking, in this case they thought that it would be wrong to alter the substance of the questions asked. A fourth category is where the facts are insufficiently clear for the Court to be able to apply the relevant legal rules. In the *Telemarsicabruzzo* case (1993) the Italian court referred two questions to the ECJ concerning the compatibility of national provisions on the distribution of TV frequencies with EC competition law. The national court provided almost nothing by way of explanation for these questions and therefore the Court decided that there was no need to answer the questions!

The Court has now incorporated the results of its case law in its *Guidance on References by National Courts of Preliminary Rulings,* published in 1997, and has recognised that there are limitations to its power to decline to take a reference. In *ICI v Colmer* (1996) the ECJ stated that 'A request for a preliminary ruling from a national court may be rejected only if it is manifest that the interpretation of Community law or the examination of the validity of a rule of Community law sought by that court bears no relation to the facts or the subject matter of the main proceedings'. However, even within this context the ECJ has begun to exercise more positive control over its own jurisdiction in the manner redolent of most superior courts.

Question 21

Crinkley plc are a large producer of potato crisps in the UK. Like all companies who are involved in manufacturing potato products, Crinkley have to purchase their potatoes from a national marketing organisation, as required by EU legislation. Under a recent Community regulation, all purchasers have to submit a tender together with a deposit of 10% of the total value of the tender.

Subsequently, Crinkley failed to take up all the supplies it had tendered for and were informed that they would, under the regulation, forfeit their deposit. This amounted to a substantial amount to Crinkley and could force them into liquidation. As a result, they are seeking to challenge the validity of the regulation, on the basis that it is contrary to the principle of proportionality. They are also suing the national potato marketing organisation to recover their deposit.

Advise Crinkley plc.

Answer plan

This problem question is seeking the application of Arts 230 and 234 as a means of challenging a Community act. In particular, the following points should be stressed:

- the requirements under Art 230 for *locus standi* and the grounds for annulment;
- the procedures under Art 234 and specifically the power of the ECJ under Art 234 on questions of validity; and
- remedies.

Answer

There are two ways open to Crinkley to challenge the regulation which has affected them. One possibility is a direct action under Art 230, whereby they will bring an action before the ECJ and ask them to annul the regulation. If they are successful, the Court could declare, under Art 231, the regulation *erga omnes* or, if appropriate, merely declare void that part of the regulation which is contrary to Community law and leave the rest of the regulation as lawful. Such a declaration would have an immediate impact on everyone within the Community. The alternative possibility is for Crinkley to seek to challenge the validity of the regulation in the English courts, probably in the action against the national potato marketing organisation to recover the deposit. In this situation, a successful challenge using the Art 234 preliminary ruling procedure would have an immediate impact on Crinkley.

In order to bring an action under Art 230, it is necessary to satisfy the ECJ with regard to their *locus standi*. Under Art 230, it is possible for an individual or company to institute proceedings against a regulation if it is in fact a decision and is of direct and individual concern to them. The measure in this problem is titled a regulation, although the name of the measure is not decisive in the view of the Court. A regulation under Art 249 is of general application and has direct applicability throughout the Community. It is thus the main legislative or normative measure of the European Community. The main characteristic of a regulation is that it applies generally and objectively to categories of persons, whereas a decision binds those named individuals to whom it is addressed.

As far as the Court is concerned, a true regulation may not be challenged by an individual, as it stated in *Calpak* (1980). The problem for Crinkley is that the measure they are seeking to challenge does appear to satisfy the requirements of a regulation. Merely because it has had this financial impact on Crinkley, as against its effect on other potato product manufacturers, does not stop it being a regulation. In some cases, the Court has looked at the other requirements of Art 230, namely, that the measure is of 'direct and individual concern' to the applicant and, having concluded that it is, they have held that it cannot be legislative in character, that is, not a true regulation (*Sgarlata*

(1965)). To satisfy the 'direct' requirement, it is merely necessary to show that there has been no exercise of discretion on the part of national authorities (*Toepfer v Commission* (1965)). However, 'individual concern' has been restrictively interpreted by the Court so as to make it very difficult for an individual to satisfy the Court on this matter.

In *Plaumann* (1963), a case involving the importation of clementines, the Court gives a good idea of the factors to be taken into account in deciding the criterion of 'individual concern'. If Crinkley could satisfy the requirement of *locus standi*, it would still have to satisfy the Court as to the ground for annulment specified in Art 230. Crinkley have already indicated that they wish to challenge the regulation on the basis of proportionality. This is one of the general principles of Community law, initially derived from German law but now firmly recognised as being a Community principle. One of the most widely used grounds for annulment is 'infringement of this Treaty or of any rule of law relating to its application', which encompasses the claim that the principle of proportionality has been breached. The principle of proportionality requires that the means used must not be excessive in the context of the aim which it is intended to achieve. It has been successfully pleaded in a number of cases, including the *Skimmed Milk* case (1977). In this case, the ECJ had declared invalid an EC regulation which compelled producers of animal feeding stuff to add milk powder to their products in place of soya.

As an action under Art 230 looks unlikely to materialise because of the problem of *locus standi*, it is necessary to look at an alternative possibility before the national courts. In order for Crinkley to use Art 234, a case must be brought before a court. This will be possible if the action is brought against the potato marketing organisation in an English court, probably the High Court. The judge hearing the action will have the discretion as to whether or not to make a reference to the ECJ. Under Art 234, the Court can give definitive answers to questions of interpretation and validity of Community acts, which includes regulations. As the Court hearing the case will come within Art 234, the judge will have a discretion as indicated above. There are guidelines from previous cases heard in the UK to assist the judge in deciding whether to make a reference or not. The main one which is supported by the European Court is that it is important to ascertain the facts first. The Court prefers any reference to be set in the appropriate legal context. With regard to other factors, Lord Denning suggested, in *Bulmer v Bollinger* (1974), that time, cost, the workload of the European Court and the wishes of the parties should be taken into account. A number of references have been made by UK courts to the European Court on the validity of Community acts, including regulations. In *R v Intervention Board for Agricultural Produce ex p ED and F Man (Sugar) Ltd* (1985), a large firm of sugar traders brought proceedings for judicial review of a decision based upon a Commission regulation. The grounds for the review included that the regulation was contrary to the principle of proportionality. On an Art 234 reference, the Court answered that the regulation did contravene the principle and, to that extent, was invalid.

Does it make a difference to Crinkley that they probably do not have *locus standi* under Art 230? In the *Berlin Butter* case of *Rau v BALM* (1987), the Court stated, in response to an Art 234 reference on the validity of a decision addressed to the German Government, that it is irrelevant whether the plaintiff would have *locus standi* under Art 230, or if, in fact, such an action had been initiated. Thus, it should not influence the judge in deciding whether to make a reference or not that an Art 230 action is not possible. Is it possible, therefore, for the judge hearing the case in the national court to declare the regulation invalid without an Art 234 reference? In the *Sugar* case (1985) mentioned above, the Divisional Court recognised that it could not make an order that the regulation was invalid. This view was clearly stated by the ECJ case of *Firma Foto-Frost* (1988). In this important case, the Court held that national courts could reject an argument based on invalidity of a Community measure, but they could not declare a measure invalid. National courts had a discretion whether or not to make a validity reference, but only the ECJ was competent to declare invalid the acts of Community institutions. One of the reasons given by the Court for this was that under the rules of procedure of the Court, Community institutions whose acts were being challenged were entitled to participate in the reference proceedings before the Court. Thus, they had the chance to defend their action before the Court before the measure was declared invalid.

What if the Court considers that Crinkley's view is well founded and agrees that the regulation is invalid? A special feature of invalidity rulings is the immediate consequence they may have outside the context of the actual case in which the question of validity is raised. In *International Chemical Corp SpA v Amministrazione delle Finanze dello Stato* (1981), the European Court held that, once an act had been declared void, a national court could not apply the act without creating serious uncertainty as to the Community law applicable. Therefore, although a judgment of the ECJ under Art 234 declaring a regulation void is directly addressed only to the national court which referred the question, it is sufficient reason for any other national court to regard that act as void for the purposes of a judgment which it has to give. Thus, Crinkley will recover their deposit under national law if the regulation is declared invalid. However, the Court may decide to limit the retrospective effect of its rulings in order to leave previous transactions unaffected. The Court claimed jurisdiction to do this in proceedings under Art 234, by analogy with the power conferred upon it by Art 231, whereby the Court may state which of the effects of the regulation it has declared void (*Maize and Starch* cases (1980)).

My advice to Crinkley is that there is a presumption under Community law that a regulation is valid. Therefore, in order to defeat this presumption, an action must be brought which allows the European Court the opportunity to deliver its view on this matter. As an action under Art 230 is unlikely, given its restrictive nature, a reference by a national court under Art 234 seems the best way to challenge the regulation.

Although the national court under Art 234 has a discretion as to whether or not it makes a reference, if a *prima facie* case can be made out by Crinkley, it is probable that a reference will be made. In the *Firma Foto-Frost* case, the ECJ suggested that a national court might grant interim relief even pending a ruling on validity, as happened in *Factortame Ltd v Secretary of State for Transport (No 3)* (1991). It has to be remembered that the national court cannot declare the regulation invalid, but merely uphold its validity. If a reference is refused, Crinkley will have to be prepared to appeal, in the hope that a court which comes within Art 234 will be obliged to make a reference to the European Court.

Question 22

Critically discuss the application of *acte clair* to Community law.

Answer plan

As well as appearing in problem questions concerning cases before courts within the Art 234 definition, essay questions like this one can be set. You need to cover the following points:

- the role of Art 234;
- the specific interpretation of Art 234;
- the relationship between Art 234(2) and 234(3) courts (formerly Art 177(2) and (3) respectively, but referred to throughout this answer using the new, post-Amsterdam Treaty numbering);
- the doctrine of *acte clair*;
- the impact of the decision in *CILFIT*; and
- the approach of UK courts.

Answer

The principle of *acte clair* is derived from French law. Its origin lies in the principle that the ordinary courts must seek a ruling from the Ministry of Foreign Affairs where a question of Treaty interpretation arises, unless the point of Treaty interpretation is clear. In such circumstances, no question of interpretation arises. It was not surprising, therefore, that the first courts to apply the doctrine to Community law were the French *Conseil d'Etat* and the *Cour de Cassation*. In *Re Shell-Berre* (1964), the *Conseil d'Etat* was concerned with the application by some oil companies for the annulment of a ministerial decree affecting garages selling petrol, contrary to Art 31. The *Conseil d'Etat* refused to make a reference under Art 234, because that would only happen if there was any doubt as to the meaning or scope of the Treaty as it applied to the facts of the case.

The ECJ has accepted that a national court of last resort is not under a duty to make a reference under Art 234 in certain circumstances. These are that the provision in question has already been interpreted by the Court, or where the correct application of European law is so obvious as to leave no scope for any reasonable doubt. This echoes the principle of *acte clair*. In *Da Costa en Schaake* (1963), the Court stated that the same question in this case had been referred in the case of *Van Gend en Loos* (1963) and had been answered to the effect that Art 25 had direct effect. Therefore, the ECJ merely referred the Dutch administrative court to its previous decision. It went on to say that, if the Court had already pronounced on a question of interpretation, it may deprive the obligation to refer of its purpose and empty it of its substance. Prior to the case of *CILFIT SA v Ministry of Health* (1982), the ECJ had treated the obligation under Art 234 as being a strict one, subject to only these derogations.

However, in the case of *CILFIT* (1982), the European Court appears to have accepted the principle of *acte clair*. The plaintiffs in this case were Italian companies which imported wool from non-member countries. Since 1968, they had been paying health inspection charges on those imports under Italian law. They now sought to argue that the Italian law was inapplicable by virtue of an EC regulation. The defendant, the Italian Ministry of Health, simply replied that the regulation did not apply to wool, as wool was not listed in Annex II to the Treaty. In spite of losing at first instance and on appeal, the plaintiffs took the case up to Italy's highest court, 'against whose decisions there is no judicial remedy under national law'. They claimed that this court was obliged by Art 234(3) to make a reference to the ECJ, although the Ministry of Health resisted the reference. They maintained that the solution was so obvious that it excluded any possibility of doubt as to the interpretation of the regulation and, hence, there was no need for a reference.

In these circumstances, the Italian court did make a reference asking about the obligation to refer under Art 234(3).

The Court said that, under Art 234(3), the obligation to refer was based on co-operation between the national courts and the ECJ. This had been established with a view to ensuring the proper application and uniform interpretation of Community law in Member States and between national courts, in their capacity as courts responsible for the application of Community law. More particularly, it seeks to prevent divergences in judicial decisions on questions of Community law. The scope of the obligation to refer must be assessed in view of these obligations.

The Court went on to say that it follows from the relationship between Art 234(2) and (3) that courts and tribunals referred to in Art 234 have the same discretion as any other national court or tribunal to ascertain whether a decision on a question of Community law is necessary to enable them to give judgment. Accordingly, these courts and tribunals are not obliged to refer to the ECJ a question concerning interpretation of Community law raised before them if that question is not relevant, that is to say, if the answer to that question, regardless of what it may be, can in no way affect the outcome of the case. The same effect, as regards the limits set to the obligation laid down by Art 234, may be produced where previous decisions of the ECJ have already dealt with the point of law in question, irrespective of the nature of proceedings which led to those decisions, even though the question at issue is not strictly identical.

Finally, the Court dealt with *acte clair*. It stated that the correct application of Community law may be so obvious as to leave no scope for any reasonable doubt as to the manner in which the question raised is to be resolved. However, before a court within Art 234(3) comes to the conclusion that such is the case, the national court or tribunal must be convinced that the matter is equally obvious to the courts and tribunals of other Member States and to the ECJ itself. It is only if these conditions are satisfied that the national court or tribunal may refrain from submitting the question to the ECJ and take upon itself the responsibility for resolving the point of Community law.

This apparent acceptance of the principle of *acte clair* must be treated with great circumspection. As the Court pointed out in its *CILFIT* judgment, the matter must be assessed on the basis of the characteristic features of Community law and the particular difficulties to which it gives rise. First, Community legislation is drafted in several languages and the different language versions are all equally authentic – interpretation, therefore, involves the comparison of different language versions. Secondly, Community law uses terminology which is peculiar to itself – also, legal concepts do not necessarily have the same meaning in Community law as in the law of various Member States. Thirdly, every provision of Community law must be placed in its context and interpreted in light of provisions of Community law as a whole, regard being had to the objectives thereof and to its state of evolution at the date on which the provision in question is to be applied.

In light of all these considerations, the Court concluded that the answer to the Art 234(3) question is that it is to be interpreted as meaning that courts and tribunals, against whose decision there is no judicial remedy under national law, are required, where a question of Community law is raised, to comply with their obligations to bring the matter before the ECJ, unless it was established that the question raised is irrelevant or the Community provision in question has already been interpreted, or that the correct application of Community law is so obvious as to leave no scope for any reasonable doubt.

In the UK, the House of Lords had adopted the approach recommended by the European Court in *CILFIT*. In *Henn and Darby v DPP* (1981), Lord Diplock stated that, in the light of the established case law of the European Court, which was so free from any doubt, there was no need for an interpretation of Art 28 (then Art 30). However, because the interpretation of the Court of Appeal was contrary to this view, a reference was made to the ECJ. The Court of Appeal had held that a total import ban did not constitute a 'quantitative restriction on imports' within Art 28 (then Art 30), because it did not relate to quantities! In fact, it was already well established in the case law of the ECJ that the term 'quantitative restriction' covered not only reductions in permitted levels of imports, but also outright bans. In *Garland v BREL* (1983), the House of Lords made a reference, not because of any doubt regarding the answer likely to be given by the ECJ, but because there was no consistent line of case law on Art 266 (then Art 199) which would make the answer too obvious and inevitable.

There are dangers associated with the principle of *acte clair*, as the Court of Appeal aptly demonstrated in *Henn and Darby v DPP*. However, there are other examples where its possible misuse could lead to the misapplication or non-application of Community law by national courts. The case of *Cohn-Bendit* (1980) illustrates this point, where the *Conseil d'Etat* held, contrary to the case law of the ECJ, that a directive could not have direct effect. To counter such possibilities happening in Germany, the German Federal Constitutional Court emphasised in *Re Patented Feedingstuffs* (1989) that it will review any arbitrary refusal by a court subject to Art 234(3) to refer to the European Court.

Professor Rasmussen believes that the *CILFIT* judgment means something very different from what it *prima facie* establishes. For him, the real strategy of *CILFIT* is not to incorporate an *acte clair* concept into Community law, but to call the national judiciaries to circumspection when they are faced with problems of interpretation and application of Community law. 'The reins are not cut loose, although that might seem to be what the court ruled in *CILFIT*.' However, it must not be forgotten that, in all such circumstances, national courts and tribunals, including those in Art 234(3), remain entirely at liberty to bring the matter before the ECJ if they consider it appropriate to do so. If the principle of *acte clair* is to be invoked in the context of European Community law, it must be on the basis of the criteria supplied by *CILFIT*.

CHAPTER 6

THE FREE MOVEMENT OF GOODS

Introduction

This is one of the fundamental freedoms of the European Community and is perhaps the most important one as far as examination questions are concerned.

Examiners set both problem and essay questions on this area of Community law and it is one which you are strongly advised to revise thoroughly. The benefit of this hard work is that many important principles have been developed through cases associated with the free movement of goods, so that you can use them as examples in answering questions on other topics, such as preliminary references or general principles of Community law.

Checklist

You should have a clear idea of the principles of a customs union (Art 23) and the following specific points:

- prohibition of import duties on imports and exports within the EU and of all charges of equivalent effect (Art 25);
- prohibition of discriminatory taxation (Art 90);
- prohibition of quantitative restrictions and measures having equivalent effect on imports (Art 28) and exports (Art 29);
- the *Dassonville* formula and *Cassis de Dijon* principles; and
- derogation from Arts 28 and 29 via Art 30.

Question 23

Critically review the role played by the European Court of Justice (ECJ) in the removal of non-pecuniary barriers to trade between Member States.

Answer plan

This essay question requires an answer which covers the following points:

- Arts 28 and 29, as they affect barriers to trade;
- Directive 70/50 EC;
- the *Dassonville* formula;
- the first principle from *Cassis de Dijon* and the rule of reason and mandatory requirements; and
- the second principle of the *Cassis de Dijon* case on the marketing of goods in Member States.

Answer

The European Community is based upon free trade between Member States, brought about by the abolition of customs duties and charges of equivalent effect. However, there are other barriers to trade of a non-pecuniary nature which have to be removed. Articles 28 and 29 are designed to eliminate these barriers. These Articles are addressed to the Member States, but neither the Community institutions nor individuals are free to act in breach of them. Even if the measure concerned is not binding, these Articles will apply. This was provided for by the European Commission in the Preamble to Directive 70/50 and confirmed by the ECJ in the *Commission v Ireland* case (1982). The most important one is Art 28, which prohibits quantitative restrictions and all measures having equivalent effect on imports. 'Quantitative restrictions' was interpreted by the ECJ in *Riseria Luigi Geddo v Ente Nazionale Rise* (1974) to include any measures which amount to a total or partial restraint on imports, exports or goods in transit.

Measures having equivalent effect to quantitative restrictions is a wider concept than that of quantitative restrictions. More importantly, the concept has been given a very generous interpretation by both the European Commission and the European Court. It has been held to include not just those measures which are overtly protective or applicable to imports or exports, which are referred to as distinctly applicable measures, but also measures which are applicable to imports, exports and domestic goods alike. These measures are called indistinctly applicable measures, and are often introduced for the most worthy of reasons. They range from regulatory measures designed to enforce a minimum standard, such as weight, size, quality, price or content for products, to tests and inspections or certification requirements to ensure goods conform to the set standard. They also include activity capable of influencing the behaviour of traders, such as promoting goods by reason of their national origin. This occurred in the *Commission v Ireland* case (1987), where an agency of the Irish Government promoted a 'buy Irish' campaign to promote Irish goods within the Irish Republic, which was held to be contrary to Art 28.

To assist Member States in the identification of measures having equivalent effect to quantitative restrictions, the Commission passed Directive 70/50. Although this directive was aimed at the transitional period during which time such measures were to be abolished, the directive has been seen as providing some non-binding guidelines to the interpretation of Art 28. The directive was not intended to provide an exhaustive list of measures capable of having equivalent effect to quantitative restrictions. The directive used the terminology indicated above by dividing such measures into two categories. The first was distinctly applicable measures, which hinder imports which could otherwise take place, including measures which make importation more difficult or expensive than domestic production (Art 2(1) of the directive). The other category covers indistinctly applicable measures (Art 3 of the directive), which are only contrary to Art 28 'where the restrictive effect of such measures on the free movement of goods exceeds the effects intrinsic to trade rules', or where 'the same objective cannot be attained by other measures which are less of a hindrance to trade'. Thus, such measures appear to be acceptable if they comply with the Community general principle of proportionality.

The ECJ has developed its own definition of measures having equivalent effect to quantitative restrictions. This was first achieved in the case of *Procureur du Roi v Dassonville* (1974), and has been applied consistently by the Court. The *Dassonville* 'formula' is that all trading rules enacted by Member States which are capable of hindering, directly or indirectly, actually or potentially, intra-Community trade are to be considered as measures having an effect equivalent to quantitative restrictions. From this formula, it can be seen that it is not necessary to show that the measure is an actual hindrance to trade between Member States, as long as it is capable of such effects. It is necessary, however, to show some proof of a hindrance to trade, because a measure which is not capable of hindering trade between Member States will not breach Art 28; for example, where the measure merely affects the flow of trade, as in the *Oebel* Belgian bakery case (1981).

The measure in *Dassonville* was a requirement under Belgian law that imported goods should carry a certificate of origin issued by the State in which the goods were manufactured. Dassonville imported a quantity of Scotch whisky from France. Unfortunately, the seller did not have the required certificate, so he produced a 'home made' one, and was subsequently charged with forgery. In his defence, he claimed that the Belgian law was contrary to Community law. The national court made a reference under Art 234 (then Art 177) to the ECJ, which applied the *Dassonville* formula and found that the Belgian measure was capable of breaching Art 28 (then Art 30).

The *Dassonville* formula was developed further in the *Cassis de Dijon* case, which identified two principles. Having applied the *Dassonville* formula to the facts of the case, the Court stated that obstacles resulting from disparities between the national laws relating to the marketing of products must be accepted in so far as they may be recognised as being necessary in order to satisfy mandatory requirements. Such requirements were listed as those relating to the effectiveness of fiscal supervision, the protection of public health, the fairness of commercial transactions and the defence of the consumer. This is known as the first *Cassis de Dijon* principle. Thus, certain measures may be within the *Dassonville* formula, but will not breach Art 28 if they are necessary to satisfy such mandatory requirements. This principle has come to be known as the 'rule of reason'. Before the *Cassis* case, it was assumed that any measure which fell within the *Dassonville* formula was a breach of Art 28, and could only be saved by the permitted derogation under Art 30. Since *Cassis*, as far as indistinctly applicable measures are concerned, the rule of reason may apply and save them from Art 28. If the measure is necessary in order to protect mandatory requirements, it will not be a breach of Art 28. This is significant, since the mandatory requirements permitted under the *Cassis* principle are wider than the grounds provided under Art 30. For example, in *Commission v Denmark* (1986), regarding disposable beer cans, the protection of the environment was held to constitute a mandatory requirement. However, where the mandatory requirement falls under one of the specific heads of derogation provided by Art 30, the Court may prefer to rely on the express provision of that Article. This happened in *Commission v Germany Re German Sausage* (1989), where the derogation was on health grounds. In the *Cassis* case itself, it was felt that the derogation was not necessary.

The word 'necessary' has been interpreted to mean no more than is necessary and is subject to the principle of proportionality. Other measures could have been used to protect the consumer regarding the alcoholic content of Cassis, such as labelling, which would have been less of a hindrance to trade. It would also have been fair to the domestic producer. The second principle from the *Cassis* case has far-reaching implications. It is suggested that there is no valid reason why, 'provided that goods have been lawfully produced and marketed in one of the Member States, they should not be introduced into any other Member State'. This principle gives rise to the presumption that goods which have been lawfully marketed in another Member State will comply with the 'mandatory requirement' of the importing State. This can be rebutted by evidence that further measures are necessary to protect the interest concerned. It is hard to rebut this presumption. The burden of proving that the measure is necessary is a heavy one, particularly when, although justifiable in principle, it clearly operates as a hindrance to intra-Community trade. Any evidence submitted in support of the measure will be closely scrutinised by the Court. In the case concerning additives in beer (*Commission v Germany* (1985)), evidence was taken concerning the medical effect of such additives from the World Health Organisation and the Food and Agriculture Organisation.

The ECJ has played an important part in removing the barriers to trade associated with measures having an equivalent effect to quantitative restrictions. By the introduction of the 'rule of reason' to such measures and the extension of the two principles stated in the *Cassis de Dijon* case, the Court has to try to balance the need of applying Art 28 with the need to respect the mandatory requirements justified under Art 30. Instead of the slow process of seeking Community-wide standards under the harmonisation procedures, where the interests of Member States could delay progress, the case law of the Court moved the Community forward in the direction of achieving its goal of a common market.

Question 24

James is an English farmer living 10 miles from the Channel Tunnel. He breeds special varieties of pigs and sheep for slaughter and subsequent sale to butchers. As a marketing advantage, he sells prepacked joints of meat and special sausages to butchers for resale.

With the opening of the tunnel, James decided to develop links with butchers in northern France. However, he has received a letter containing the following points from French officials:

- as his packs of meat are not labelled in French, they cannot be sold in France;

- the prepacked joints of meat do not comply with French standards of consumer protection with regard to weight;

- the price he is selling his packs at is below the minimum price set in France; and

- the sausages contain additives which, although permitted under English law, are not allowed by French legislation.

James seeks your advice as to his position under EU law.

Answer plan

This question represents the typical problem associated with the free movement of goods. The approach you should take is to state the principles and then apply them to the individual aspects of the problem.

You should deal with the following points:

- Art 28 and barriers to trade;
- definitions and examples of quantitative restrictions and measures having equivalent effect;
- the *Dassonville* formula;
- the principles of *Cassis de Dijon*; and
- remedies.

Answer

The European Community is based upon a customs union whereby there is a common external tariff for goods coming into the Community and the removal of barriers to intra-Community trade. It has been relatively easy for the Community to deal with the more obvious barriers to such trade, such as tariffs. It has been the non-pecuniary barriers, which are more subtle and disguised, which have caused problems, such as those experienced by James. Article 28 provides that barriers to trade which amount to quantitative restrictions and all measures having equivalent effect are prohibited. Such quantitative restrictions have been interpreted by the ECJ in *Riseria Luigi Geddo v Ente Nazionale Risi* (1974) to cover any measure which amounts to a total or partial restraint on trade between Member States.

The concept of measures having equivalent effect to quantitative restrictions has been given a wide interpretation by the ECJ. It is much wider than mere quantitative restrictions. To assist with the application of the concept, it is divided into those measures which are indistinctly applicable and those which are distinctly applicable. Indistinctly applicable measures are often introduced by governments for seemingly the most worthy of purposes. As such measures are applied to both imported and domestically produced goods alike, they are often thought by the government concerned not to discriminate in any way and not to fall within the prohibitions of Art 28. Such measures include regulatory controls designed to enforce minimum standards, such as price, which occurs in

James's problem. Distinctly applicable measures are those which are applicable only to imported goods.

In the problem the French government has introduced standards for packaging any meat product. This was introduced to protect consumers. This measure comes within the category of indistinctly applicable measures, as it applies to both French and imported products of this type. It was Directive 70/50 which introduced the categories of measures having equivalent effect to quantitative restrictions in order to help Member States to identify and eliminate such measures in the transitional period. Although this period has passed, the directive is still seen as providing non-binding guidelines to the interpretation of Art 28. It is Art 3 of the directive which deals with indistinctly applicable measures. Such measures are said to be only contrary to Art 28 if they do not satisfy the principle of proportionality, that is, if the same objective cannot be attained by other measures which are less of a hindrance to trade.

However, it is the case law of the European Court which is of most importance to James. Building upon the directive, the Court has given some very important judgments in this area of Community law. The first case was *Procureur du Roi v Dassonville* (1974), which led to the development of the *Dassonville* formula. Dassonville had imported some Scotch whisky from France. Under Belgian law, it was necessary to have a certificate of origin from the State in which the goods had been manufactured. As the seller did not have such a certificate, he produced one of his own. When he was subsequently charged with forgery, he claimed that the Belgian law was contrary to Community law. From its answers to the Art 234 (then Art 177) reference made by the Belgian court, the *Dassonville* formula was developed, which stated that the Belgian measure was capable of breaching Art 28 (then Art 30). The formula is that all trading rules enacted by Member States which are capable of hindering, directly or indirectly, actually or potentially, intra-Community trade are to be considered as measures having an effect equivalent to quantitative restrictions.

In the *Cassis de Dijon* case (1978), the *Dassonville* formula was extended. In this case, a German law required the minimum alcohol content of Cassis to be 25%, whereas that imported from France was 15–20%. When it was challenged by the importer, the Court applied the *Dassonville* formula and held that the German law contravened Art 28 (then Art 30). In rejecting the claim that they were protecting public health and the consumer, the Court stated that this could be achieved by the alcoholic content of the different products being stated on the label. Under the first principle, certain measures may fall within the *Dassonville* formula, but will not breach Art 28 if they are necessary to satisfy mandatory requirements of the public interest. These include protection of public health and the defence of the consumer, and are wider than those listed in Art 30. This principle has become known as the 'rule of reason'. However, the national measure must be proved to serve a purpose which is in the general interest and has to take precedence over the requirements of the free movement of goods. Thus, if the measure is necessary in order to protect mandatory requirements, it will not breach Art 28.

The second principle derived from the *Cassis de Dijon* case gives rise to a presumption that goods which have been lawfully marketed in one Member State will comply with the 'mandatory requirements' of the importing State. This presumption can be rebutted, but it is very difficult to do so. The burden of proving that the measure is necessary to protect the interest concerned falls on the Member State which imposed it. Although the measure may be justifiable in principle, such measures clearly operate as a hindrance to intra-Community trade.

Obviously, James wishes to challenge the French law and obtain a judgment that it is contrary to Community law. The most direct way to do this is to seek to sell a quantity of his meat and sausages in France and to be charged with contravening the domestic legislation. Once the case is before a court, he can request them to declare the legislation to be contrary to the provisions of Community law. The court will probably be reluctant to do this without a reference being made to the ECJ under Art 234. The discretion to make such a request under Art 234 belongs to the court alone, but having raised the matter of Community law, the court can either decide the point itself or make a reference. It may be in James's interest for the court to decide the matter itself, as a reference can take up to 18 months. Whatever the court decides to do, it is the principles of Community law outlined above which will be applied. It will be necessary to apply the principle of proportionality to ensure that the measures that go beyond what is strictly necessary to achieve the desired end are held to be contrary to Community law. It is therefore important to see how the ECJ has dealt with cases similar to James's.

With regard to the fact that the meat is labelled in English and not French, although this may be a marketing disadvantage for James, it should not stop him selling it in France. His meat is marketed in the UK and, therefore, under the second *Cassis* principle, it must be admitted to the French market. For the second point listed by the official, an obvious question is: why is it a requirement of French consumer protection that meat must be packed in particular weights? This measure appears to be indistinctly applicable, and since the *Cassis* case, it is necessary for any court hearing the case to apply the rule of reason to Art 28. Is the measure necessary to protect the mandatory requirement of consumer protection? If it is, then it will not breach Art 28.

However, the ECJ case law has shown that the word 'necessary' has been interpreted to mean no more than is necessary by applying the principle of proportionality. As indicated above, the German Government in the *Cassis* case did not succeed with their defence, because the consumer could have been protected by some other means. For example, in *Commission v Germany* (1989), German law on the meat content of sausages could not be enforced against imported sausages where there was no threat to health to invoke Art 30 (then Art 36). This was held to be in breach of Art 28 (then Art 30), because the objective could have been achieved by other means, such as labelling, which would be less of a hindrance to trade. Here again, it would seem that James can defeat any attempt by the French Government to justify the measure as being a mandatory requirement.

In *Commission v Germany* (1985), a case was brought against the German prohibition of additives in imported beer. The European Court held that the prohibition of marketing products containing additives authorised in the Member State of production, but prohibited in the Member State of importation, is permissible only if it complies with the requirements of Art 30 (then Art 36). But, the Court emphasised the last sentence of Art 30 (then Art 36), which states that such prohibitions should not constitute a means of arbitrary discrimination or a disguised restriction on trade between Member States. The Court concluded that the use of a specific additive which is authorised in another Member State must be authorised in the case of a product imported from that Member State.

It would seem that the French Government cannot use the domestic law to stop the importation of James's sausages.

In *Keck and Mithouard* (1993), the European Court had to deal with a reference concerning the prohibition in France of resale at a loss. Although the facts are not exactly as those affecting James, the Court's judgment is applicable. In clarifying its case law, the Court said that the application to products from other Member States of national provisions restricting or prohibiting certain selling arrangements was not such as to hinder directly or indirectly, actually or potentially, trade between Member States within the meaning of the *Dassonville* judgment. This was provided that those provisions applied to all affected traders operating within the national territory and affected them the same way, both legally and factually. In these circumstances, Art 28 is not breached and James can raise his prices to conform to the set minimum.

Question 25

Robson Pharmaceutical plc developed some time ago a new product to relieve flu symptoms and granted the right to sell under the Robson trade mark to two companies: one in Germany and one in The Netherlands. Robson Pharmaceutical plc kept the UK market and exports outside the European Economic Area (EEA).

Three months ago, the German company reported to Robson that their products were appearing on the German market. The goods had been purchased in the UK and Malaysia from pharmaceutical wholesalers and transported to Germany where the packaging had been altered to conform to German drug laws. The German price for the Robson product is 30% higher than the price in the UK.

Robson Pharmaceutical have discovered that an English company, PharmaJones Ltd, are responsible for the exports to Germany. They have complained to the UK Government, as have the German company to their Government, and a joint approach was made to the Commission to stop this movement under Art 30. Robson Pharmaceutical has also contacted PharmaJones Ltd direct, but their response was that any action against them would be contrary to the free movement of goods.

Advise Robson Pharmaceutical plc.

Answer plan

As you read this question, you should mark those passages which you feel cover the facts which are relevant to the law and make sure that you deal with them in your answer. The main points to cover are:

- Arts 28 and 29, stating the policy of free movement for imports and exports;
- the principles from *Cassis de Dijon*;
- derogation under Art 30;
- rights associated with trade marks;
- the Trade Mark Directive (89/104/EEC).

Answer

This question concerns the free movement of goods, one of the fundamental principles of the European Community. The Community is based upon a customs union which provides for a common customs tariff to goods coming from outside the EC and the removal of barriers to the free movement of goods within the EC. This applies to both imports (Art 28) and exports (Art 29) between Member States. These Articles are aimed at the governments of Member States, but have implications for individual business organisations. The EC does not want to have the situation where governments remove barriers, only for companies to organise their operations so as to set up new ones. If a number of companies operate in this way, competition policy under Arts 81 and 82 may be involved. However, in this problem, Robson Pharmaceutical plc do not appear to be acting in agreement with other undertakings or in a dominant position, so I will not look at the competition aspects of this problem in detail. What is more applicable is Art 30, which allows derogation from Arts 28 and 29 on specific grounds with the overall requirement that there is not an arbitrary discrimination or a disguised restriction on trade between Member States. The essential function of a trade mark is to guarantee to consumers the real origin of goods or services (*Arsenal Football Club plc v Reed* (2002)).

There is a presumption in favour of goods lawfully marketed in one Member State of the Community being accepted in another Member State. This was clearly stated in the second principle identified by the Court in the *Cassis de Dijon* case (1978). If a company or State is seeking to rebut that principle, it must prove that the conditions are such that Art 30 is applicable. This Article gives a number of grounds that are only available to the government of a Member State, for example, where it is claimed that restrictions are justified on the grounds of public policy or public security. However, it is possible for a business to seek derogation under Art 30 on the ground of 'protection of industrial and commercial property'. This includes such intellectual property rights as patents, copyright and trade marks. This supports the recognition given in the Treaty that property rights have not been affected by the establishment of the EC. Article 295 states that the Treaty shall in no way prejudice the rules in the Member States governing the system of property ownership.

If Robson Pharmaceutical plc are to achieve a solution to their problem, they must seek assistance from Art 30. How much protection will this Article give to them?

In *Deutsche Grammophon* (78/79), concerning copyright, the ECJ stated that Art 30 (then Art 36) permitted prohibitions or restrictions on the free movement of goods only to the extent that they were justified for the protection of the rights that form the specific subject matter of the property. In other words, it is necessary to look at what the owner of the property right is seeking to protect. Given that Art 295 (then Art 222) clearly states that property rights have not been affected by the Community, the Court could not dispute this. However, the Court went on to draw a distinction between the existence of industrial property rights and their exercise. It was this latter aspect of property rights which could interfere with the free movement of goods and which the Court wanted to ensure was not in conflict with the integration of the 'common market'. This principle does not only apply to copyright, but to all intellectual property.

In the pharmaceutical case of *Centrafarm BV v Winthrop BV* (16/74), a claim was made by Winthrop that their trade mark had been infringed. What right did the trade mark holder have? The Court held that they had the exclusive right to use the trade mark for the purposes of putting into circulation products protected by the trade mark for the first time. They might either do this themselves or transfer that right to a third party by way of licences, etc. Once the protected product has been put onto the market in a particular State by or with the consent of the owner, he can no longer be allowed to rely on his national property rights to prevent the importation of that product from that State into other Member States. The rights that are associated with the trade mark are exhausted. This doctrine of exhaustion of rights has been applied by the court to all types of property rights, including trade marks, patents and copyright – for example, see *Pharmacia & Upjohn SA v Paranova SA* (379/97).

In this problem, Robson Pharmaceutical are the owners of the trade mark and therefore have the rights described above. They exercise these rights themselves in certain countries, but have consented to two companies exercising this right on their behalf in Germany and Holland. If a product like flu remedy has been lawfully put onto the market with the owner's consent in one Member State, the importation of that product into another Member State cannot be restricted. This will apply even if, as in Robson Pharmaceutical's case, the purpose is to prevent parties taking advantage of price differences in different Member States. This is after all what was attempted in *Centrafarm v Winthrop*. (The emphasis in that case was to ask what makes a trade mark valuable – the reservation to the owner, through his exclusive right to put marked products into circulation, or the goodwill associated with the mark.)

There have been cases where importers have sought to take advantage of the price differentials which apply in different Member States and the exhaustion principle, but the product has had to be repackaged or labelled to meet the requirements of that particular market. This is what has happened in this problem to meet the specification of the German drug laws. In the case of *Hoffman-La Roche v Centrafarm* (102/77) a similar situation arose regarding the product 'Valium'. In the UK a subsidiary of the Roche group marketed the product in packages of 100 or 500 tablets at lower prices than in Germany.

Centrafarm purchased these UK products and repackaged them in 1,000 tablets, affixed the Hoffman-La Roche trade mark and sold them in Germany. Obviously, Hoffman-La Roche sought to protect what they saw as an infringement of their trade mark. In this important case, the ECJ laid down certain conditions which, if met by the importer, means that the repackager cannot be restrained by the trade mark holder from importing the product. The conditions illustrate the possibility that the holder of the trade mark may seek to organise the marketing of his product so as to constitute a disguised restriction on trade between Member States. In *Centrafarm v American Home Products* (3/78), the Court recognised this danger even though the use of different marks in the UK and The Netherlands could be justified under Art 30 (then Art 36). The importer in *Pfizer Inc v Eurim-Pharm GmbH* (1/81) followed these guidelines when importing Vibramycin tablets manufactured by Pfizer in the UK into Germany. In this case, the Court held that the plaintiff company could not rely on its trade mark and Art 30 (then Art 36) to prevent the importation under these circumstances.

However, the principle of 'exhaustion of rights' only applies within the Community. The ECJ has been concerned that individual Member States cannot create their own rules regarding exhaustion of rights where the goods are imported from outside the EC. In the important case of *Silhouette International* (335/96), the ECJ stated that the exhaustion of rights does not and cannot apply where goods placed on the market outside the EEA are brought into and sold within the EEA, which obviously includes the EC. The only exception to this appears to be where the trade mark owner can be said to have consented to the importation, circulation and sale. This was the view applied by the High Court in *Zino Davidoff SA v A&G Imports Ltd (No 1)*.

My advice to Robson Pharmaceutical plc is that they have a difficulty, in the sense that the ECJ has given a very narrow interpretation to Art 30, because it has given greater significance to the last sentence of the Article. Robson are seeking to protect their trade mark, whose essential function is to guarantee to consumers or final users the original identity of the marked product, so as to avoid confusion. They could bring an action in the national court seeking to enforce this right by a request for an injunction against PharmaJones Ltd and damages for the infringement of their right. However, as has been shown above, the ECJ has developed a clear principle in these cases in such examples as *Hoffman-La Roche v Centrafarm*. Whether the national court decides or makes a preliminary reference to the ECJ, it is this principle which will be applied. The problem does not indicate the form of the repackaging or what information is printed on it. However, it is clear from the question that PharmaJones Ltd did not communicate with Robson Pharmaceutical about their intention to repackage and import into Germany.

This is one of the conditions laid down in *Hoffman-La Roche v Centrafarm* and met successfully in the *Pfizer* case. It is possible that on PharmaJones Ltd failing to meet all the conditions, Robson Pharmaceutical may be able to protect how they currently operate if it is not considered to be a means of arbitrary discrimination or a disguised restriction on trade between Member States. If the repackaging had led to defacing or removal of important information, this form of repackaging would not be considered appropriate, as was decided in the *Zino Davidoff* case.

However if PharmaJones Ltd gives the appropriate notice, assuming the packaging is acceptable, they will then meet all the conditions laid down by the ECJ with regard to exhaustion of trade mark rights within the EC. However, the 'grey or parallel import' market is a very profitable one and is worldwide. Thus with regard to the importation from Malaysia the rights of the trade mark owner have not been exhausted and Robson Pharmaceutical can take action to enforce their rights, as happened in *Sebago Inc v GB Unic SA* (173/98) and *Bristol Myers Squibb v Parnova* (427/93).

Question 26

Analyse TWO of the following cases which came before the ECJ, and explain their importance in the development of Community law:

(a) *Cassis de Dijon* – Case 120/78;

(b) *Commission v Ireland* – Case 249/81;

(c) *Centrafarm v Sterling Drug* – Case 15/74.

Answer plan

When approaching a question like this, the temptation is to produce too descriptive an answer. The facts are important, but are only one element of the answer. You should try to deal with the following:

- the facts, the legal points raised and the decision of the Court;

- what kind of case was it? A preliminary reference or a direct action? What Article of the Treaty was it based upon?; and

- the cases chosen for this type of question have usually played their part in developing or reinforcing European Court judgments – what part has this case played?

(a) Cassis de Dijon – Case 120/78

This action was brought in a German court because of the application of a German law which forbade the marketing of liqueurs with a low alcohol content. The French liqueur called Cassis de Dijon had a maximum strength of 20% alcohol by volume, whereas German law required a minimum content of 25%. The French company claimed that the German law was contrary to Art 28 (then Art 30), as it interfered with the free movement of goods. Although the German authorities were not affecting the free movement of goods by imposing quotas, their actions were still covered by Art 28 (then Art 30). This is because the Article also forbids measures having an equivalent effect to quotas.

The German authorities claimed that the law did not discriminate against the French liqueur, as the same minimum content also applied to German producers. To allow the 'milder' French drink to be treated as a liqueur would lead to a reduction in alcohol content applied to German producers and thus a lowering standard. In order to avoid the application of Art 28 (then Art 30), the German Government had to plead Art 30 (then Art 36). This Article allows a government of a Member State to derogate from its obligations under Art 28 on such grounds as public policy, public morality, public security or the protection of the health and life of humans, animals and plants. Specifically, the German Government argued that its minimum standard law was aspired by the wish to protect the consumer from alcoholism, that is, public health. However, Art 30 ends by saying that it shall not be used as a means of disguised restriction of trade.

The ECJ said that, in the absence of common rules to the production and marketing of alcohol, it is for the Member State to regulate, in that they are necessary to satisfy fiscal supervision, the protection of public health, the defence of the consumer and the fairness of commercial transactions. These points were raised by the German Government. They said that public health was protected by fixing a minimum alcohol content, as beverages with a low alcohol content more easily induce a tolerance towards alcohol. There would be a general lowering of standards, as the lowest alcohol content permitted in any Member State would become the Community standard. This was rejected by the Court, as stronger beverages were generally consumed in a diluted form. They also rejected the claim that lower alcohol contents would lead to unfair practices against consumers.

As far as the Court was concerned, the requirements set by the German Government relating to the minimum alcohol content did not serve the general interest and interfered with the fundamental principle of the free movement of goods. It would be a much simpler matter to ensure that suitable information is conveyed to the purchaser by requiring the display of an indication of origin and of the alcohol content on the packaging of products.

(b) Commission v Ireland – Case 249/81

Faced with economic problems, the Irish Government announced in 1978 a programme to create jobs in Ireland's manufacturing and service industries. The main platform for this policy was to persuade individuals to purchase Irish goods. Supported by public funds, a 'Buy Irish' campaign was launched, involving the Irish Goods Council and the use of a 'Guaranteed Irish' symbol. In 1981, the European Commission delivered its Reasoned Opinion that the campaign was equivalent to a quantitative restriction in imports and in breach of Art 28 (then Art 30). This Article prohibits all quantitative restrictions on imports and all measures having equivalent effect. The concept of measures having an equivalent effect has been interpreted very generously by the Court, to include any activity capable of influencing the behaviour of traders.

The Reasoned Opinion is a requirement when the Commission is seeking to exercise its powers under Art 226 against a Member State which is failing to fulfil its obligations under the Treaty. It is the final step in the administrative stage before the Commission decides whether to take the Member State before the ECJ. The Reasoned Opinion has to provide details of the failure on the part of the Member State, the action required to be taken and the timescale in which this must be done.

The Irish Government argued that the campaign was not contrary to Art 28 (then Art 30). They did so by arguing that the prohibition only applies to measures which are binding. All that the campaign did was to give moral support and some financial aid for advertising the activities pursued by the Irish industries. The aid was compatible with Art 87 (then Art 92), which permits State aid to industry for such purposes as combating unemployment. They also claimed that there had been no restrictive effect on trade, as the campaign had failed. During the campaign, the proportion of Irish goods to all goods sold on the Irish market fell from 49.2% to 43.4%!

The Court rejected these arguments, because they believed that the Irish Government's considered intention was to substitute domestic products for imported products on the Irish market and thereby to check the flow of imports from other Member States. Even though the campaign did not have any significant success, the Court could not overlook the fact that the activities formed part of a government programme which was designed to achieve this substitution of domestic products for imported products and, as such, was liable to affect the volume of trade between Member States. The 'Buy Irish' campaign was discriminatory and had a potential effect on imports from other Member States as if it were one of a binding nature.

A measure like this cannot escape the prohibition laid down in Art 28 solely because it is not based on decisions which are binding on businesses.

Even measures which are not binding may be capable of influencing the conduct of traders and consumers and thus of frustrating the aims of the Community set out in Arts 2 and 3. The action of the Irish Government was a restrictive practice which represented the implementation of a programme defined by the Government and which affected the economy as a whole by encouraging the purchase of domestic products. Given that the Irish Government had provided some financial funding for the campaign, they were in breach of their obligations under the Treaty. The judgment in this case should not have come as a surprise to the Irish Government, as they had already been the subject of an Art 226 (then Art 169) action by the Commission in Case 113/80. In that case, the Court had held that the Irish Government had breached Art 28 (then Art 30) by imposing a legal requirement that imported 'souvenirs of Ireland' should bear either the name of their country of origin or the word 'foreign'.

(c) Centrafarm v Sterling Drug – Case 15/74

Sterling Drug was the parent company holding a number of patents in several countries, including The Netherlands and the UK, for a treatment of infections of the urinary passages. The trade mark Negram is used for this product. In the UK, the trade mark was the property of Sterling-Winthrop Group Ltd and, in The Netherlands, Winthrop BV, a subsidiary of the UK company.

Centrafarm imported into The Netherlands from England and Germany some of the medicinal preparations manufactured according to the patent method and put onto the market by subsidiaries of Sterling Drug, some of which carried the trade mark Negram. They did this without the agreement of Sterling Drug. By importing from the UK, Centrafarm had been able to take advantage of a considerable price differential. This was almost 50% of the price charged in The Netherlands.

In June 1971, Sterling Drug submitted an application to a Dutch judge sitting in chambers requiring Centrafarm to refrain from any further infringement of their patent. The judge refused, on the basis of his interpretation of the patent law. Sterling Drug succeeded on appeal, and the case finally came to the Dutch Supreme Court on appeal by Centrafarm. This court used the preliminary reference procedure of Art 234 (then Art 177) to ask certain questions on patent rights in relation to the provisions of the Treaty.

The European Court accepted that the main issue was whether the Treaty rules on the free movement of goods prevented the patentee from ensuring that the product protected by the patent is not marketed by others. It referred to Art 28 (then Art 30) and the prohibition on quantitative restrictions on imports and all measures having equivalent effect. However, it recognised that Art 30 (then Art 36) did allow such restrictions or prohibitions on the grounds justified for the protection of commercial or industrial property, which would include patents. This had to be read in conjunction with the last sentence of Art 30 (then Art 36), which states that such restrictions shall not constitute a means of arbitrary discrimination or a disguised restriction on trade between Member States.

Given that the EC Treaty does not interfere with property rights, the Court looked at the exercise of those rights. Article 30 allows for the derogation from one of the fundamental principles of the Community, but only where the derogation is justified for the purposes of safeguarding rights which constitute the specific subject matter of the property. What are these rights in relation to patents? The Court answered that the specific subject matter of a patent was the guaranteed right of the patentee, as a reward for their creative effort, to manufacture and put into circulation their product for the first time. This could be done directly by the company or by the grant of licences to third parties. In relation to this right, the patent holder could seek enforcement of their rights.

What the Court was concerned to do was not to allow the exercise of a patentee's right to interfere with the development of the Community. If the patentee could prevent the importation of protected products marketed by him or with his consent in another Member State, he would be able to partition off national markets and thereby restrict trade between Member States. Therefore, the action of Sterling Drug, given that it was not necessary to protect their exclusive rights flowing from their patent, was incompatible with the Treaty provisions concerning the free movement of goods. This principle has been applied in subsequent cases, especially where drug companies have sought to use their property rights to block parallel imports from other Member States.

CHAPTER 7

COMPETITION POLICY

Introduction

The competition policy of the European Community is seen as a very important safeguard to its development. Many of the questions set on this topic are of the problem type, notably on the application of Arts 81 and 82. However, there are possible essay questions on the main principles, as illustrated by some of the questions in this chapter. It is also possible for questions to be set which have a competition element and relate to the free movement of goods, for example, the Robson Pharmaceutical problem on p 102. In such circumstances, you can either split your answer between the topics or indicate the possible involvement of one but concentrate on the other.

Checklist

You should have a clear knowledge of the differences between Arts 81 and 82 and the role each plays in the competition policy of the EU.

More specifically, you should understand the following points:

- the type of agreements dealt with by Art 81;
- the possible exemptions under Art 81;
- the meaning of dominant position under Art 82;
- the control of mergers within the EU;
- the sanctions for anti-competitive behaviour;
- the control of public anti-competitive behaviour under Arts 87 and 88;
- the role and powers of the European Commission; and
- the remedies available, including those provided by the national courts.

Question 27

Dicero plc have been purchasing large quantities of manopull textiles from Smart International, a German company, for five years. They are the only manufacturers of this product and they control world sales by a system of licensing agreements.

Two years ago, they began imposing retail prices on all purchasers, including Dicero, and restricted the distribution areas any company could control. Dicero were allocated the UK market, whereas companies in France and Italy were given their domestic market plus a share of the world market.

For the last 12 months, Dicero have had discussions with Smart International to try to obtain some of the necessary export markets to allow for viable production levels. They have conceded nothing. In fact, they have stated that, unless Dicero sign a new agreement with them, they will give the UK market to the French company.

Advice Dicero.

Answer plan

This traditional problem question requires the application of Art 81, and the following specific points:

- the relationship between Community and national competition law;
- a definition of 'dominance' within the meaning of Art 82;
- factors associated with dominance in fact;
- abuse of a dominant position; and
- remedies.

Answer

This problem is concerned with one undertaking, Smart International, acting in a way which appears to be anti-competitive. The EU, having as one of its objectives the removal of barriers to trade between Member States, takes a strong policy against any undertaking which seeks to exercise economic power in the market in a way which sets up barriers to such trade. Under Art 82, monopolies in themselves are not prohibited, but it does prohibit certain anti-competitive conduct by such organisations. The Article applies to either goods or services and has a scope which is not limited to those businesses which are established in the EU.

It would seem that Dicero Products may have a remedy under this provision of the Treaty. If it can prove that Smart International are acting in breach of Art 82, such action is prohibited by the Article. In order to satisfy Art 82, three essential ingredients must be proved. The undertaking must have a dominant position in the market, there must be an abuse of that position and that abuse must affect trade between Member States. If this last requirement is not met, the matter is left to be dealt with by the national competition laws of the Member State concerned.

In order to prove that Smart International are in a dominant position, Dicero need to satisfy the definition of dominance laid down by the ECJ in *United Brands Co v Commission* (1976). This case involved United Brands' position in the banana market. The Court said that dominance means a position of economic strength enjoyed by an undertaking which enables it to prevent effective competition in the relevant market because its strength allows it to act independently of its competitors, customers and ultimately its consumers. The Commission added to this, in the *AKZO Chemie BV* case (1986), that it may also involve the ability to eliminate or seriously weaken existing competitors, or to prevent potential competitors from entering the market.

Although this is the principle of dominance, it has to be looked at more closely if the rules of the Court are to be satisfied. It may be possible to say that this is the way that Smart International are acting, but are they in a dominant position?

Specifically, what is the market in which Dicero are claiming that Smart International are dominant? This is not as straightforward as it may appear, as the European Commission has found when seeking to apply Art 82. It is necessary to identify the relevant market. As far as the Court and Commission are concerned, this is a matter of product substitution. In the *Continental Can* case (1972), a large Dutch packaging company was being taken over by a subsidiary of the Continental Can company based in the USA.

The Continental Can company was a large organisation in the packaging industry, controlling 86% of a German metal containers company, which it intended to transfer to the Dutch company if it acquired it. This would have meant that Continental Can would have had significant market power in Europe and specifically in Germany. However, although the Court agreed with the Commission that the takeover could be an abuse, the Commission had not looked at the relevant market. It had not taken into account product substitution. In other words, alternative suppliers of cans could adapt their production to produce cylindrical cans suitable for fish or those who purchased the cans could swap to a different shape or design. Such product substitution can be assessed by reference to the characteristics of the product, its price or the use to which it may be put. Are there any substitutes for manopull? What market is it in?

Although the Commission got the market wrong in *Continental Can*, in the bananas case of *United Brands* it satisfied the Court that the banana market was distinctive. In that case, United Brands had argued that the correct market was the fresh fruit market, in which they were not dominant. However, by means of information about buying habits of consumers and the special characteristics of bananas, the Commission was able to defeat this argument. Could Smart International argue that the consumer had alternative textiles to select from and therefore would not be disadvantaged by their actions? In the *Commercial Solvents* case (1974), the Court stated that Art 82 (then Art 86) was concerned not only with abuses which prejudiced consumers directly, but also those abuses which impair the competitive structure of the market and thus affect consumers indirectly. It would appear that Smart International's action falls into this type of category. The Commission, supported by judgments of the Court, takes a hard line in seeking to protect competition in manufacturing and, in particular, to prevent smaller firms suffering at the hands of more powerful competitors. We are not told the size of Smart International or Dicero, but even where the relevant market has been quite small, as in the *Hugin Cash Registers* case, Art 82 has been applied, provided an undertaking has been dominant in the particular market.

If it is assumed that it is possible to identify the relevant market, are Smart International behaving in a way which does not need to take into account their competitors, purchasers or consumers? In other words, are they dominant in fact? This requires a wide ranging economic analysis of the market and Smart International. Following previous Commission decisions, four factors are taken into account. The first of these, and the most important, is market share. How big a share of the market do Smart International have? Secondly, how long have Smart International held this position in the market? Obviously, the longer the period of time, the greater the barriers to entry for new competitors or entrants to the market will be. Thirdly, the financial and technological resources of Smart International: can they use their resources to use predatory pricing to undercut potential rivals or to maintain their technological advantage? Lastly, access to raw materials and outlets may give Smart International more power. Do they control not only raw materials and production, but also applications or retail outlets? This form of vertical integration within their business will be evidence of a dominant undertaking.

Finally, in order to come within Art 82, it must also be proved that Smart International are dominant within the common market or in a substantial part of it. We are told that Smart International control sales in the world but, more importantly, within the European Community by means of licensing agreements. It is clear, therefore, that this criterion is satisfied.

Having identified that there is a dominant position, this does not mean that Art 82 has been satisfied. It is not the fact that an undertaking is in a dominant position which is sufficient; Dicero must show that there has been an abuse.

Article 82 itself provides a number of examples of abuse. This list is not to be considered exhaustive, but it does illustrate what Dicero could prove. The problem states that Smart International are restricting the distribution area of each company granted a licence. More importantly, they have threatened to refuse to supply Dicero if it refuses to sign the agreement. The refusal to supply in *United Brands* was found to be an abuse. In *Commercial Solvents*, the anti-competitive refusal to supply also amounted to an abuse. This will not always be the situation if the refusal is based on objective criteria and is non-discriminatory. It does not appear that this would be the case with Smart International.

If an undertaking is found to be abusing its dominant position, there is no possibility of exemption as there is with restrictive practices under Art 81. Fines can be imposed by the Commission for breach of Art 82, ranging from 1,000 to 1 m euros, or 10% of the undertaking's turnover. Substantial fines have been imposed in the past, for example, 60 m euros in the *Polypropylene* case (1986). The threat over Dicero may make them reluctant to wait for action to be taken by the European Commission against Smart International. Article 82 is directly effective and can be applied in the national courts. There has been some reluctance in national courts to do this, because of the detailed economic analysis indicated above, which is often necessary with Art 82 cases. However, breach of Art 82 should lead to the application of the same remedies as are available for similar breaches of national law. Therefore, it would be appropriate for Dicero to seek an injunction or a declaration in interlocutory proceedings. As was indicated in *Garden Cottage Foods* (1984) by the House of Lords, English courts are reluctant to award damages in such cases.

Question 28

Jamesons Ltd are a small chain of retail chemists. Until five years ago, they owned eight shops, but they now have 30. As they have expanded in number, they have also increased the size of the shops. This allows them to offer a greater selection of merchandise for sale.

Recently, a problem has developed concerning the supply of perfume. Oddwax SA (Paris) refuse to supply any of their exclusive brands of perfume, because they claim that Jamesons Ltd are not one of their recognised distributors, and also that when supplies of Oddwax products have been obtained from third parties, Jamesons have sold them below the prices indicated by Oddwax.

Jamesons have written to Oddwax stating that they consider the refusal to be contrary to EC competition law, and that legal action will be taken, if necessary, to obtain supplies from Oddwax.

Oddwax have replied that they received a letter from the Commission three years ago about these matters which stated that 'on the information available the Commission can see no reason to intervene under Art 81', and had 'consequently closed the file'. Oddwax considered that this legitimised their activities.

Advise Jamesons.

Answer plan

This question concerns Art 81 and the kinds of restrictive practices which have been identified under EC competition policy as being anti-competitive.

You should cover the following points:

- the relationship between Arts 81 and 82;
- types of agreements covered by Art 81;
- the effect of Art 81;
- possible exemption under Art 81;
- comfort letters;
- the role of the national courts;
- remedies.

Answer

In the context of EC law, a possibility for Jamesons Ltd is to seek to utilise the competition policy of the Community. Under Arts 81 and 82, certain action is considered anti-competitive and therefore contrary to EC law. The Community is very concerned to safeguard legitimate competition undertaken by businesses such as Jamesons. It does this by dealing specifically with restrictive trade practices (Art 81) and monopoly situations (Art 82). The latter deals with 'an undertaking which is in a dominant position' in the market for particular goods and abuses that position. As Oddwax SA (Paris) do not appear to have such a position in the market, I will concentrate on Art 81.

Article 81 provides a very broad base of liability, subject to the possibility of exemption. It covers agreements which have as their object or effect the prevention, restriction or distortion of competition within the common market. Is there an agreement between Oddwax and its distributors which is making it difficult for Jamesons to get supplies? The agreement does not have to be a formal written one to fall within Art 81, because it also covers concerted practices, which include 'gentlemen's agreements'. In *ICI v EC Commission* (1972), the ECJ defined such practices as a form of co-ordination between enterprises that has not yet reached the point where there is a contract in the true sense of the word, but which in practice consciously substitutes a practical co-operation for the risk of competition. Therefore, because there are a number of recognised distributors for Oddwax products, there must be an agreement between the parties, even if we are not told what form it takes.

It is clear that such agreements come within the scope of Art 81, but are they amongst those which are identified as being incompatible with the common market? Article 81 lists a number of examples of such agreements which impede the free movement of goods or services throughout the Community and thus distort competition with the market. The list is not exhaustive, but it does include one which seems to apply to the situation facing Jamesons Ltd.

This is where the agreement directly or indirectly fixes purchase or selling prices or any other trading conditions. It would seem from this that there is one aspect of the problem facing Jamesons which is covered, namely, selective distribution agreements. This is the term used by the European Commission for sales conducted through a network of authorised dealers or outlets. Only certain selected dealers are admitted to the network, and only they may receive supplies. This type of agreement is often very attractive to manufacturers because, quite legitimately, it gives them control over the way in which their product is sold, and can help them maintain an upmarket image. However, it is also a way of maintaining high retail prices. It is stated in the problem that one of the reasons for Oddwax refusing to supply Jamesons is the fact that they had previously sold the products at below the price indicated by Oddwax. If an agreement comes within Art 81, it is automatically void. This means that the agreement can only be implemented at the risk of the parties to it. It can also mean that if action is taken by the European Commission under the procedure of Regulation 17/62, the parties to the agreement, notably Oddwax in this problem, could be heavily fined by the Commission. The fine could amount to 1 m euros, or 10% of the company's worldwide turnover, whichever is the greater.

However, although Art 81 states that all such agreements are void, it gives the power to the Commission to grant exemptions. What the Commission looks for in the agreement is a contribution to the improvement of production or distribution of goods, or the promotion of technical or economic progress, with the proviso that customers are allowed a fair share of the resulting benefit. It is also necessary that the restrictions in the agreement go no further than is necessary for the objectives to be achieved and it does not provide the possibility of eliminating competition in respect of a substantial part of the products in question. If Oddwax had sought an individual exemption, they would have had to prove that the agreement with the outlets met these conditions. However, obtaining an individual exemption is a lengthy process, so the European Commission introduced various block exemptions which allow the parties to draft their agreements to fall outside the scope of Art 81. However, although there have been eight regulations issued granting exemptions, none would apply to this problem. In the letter received by Jamesons from Oddwax, reference is made to the comment from the Commission that, on the information available, it saw no reason to intervene under Art 81 and had closed the file. This does not mean that an exemption has been granted. It is more likely to be what is termed a 'comfort letter'. These were introduced by the Commission in an attempt to reduce its workload and to speed up the decision making process. However, it has been held by the ECJ to be merely an administrative letter and not binding on the national courts because it is outside the framework of Regulation 17/62. This was stated by the Court in a number of judgments referred to as the *Perfume* cases (1980). The file indicated to be closed three years ago by the Commission can be re-opened, especially when new information or a change in circumstances is brought to its attention.

It would seem that the refusal by Oddwax to supply Jamesons is contrary to Art 81 and does not fall within any possible exemption. Under European Community competition law, the Court has introduced the *de minimis* principle. This states that, to come within Art 81, competition must be affected to a noticeable extent, judged by taking into account the position of the parties, indicated by their size and share of the market. If the principle applies, then Art 81 will not be breached and Jamesons must look to national law to provide a remedy. However, it is unlikely on the facts in the problem that it will apply in this case. Is there any action open to Jamesons? It would be possible to complain to the European Commission on the expectation that they will utilise the machinery under Regulation 17/62 to enforce Art 81. However, this will be a lengthy business and a speedier remedy should be considered. Jamesons have threatened legal action, so this may be a possibility. As the 'comfort letter' mentioned above is not legally binding, it is not possible to go to the ECJ to seek its annulment under Art 230, but national courts are required to apply Art 81 as it is directly effective, thus providing the best course of action for Jamesons. The national court will be able to use the European rule of reason devised by the ECJ to decide if the agreement is compatible with Art 81. If it is found to be incompatible by the Court, then it is void, because only the European Commission can grant an exemption, not the Court. Thus the remedies available in national courts for breach of Art 81 are those remedies available for similar breaches of national law (*Rewe-Zentralfinanz* (1976)), although the Court will not have the power to order fines. In the case of Jamesons, the remedy will be an injunction or a declaration in interlocutory proceedings. In the UK, the possibility of the court awarding damages to Jamesons is unclear. In *Garden Cottage Foods Ltd v Milk Marketing Board* (1984), the House of Lords left it unclear as to whether a breach of Art 81 (then Art 85) could give rise to a remedy in damages. However, recent cases following on from *Francovich* may provide a new opportunity to the House of Lords to reconsider this view.

Question 29

Critically review the powers of the Commission under the competition law of the EU.

Answer plan

This straightforward essay question requires the following points to be covered:

- what is the basis of the EU competition policy?;
- Arts 81 and 82–86;
- procedures under Regulation 17/62;

- power to issue decisions and levy fines;
- control of the Commission's exercise of powers via actions for annulment (Art 230) and damages (Art 288).

Answer

According to the European Commission, competition is the best stimulant of economic activity, since it guarantees the widest possible freedom of action. The Treaty does not define the concept of 'competition', but refers to certain measures which interfere with competition and are therefore prohibited, subject to exemptions granted by the Commission. Thus, Art 3(f) sets, as one of the objectives of the Community, the institution of a system ensuring that competition in the common market is not distorted. Competition policy is another instrument which the Community can use to ensure that objectives set out in the Treaty are obtained, for example, that economic integration will take place to produce 'one common market'.

The chapter of the Treaty dealing with competition contains mainly two sets of rules, reflecting the private and public economic activity which takes place. Articles 81 and 82 apply to enterprises which might be involved in restrictive practices or which are abusing a dominant position within the market. Articles 87 and 88 cover aid granted by Member States. The European Commission has a central role in enforcing Community competition policy. It has the power to issue decisions which, under the definitions in Art 249, are binding upon those to whom they are addressed.

The Commission's powers relate to four main areas. It has the power to collect information, to grant exemptions under Art 81, to impose fines and to make interim measures. The powers it has and the procedures it must follow are laid down in Regulation 17/62. These substantial powers are necessary if the Commission is to fulfil its role. However, the procedural requirements are strict under Regulation 17/62, and there is a general duty of confidentiality. A breach of these duties or procedures can result in an action being brought under Art 230 before the ECJ, and ultimately, the Commission decision can be annulled. It is also possible for an action for damages to be brought against the Commission, as happened in the *Adams* case (1986). Adams brought an action under Art 288 (then Art 215) against the Commission for breach of confidentiality when it allowed the fact that he had assisted the Commission to be disclosed to his employers, Hoffman-La Roche.

With regard to Art 81, dealing with restrictive practices, the Commission's task is to monitor agreements with a view to granting negative clearance or exemption. This is done on the basis of information supplied by the applicant and other parties.

The Commission has the power to impose fines of up to 5,000 euros where applicants intentionally or negligently supply incorrect or misleading information. The power of granting exemptions under Art 81 is only given to the Commission. Before doing so, the Commission must publish a summary of the relevant application or notification and all interested parties must be invited to submit their comments. If the final decision is adverse to the applicant, the Commission must give him an opportunity to be heard on the matters to which he objects. Owing to the need to speed up the process of considering applications for exemption, the Commission has issued a number of block exemptions, which allow undertakings to arrange their business affairs so as not to be in breach of competition policy.

In order to make a decision related to Community competition policy, the Commission normally needs further information in order to come to an opinion on the legality of the behaviour in question. There are two basic ways to obtain this information: either by investigations or by written requests for information. For example, if the Commission is investigating the behaviour of a dominant firm, it may write not only to the company concerned, but also to the smaller undertakings who have dealings with the company.

If the replies from the undertakings are incorrect or incomplete, the Commission has the right to impose fines of up to 5,000 euros. On some occasions, it is necessary to undertake detailed market analysis, and to this end the Commission has been given exhaustive powers. The Commission may conduct general inquiries into whole sectors of the economy if economic trends suggest that competition within the common market is being restricted or distorted. To achieve this task, the Commission may request every undertaking in a particular sector to supply details of agreements or concerted practices considered exempt. Undertakings or groups which may be in a dominant position may also be required to supply information concerning their structure and practices. Additional information may be requested from governments or competent authorities in Member States. In all these instances, the Commission may request any information which it considers 'necessary' to enable it to carry out its tasks. In addition to requesting information, the Commission may seek it by carrying out on-the-spot investigations. These include the power to enter premises, examine books or business records, to copy such records and to conduct oral examinations. These investigations may be 'voluntary' or 'compulsory'. Where they are compulsory, Commission officials are required to produce written authority in the form of a Decision, specifying the subject matter and purpose of the investigation. Normally, the Commission will resort to an unannounced visit where a serious risk exists that the undertakings, if forewarned of the inspection, will destroy any incriminating evidence. In *National Panasonic* (1980), a 'dawn raid' had taken place at National

Panasonic's offices, with a search and seizure operation taking place before the company's lawyers could arrive. National claimed that, although the raid was authorised by a decision under Regulation 17/62, some prior warning should have been given. The ECJ, hearing an action under Art 230 (then Art 173) to have the decision annulled, disagreed. It held that, under the regulation, the Commission was entitled to undertake such investigations as are necessary to bring to light any breaches of Arts 81 and 82 (then Arts 85 and 86). However, it is for the Court to control the investigative powers of the Commission, as was stated in another case involving a 'dawn raid' (*Hoechst* (1989)). In some instances, the Commission may request the competent authority of the Member State, such as the Office of Fair Trading, to carry out necessary investigations on its behalf. All undertakings are bound to comply with the legitimate demands of the Commission, even if the information is self-incriminating. If they fail to co-operate, or give false or misleading information, they are liable to penalties.

Obviously, in the exercise of its powers to collect information a great deal of commercially sensitive data comes before the Commission officials. The Commission has a general duty of confidentiality and must have regard to the legitimate interests of undertakings in protecting their business secrets. However, the ECJ held, in *AKZO Chemie v Commission* (1976), that it is for the Commission to decide which particular documents contain business secrets. The Commission has to issue a decision informing the undertaking, if it intends to communicate documents containing alleged secrets to third parties. This allows the undertaking to challenge the decision before the ECJ.

The Commission has the power to impose fines of up to 1 m euros, or 10% of the world annual turnover of the undertaking, whichever is the larger, where Art 81 or Art 82 has been infringed. This applies whether the infringement has arisen intentionally or negligently. The amount of the fine will depend upon the seriousness of the behaviour, its duration and the size of the undertaking involved. A deliberate infringement will normally deserve a heavier fine than where an undertaking has been purely negligent. The Commission has not been hesitant in using its power to impose fines. In the *Pioneer Hi-Fi* case (1980), a fine of almost 7 m ECU was imposed for a breach of Art 81 (then Art 85(1)), although it was subsequently reduced on appeal to the Court. Any fine levied is paid to the Commission and none of it goes to the injured victim of the anti-competitive practice. They must seek a remedy in their national courts. The Court of First Instance, under Art 229, has unlimited jurisdiction with regard to fines. Where the amount of the fine is being challenged, this will normally be done by way of proceedings under Art 230 to annul the decision imposing it.

The work of the Commission with regard to competition policy raises complex issues, which may take up to two years to be resolved. In some instances, such a delay may cause irreparable damage to some of the undertakings. To deal with this possibility, the Commission is given the power to take immediate action in the form of interim measures to stop objectionable behaviour. This power was implied by the Court under Regulation 17/62 in the *Camera Care* case (1980). These measures are of a temporary nature aimed at safeguarding the status quo. The Court of First Instance has also introduced an expedited procedure to hear cases 'within months' to assist in this process.

It can be seen that, in relation to the competition policy of the European Community, the Commission does have very wide powers. In the exercise of these powers, the Commission is subject to the law of the Community, including the general principles of Community law which have been identified by the Court. The Court of First Instance has the power to confirm, reduce, cancel or increase fines and penalty payments imposed by the Commission. As all legally binding actions by the Commission are required to be made by decisions, these can be challenged before the ECJ via an action under Art 230. There is, therefore, clear judicial control of the Commission to ensure that it exercises its powers within Community law. Recent cases have seen Commission Decisions annulled by the CFI because the Court was not satisfied with the economic analysis of the anti-competition effects produced by the Commission (*Tetra Laval BV and Schneider Electric SA* (2002)). Given the identified need in Art 3(f) to have a machinery to ensure that competition within the Community is not distorted, the powers given to the Commission are necessary to achieve this, but the practical difficulties are large.

Note

This answer concentrates on the powers associated with Arts 81 and 82. It would be possible to concentrate more on Arts 87 and 88, although most of the powers of the Commission are exercised against private undertakings.

Question 30

What is meant by 'an abuse of a dominant position'?

Answer plan

This is a very popular type of question. It is straightforward, but you should cover the following points:

- Art 82 and the EU competition policy;
- the role of the Commission;
- definition of 'dominant position' from *Continental Can*; and
- the decision in *United Brands*.

Answer

The term 'dominant position' is associated with Art 82 and the policy against anti-competitive behaviour by businesses. There is nothing in Community law which does not allow for a dominant position to be established. What Art 82 is concerned with is the abuse of that dominant position within the common market or a substantial part of it. It is designed to restrain the conduct by a dominant firm that harms those with whom it deals. Such an abuse is prohibited, in so far as it may affect trade between Member States.

In *Continental Can* (1972), the Commission defined its view of a dominant position. It said that undertakings are in a dominant position when they have the power to behave independently without taking into account their competitors, purchasers or suppliers. This arises due to the undertaking's share of the market or because of the availability of technical knowledge, raw materials or capital in addition to market share. It does not mean that there should be an absolute domination, in the sense that the undertaking can eliminate all other competitors. It is enough that their market strength allows them an overall independence of behaviour. The concept of dominance was developed further in *AKZO Chemie BV* (1986), in which the Commission stated that the ability to eliminate or seriously weaken existing competitors or to prevent potential competitors from entering the market may be involved in a dominant position.

In *Continental Can*, the Court insisted that the Commission analyse an undertaking's market power in two steps. First, it needed to define the relevant market and, secondly, it should assess their dominance within that market. This is not an easy exercise, because markets are not always easy to identify. If the market is given a narrow definition, perhaps ignoring the possible substitutes available, it may indicate a large market share, which overstates the market power of the undertaking's product. If a wide definition is given to the market, the undertaking's market share is understated. The Court is quite stringent in requiring the Commission to define the relevant market and to give reasons for its definition. In the *Continental Can v Commission* case, the Commission's finding that the Continental Can company was in a dominant position over the supply of cans and closures used for meat and fish products was not accepted by the Court.

The main problem was that the Commission had not paid sufficient attention to substitute products. The meat and fish suppliers could turn to glass or plastic containers, or the manufacturers of cylindrical cans could move towards the production of the flat cans traditionally used for meat and fish products. In the *United Brands* case, the company sought to prove that the Commission had got the market wrong once more. However, the Court accepted that the Commission was right in identifying the relevant market as that of bananas. Although United Brands said that the relevant market was that of fresh fruit, in which they were not dominant, the Commission showed that bananas were consumed particularly by the very young, the old and the sick and were little affected by the pricing and consumption of other fruit.

It is clear that establishing dominance within a particular product market requires detailed economic analysis. From this analysis, a number of factors are used to determine dominance. The market share held by the undertaking is a crucial factor when determining dominance. In the *Continental Can* case, for example, the company had 80% of the German market. *United Brands* had 45% of the banana market, so it is possible to see the wide variation in market share which can be involved. The Commission considers that a share of between 20–40% may amount to dominance in certain markets. The period of time in which the undertaking has held its position in the market will be important. What are the financial and technical resources of the 'dominant' undertaking? Can it eliminate competitors by intensive advertising campaigns or by predatory pricing? The access to raw materials and markets can also be important. In the *United Brands* case, the company was vertically integrated, owning plantation, shipping, storage and distribution businesses for bananas. In *Commercial Solvents*, the company, which refused to supply another Italian company with aminobutanol, had a near-monopoly in its production. The refusal to supply in this case is an example of the final factor which may determine dominance, namely, the behaviour of the firm. A firm's behaviour may indicate that it is dominant within the definition given above from the *Continental Can* case, that is, it is able to act independently of its competitors, customers and, ultimately, consumers. Another example would be the discriminatory pricing system used by United Brands.

Article 86 is only infringed where dominance is within the common market or a substantial part of it. It is not entirely clear how large an area, or what proportion of supply, amounts to a 'substantial part of the common market'. In *Sugar* (1975), the Court stated that the pattern and volume of the production and consumption of a particular product as well as the habits and economic opportunities of vendors and purchasers must be considered. The Commission provided some useful guidance on the relevant geographical market in its Notice on Agreements of Minor Importance, where it noted that the cost of transport is particularly important. It is also necessary to consider the temporal aspect when looking at the question of dominance. The time of year can have a large impact on a particular market, especially when looking at fresh produce.

As indicated earlier, it is not the dominance in fact which Art 82 is designed to deal with, but the abuse of that dominant position. What amounts to an abuse under Art 82? The Article itself does give some examples of anti-competitive behaviour, but the list is not intended to be exhaustive. There are two main categories of abuse: exploitative and anti-competitive. Exploitative abuses arise where the dominant undertaking takes advantage of its position by imposing harsh or unfair trading conditions. The most common examples of these are unfair prices, unfair trading conditions, discriminatory treatment and refusal to supply. Unfair price was defined in *United Brands* as a price which bears no reasonable relation to the economic value of the product. Although the Court did not state its opinion on the point, the Commission argued that United Brands were charging excessively high prices for its Chiquita brand of bananas. When United Brands refused to allow importers to sell the bananas when they were still green, they were found to be imposing unfair trading conditions. This was despite United Brands' argument that they imposed this requirement to ensure that the consumer obtained a better product. Some of the prices charged by United Brands differed by up to 100% in different Member States, such was their power to impose discriminatory pricing. Finally, United Brands refused to supply one of its main customers who had invested heavily in the appropriate plant and buildings, because it had taken part in an advertising campaign for a competitor. Such is the power of the undertaking in a dominant position.

Anti-competitive abuses are less easy to prove than exploitative abuses. They are not usually so harsh, but they have the same effect, in that they reduce or eliminate competition, for example, the tying-in agreement which came before the Court in *Hoffman-La Roche* (1977). This undertaking had a dominant position in seven separate vitamin markets. Customers undertook to buy all or most of their requirements from La Roche as part of tying-in agreements. As a 'reward', such companies received fidelity rebates in the form of discounts. The agreements also included 'English' clauses, which allowed a customer who found suppliers offering similar products elsewhere to ask La Roche to match these prices. If La Roche failed to do so, the company was free to purchase the products elsewhere. Although not oppressive for the companies concerned, the Commission found that these tying-in agreements limited their customers' freedom to buy from alternative suppliers. Once the alternative suppliers had been identified, La Roche was of a size to be able to take pre-emptive action to remove its competitor. Both the Commission and the Court found these practices to be abusive.

The kind of predatory pricing used by La Roche is another example of anti-competitive abuse. In *AKZO Chemie BV* (1986), a firm in a dominant position in the production of organic peroxides, used this strategy where prices are reduced below cost, in order to drive potential competitors out of the market. Other examples of anti-competitive abuse include refusal to supply, exclusive reservation of activities and import and export bans. In *Continental Can*, the Commission applied Art 82 (then Art 86) in the context of a proposed merger or takeover. The Commission's decision said that the proposed takeover constituted an abuse of their dominant position within the common market, that is, in Germany. Such a case is unlikely to happen now under Art 82, as there is now Regulation 4064/89, a special measure to deal with mergers and acquisitions.

Question 31

Analyse TWO of the following cases which came before the ECJ, and explain their importance in the development of Community law:

(a) *Consten and Grundig v Commission* – Cases 56 and 58/64;

(b) *ICI (Dyestuff)* – Case 48/69;

(c) *United Brands* – Case 27/76.

Answer plan

When approaching a question like this, the temptation is to produce too descriptive an answer. The facts are important, but are only one element of the answer. You should deal with the following:

* the facts, the legal points raised and the decision of the Court;

* what kind of case was it? A preliminary reference or a direct action? What Article of the Treaty was it based upon?; and

* the cases chosen for this type of question have usually played their part in developing or reinforcing European Court judgments – what part has this case played?

Answer

(a) Consten and Grundig v Commission – Cases 56 and 58/64

This case concerns attempts by private traders to carve up the internal market in the face of one of the fundamental objectives of the Community: the removal of national barriers to trade. Consten was a French firm which specialised in acting as wholesalers for electrical products. Grundig was a German firm which manufactured radio, television sets and similar products in Germany. The reason the two cases are joined is because they both arose from the exclusive distribution contract made between the two businesses in 1957. Under this contract, Grundig promised not to deliver to any other French distributor and to include in any contract they entered into with other firms elsewhere a clause preventing their goods from being transferred to France. Consten promised in return to buy Grundig's products, and not from any other competitors, and not to deliver outside France. One final fact was that the products subject to the contract all carried the trade mark GINT, that is, Grundig International. Consten registered this mark in France with Grundig's consent.

Two important events happened subsequent to this contract in 1957. First, in 1958, the Treaty of Rome, setting up the European Community, came into force and with it the Articles dealing with anti-competitive activity. In 1962, Regulation 17 was adopted, which provided the machinery for the Commission to deal with any anti-competitive behaviour. Under this regulation, agreements like the one between Grundig and Consten had to be registered. This was done by Grundig. Secondly, also at this time, French competitors were getting Grundig products into France and selling them at lower prices. Consten had sued a number of these businesses in the French courts for unfair competition and infringement of their trade mark.

Acting under Regulation 17, the Commission, in 1964, took a decision addressed to Grundig and Consten stating that their contract was in breach of Art 81 (then Art 85(1)). They were forbidden to hinder the acquisition by competitors of the goods covered by the contract for resale in France. The firms wished to challenge these decisions, which they did under Art 230 (then Art 173) in an action for annulment. Article 81 prohibits agreements which may affect trade between Member States and which have as their object or effect the prevention, restriction or distortion of competition within the common market. Grundig and Consten claimed that they were not competitors and so there was never any question of them promising not to compete with each other. Supported by the Italian Government, they argued that the word 'agreement' in Art 81 (then Art 85) only applied to contracts between competitors at the same level – horizontal agreements. However, the

Court held that Art 81 (then Art 85) refers in a general way to all agreements which distort competition within the common market. Therefore, as the Treaty does not make a distinction between the level at which the firms operate or whether they are competitors or not, such a distinction cannot be implied into the Treaty. Competition can be distorted within the meaning of Art 81 by agreements which prevent or restrict competition between one of them and third parties. The contract created an unjustified advantage at the expense of the consumer, contrary to the aims of Art 81.

The firms also argued that the Art 81 reference to 'affect' meant affect in a detrimental way, for the worse. The contract, they argued, strengthened Grundig and allowed for greater competition between them and their rival manufacturers. The Court held that what is important is whether the agreement is capable of constituting a threat, either direct or indirect, actual or potential, to freedom of trade between Member States in a manner which might harm the attainment of the objectives of a single market between States. Thus, the fact that the agreement encouraged an increase in the volume of trade between States is not sufficient to exclude the possibility that the agreement may 'affect' such trade, especially as Consten was prohibited from re-exporting to other Member States.

The final argument put forward against the Commission's decision was that Consten owned the trade mark in France. Under Art 295 (then Art 222), it is stated that the Treaty does not prejudice the rules in Member States governing the system of property ownership. Yet, the Commission's decision had stopped Consten's use of its trade mark protection to prevent parallel imports of Grundig products. The Court's view was that the GINT trade mark was intended to place an obstacle in the way of parallel imports. As the agreement is void under Art 81 (then Art 85(2)), this would be ineffective if the trade mark could still be used by Consten to achieve the same objective. There is a distinction between the rights inherent in a trade mark, which are recognised by Art 295, and the exercise of those rights. The rights of the owner of a trade mark are limited, to the extent that the exercise of those rights may infringe Art 81.

(b) ICI Ltd v EC Commission – Case 48/69

This case, which is often called the *Dyestuff* case, involves the competition policy of the European Community and, in particular, Art 81. This Article is concerned with restrictive practices arising from agreements and concerted practices which affect trade between Member States. However, what amounts to a concerted practice was one of the key questions in this case.

ICI was among the undertakings producing aniline dyestuffs who together accounted for 85% of the market. There had been three uniform price increases introduced almost simultaneously in 1964, 1965 and 1967. The increases covered the same product. In January 1964, there was a 10% increase, followed in autumn 1964 by a 10–15% increase which was to come into effect in January 1965. At a meeting in Basle in August 1967, one of the producers announced an 8% increase and two other producers subsequently announced a similar increase. The Commission concluded that there had been a concerted practice between the undertakings, and using its powers to enforce the Community's competition policy it imposed fines on all the undertakings involved. The undertakings challenged the Commission's decision by a direct action before the European Court under Art 230 (then Art 173). They claimed that the price increases merely reflected parallel behaviour associated with an oligopolistic market, where each producer followed the price leader.

The Court upheld the Commission's decision. In its judgment, the Court stated that the inclusion of concerted practices in addition to agreements between undertakings in Art 81 (then Art 85) was for a specific purpose. The object is to bring within the prohibition of the Article a form of co-ordination between undertakings which, without having reached the stage where an agreement properly so called has been concluded, knowingly substitutes practical co-operation between them for the risks of competition. The behaviour of the participants is therefore important, because it is that which is identified as the concerted practice. However, the Court recognised that this behaviour could not be conclusive, but it was strong evidence to suggest that the market was not 'operating normally', having regard to the nature of the products, the size and number of undertakings involved and the market volume they controlled. This idea of the 'normal conditions' of the market has been criticised, as it does not take into account the type of activity which occurs in oligopolistic markets, although on the facts of the case it is very difficult to find any support for the dyestuff producers.

The identification of a concerted practice requires the evidence provided by the Commission to be considered as a whole, taking into account the parties involved and the specific features of the market for the product in question, that is, the freedom of the consumers to choose their supplier. In this instance, the general and uniform increase in prices can only be explained by a common intention on the part of the undertakings. This intention was to adjust the price level and to avoid the risk which could accompany such price increases of changing the conditions of competition.

(c) United Brands – Case 27/76

United Brands Co is a conglomerate owned by a company based in the USA. It is the world's largest seller of bananas. In the opinion of the European Commission, United Brands holds a dominant position in the banana market in a substantial part of the European Community. This is based upon the fact that it handles 40% of the trade in bananas in the EC and has overwhelming economic power based upon the vertical integration of its banana business. United Brands owns numerous plantations in tropical banana-growing countries and a fleet of refrigerated banana boats. In addition, it controls banana ripening in consumer countries and takes direct charge of the advertising campaigns and sales promotion activities related to its brand, Chiquita. It is the only firm to have all these advantages in the banana market, and is thus in a position to use them to place major obstacles in the way of effective competition in the banana market.

The European Commission reached the decision that United Brands was abusing its dominant position, contrary to Art 82 (then Art 86). This was based upon a number of points, including:

(a) United Brands prohibited its distributors and ripeners from selling green bananas, which meant there was market fragmentation;

(b) it charged its customers prices which differed according to the Member State in which they were located. Such differences could amount to 100%, although there were no objective reasons for this discrimination;

(c) it charged unfair prices for sales to its customers in Germany, Denmark and the Benelux countries; and

(d) finally, for no objectively valid reason, it refused, for nearly two years, to supply one of its main Danish customers.

The Commission considered these to be serious violations of Art 82 (then Art 86) and imposed a heavy fine of 1 m euros and ordered United Brands to put an end to its infringements. The importance of this case lies in the fact that the Commission investigated United Brands' entire marketing policy in the light of Art 82, perhaps because of the problems it had experienced in the *Continental Can* case (1972). They were not attacking the commercial dynamism of United Brands, which is not contrary to Art 82, but because a dominant firm has an obligation not to indulge in business practices which are at variance with the goals of the Community's competition policy. It is not being in a dominant position which is contrary to Art 82, but the abuse of that position.

United Brands appealed to the European Court against the decision of the Commission, seeking its annulment under Art 230 (then Art 173). They claimed that the 'relevant market' identified by the Commission was too narrow and should have been the fresh fruit, rather than the banana market. The Court upheld the Commission's choice of bananas as the relevant market. However, it quashed the Commission's decision that United Brands' prices were excessive, because the Commission should at least have asked United Brands about its costs. Overall, the Court upheld the Commission's decision, including its condemnation of United Brands' refusal to supply, although the fine was reduced to 850,000 euros. The definition of a dominant position given in the Court's judgment has been followed very closely in subsequent cases involving infringements of Art 82. The definition is that a dominant position involves economic strength which enables an undertaking to prevent effective competition and to act independently of its competitors, customers and ultimately of consumers.

Question 32

Critically review the Commission's application of the Merger Directive.

Answer plan

It is quite rare to have a problem question set on mergers, although this may change as the case law on the Merger Regulation develops. Where questions are set they are generally this type of essay. The main points which should be covered in your answer are:

- the role of Arts 81 and 82 (formerly Arts 85 and 86 EC) in merger policy;
- the need for a specific merger policy;
- the Merger Regulation 4064/89 as amended by Regulation 1310/97;
- the requirements of the Regulation;
- the benefits of the Regulation;
- the case law of the Court of First Instance with regard to the Merger Regulation.

Answer

Although the competition policy of the EC has a strong emphasis towards restrictive practices or the abuse of a dominant position, these are not the only activities that EC law seeks to control. There are also activities of Member States or mergers of public companies that can be seen to be anti-competitive. EC law seeks to control or limit these in so far as they impact on the Community. The competence to deal with mergers is given to the Commission under Regulation 4064/89. This regulation has been amended by Regulation 1310/97 to facilitate greater procedural harmony in the assessment of different types of concentrations. If a proposed merger qualifies as a concentration, the next question is whether it has a 'Community dimension'. The test for this is one of sales or turnover. Initially the worldwide turnover specified was 5 m euros but Regulation 1310/97 has reduced this and in so doing has increased the supervision role of the Commission over mergers. The new Art 1(3) provides that those mergers involving a worldwide turnover of 2,500 m euros where the aggregate Community turnover is more than 100 m euros will be subject to examination by the European Commission. Such mergers must be notified to the Commission.

Mergers can be categorised into horizontal, vertical and conglomerate mergers. Horizontal mergers arise where companies make the same products and operate in the same level of the market. Vertical mergers are those where the undertakings operate at different levels but in the same product market. Lastly, conglomerate mergers are where there is no connection between the businesses in any product market. With regard to the impact on competition, it is horizontal mergers that have the most damaging potential.

It is the European Commission that has the responsibility to police the competition policy of the European Community, including that relating to mergers. Within the Competition Directorate DG IV, there is the Merger Task Force (MTF), which oversees merger control within the EC. For the policy to be effective there has to be notification by the companies concerned. Article 4(1) of Regulation 4064/89 as amended requires such notification to the MTF and failure to do so can lead to fines being imposed under Art 14(1)(a). Where the MTF considers that the notification falls within the ambit of the Merger Regulation, it must publish that notification. The MTF can instigate an investigation into the proposed merger or concentration, during which time the merger should be suspended. Failure to do so can lead to a heavy fine being imposed by the Commission (Art 14(2)).

The investigation by the MTF is conducted in two stages. In the first stage the MTF can decide under Art 6(1) whether the concentration is outside the regulation. The second stage arises where the Commission has serious doubts about the compatibility of the merger or concentration with the common market. Article 8 of the regulation provides a number of options for the Commission, including finding that the merger or concentration does not in fact breach the criteria by which such matters are judged. The regulation states that the Commission has four months from the initiation of the proceedings to make its decision. If it fails to do so the merger will be deemed to be compatible with the common market. However, if the Commission determines within the time limit that it is incompatible with the common market because competition will be significantly impeded, the Commission can issue a decision to that effect. This may stop the merger going ahead or demand the reversal of a merger that has already taken place.

The Commission has made it clear that the determination of whether or not a concentration exists will be based on issues of law and fact. However, the Commission has been criticised for some of its decisions, such as where it blocked the merger between Aerospatiale-Alenia and de Havilland. The criticism of the decision centred on the Commission's definition of the relevant product market. Those who supported the merger claimed that the Commission had taken too narrow a definition of the market as 20–70 seater aircraft. However, the Commission has resisted all attempts to re-open the case. This case can be seen as an exception in that the majority of notifications do not lead to the Commission blocking the merger. This is helped by the fact that the Commission can, where it has some concerns, impose conditions before clearing a merger, such as in the merger between Nestlé SA and Perrier SA in 1993.

However, the most recent difficulty that has arisen for the Commission relates to collective dominance. The Commission has taken the view that the Merger Regulation applies to collective dominance, where a merger creates or strengthens a dominant position between the parties and others in the market for particular goods or services. In *Gencor Ltd v Commission* there was a proposed concentration between two firms in the platinum market, which the Commission thought could lead to a dominant position between these two undertakings and another business. On appeal to the Court of First Instance, the Court confirmed that this type of collective dominance was covered by the Merger Regulation and issued guidance for its application. Following on from the tests established by the ECJ in the *Woodpulp* case, the Court of First Instance said that the extra-territoriality of the regulation was satisfied because the platinum was to be sold in the EC although it was produced in South Africa. The Court thought that under public international law it was foreseeable that the proposed concentration would have an immediate and substantial effect in the EC.

The wide interpretation given by the CFI to the regulation with regard to collective dominance has caused some problems for the Commission when it comes to proving the *existence* of collective dominance. In *Airtours plc v Commission*, the CFI held that the Commission had made errors of assessment in its analysis of competition in the 'relevant market'. In the UK the tour operator market is dominated by a small number of large operators. The operators were Thomson's with 27% of sales, Airtours with 21%, Thomas Cook with 20% and First Choice with 11%. If Airtours combined with First Choice they would have a larger share of the market, but more importantly there was the opportunity for the remaining three large operators to have a dominant position on the market as no other operator had more than 5% of sales. The Commission had not supported its assessment of the foreseeable reaction to the purchase by Airtours of First Choice plc, one of its main competitors. Therefore, the Commission's decision blocking the concentration was annulled. The outcome of this case has emphasised the role of the transparency test in deciding whether there is collective dominance. But, as with the tests for dominance under Art 82 EC, this is difficult to prove. In the case of *Schneider Electric SA v Commission*, a merger by Schneider with another French producer of low-voltage electrical equipment blocked by the Commission was annulled. The economic analysis by the Commission, in the view of the CFI, was flawed. This was followed soon after by the case of *Tetra Laval BV v Commission*, where the CFI was very critical of the Commission's analysis. The Commission overestimated the anti-competitive effects of the merger and the evidence produced by the Commission was insufficient to support its conclusion.

The Commission's powers with regard to mergers are no longer dependent on trying to use Art 82 EC as it did in the *Continental Can* case (1973) or Art 81 EC in the *Philip Morris* case (1987). The demands of business and the EC has led to the present amended Regulation 4064/89 to provide a 'one stop procedure'. This provided businesses with a clear reporting requirement showing the distinctive involvement of the Commission as against the various merger bodies within the Member States. The Commission has strong powers of investigation and the ability to impose fines. However, one large problem has been the tight time limits within which it has to act. Although it can be understood in the modern global economy that decisions have to be made swiftly, it does impose burdens and constraints on the Commission. The cases above of *Tetra Laval* and *Schneider* illustrate that to investigate the market and the likely impact of the proposed merger or concentration within the time scale of the regulation creates problems. It is likely that the Commission will be seeking the views of the Member States and the business community on reforming the application of the Merger Regulation.

CHAPTER 8

THE FREE MOVEMENT OF WORKERS

Introduction

This is perhaps the most developed area of mobility within the Community, apart from the free movement of goods. Very often, there are problem questions associated with the rights of workers and their dependants to move around the Community in order to search for work or take up offers of employment. The starting point on this topic should be Art 39, the directives and regulations adopted to provide the detail for this Community freedom and the judgments of the ECJ which have developed the principles of interpretation and application of Community law.

Checklist

You need to put this free movement policy for workers within the context of the development of a 'common market for labour' as a necessary factor of production. In particular, you should understand:

* the right given to workers under Art 39 to enter and remain in a Member State;
* the possible derogation by Member States under Art 39 and Directive 64/221;
* the possible reservation of 'public service' jobs under Art 39;
* Directive 68/360 and Regulation 1612/68 on the rights of entry and the right to remain; and
* Regulation 1251/70 and the right to remain after employment.

Question 33

Maria is a Spanish single parent living in Madrid with her young daughter and mother. She has recently lost her job due to redundancy. While she was a student, Maria had spent some time in England on an exchange programme. Remembering the vacancies she had seen advertised in the newspapers, she decides to travel to London to seek employment.

Unfortunately, she finds it hard to find employment and is considering seeking help from the social security. She is informed at the social security office that her child and mother must return to Spain immediately if she cannot support them. If she cannot find a job after three months, she will have to return to Spain herself.

Advise Maria.

Answer plan

This question requires you to apply the principles of free movement of workers to a problem involving Maria. What are we going to do about Maria? It is necessary to state the laws affecting her, her daughter and her mother and then apply them to the specific information in the problem. Obviously, the bulk of the answer will centre on Maria, because generally the rights of the daughter and mother are derived from hers. You should cover the following points:

* Art 39 and the right to accept offers of work;
* Directive 68/360 and the case of *Procureur du Roi v Royer* on searching for work;
* time limitation on searching for work and the factor of social security; and
* Regulation 1612/68 on dependants.

Answer

Maria only needed a valid passport or identity card to enter the UK. No visa or equivalent documentation could have been demanded from her or her family. However, if she wishes to remain in the UK to look for work, she will have to meet certain requirements. As there is no indication in the problem that Maria is contemplating setting up her own business or wishes to practise a profession, it is assumed that she comes within the category of 'worker' as far as the European Community is concerned. Articles 43 or 49 will not be considered, as they refer to the right of establishment and the right to provide services on a temporary basis.

Article 39 gives an individual who is a worker in one Member State the freedom to move to another Member State to accept offers of employment actually made. There is no definition of worker in the Treaty, but subsequent secondary legislation and case law have provided such a definition. In the *Lawrie-Blum* case (1987), the ECJ suggested that the essential characteristics of a worker are of someone who performs services for another during a certain period of time and under the direction of another in return for remuneration. Unfortunately, Maria has not received such an offer of employment before coming to the UK and, therefore, does not come within the definition of either Art 39 or of a worker. However, does she have any rights as an individual who is seeking employment as a worker?

In 1968, the Council adopted Directive 68/360, which deals with the abolition of restrictions on the movement and residence of workers and their families. Although this directive does not specifically cover those who enter another Member State in search of employment, it has been generously interpreted by the ECJ to facilitate such a search. In the case of *Procureur du Roi v Royer* (1976), the Court held that Art 3 of the directive included the right to enter a Member State to search for work. When the directive was being adopted, it had been minuted that individuals who moved to another Member State without a specific job offer should be allowed to enter that Member State in order to look for work. This had been pointed out in the *Levin* case (1982). However, this right was to be for a limited period of three months on the proviso that the individual could support him or herself without recourse to public assistance. Although this minute had no legal effect, the Court held, in *Antonissen* (1991), that Community law gives immigrants seeking employment the right to enter another Member State and stay there for a sufficient period of time to find out about the job market opportunities and, if appropriate, to find employment.

Thus, from the case law of the Court, Maria does have the right to enter the UK for the purpose of seeking work, but what time period does she have? In the cases above, the period of three months was indicated. This was perhaps due to the reference, in the EC legislation on social security in Regulation 1408/71, to the fact that payment of unemployment benefit for up to three months could be paid in another Member State while the claimant is looking for work. In fact, under UK law, the period is stated to be a period of six months. However, in the *Antonissen* case mentioned above, the Court went on to say that if, after this period, the immigrant provides evidence that they have a genuine chance of obtaining employment, they should not be subject to immediate deportation. The corollary of this is that if they have not found employment and cannot satisfy the authorities that they have any genuine job opportunity, they can be deported.

It would appear that Maria does have a period in which she can seek employment in the UK, but what of her mother and daughter? Obviously, the daughter does not come within the category of someone seeking to exercise her rights as a worker within the Community. The mother may be of such an age that she too could claim the same right as Maria, that is, to remain for six months whilst she is seeking employment. However, if we assume that she is dependent on Maria, what are her rights? The situation seems to be a little complicated, in that the rights of members of a worker's family and dependants are dependent upon the status of worker being granted to an individual, such as Maria. Those who may be identified as having the right to install themselves with the worker are defined in Art 10(1) of Regulation 1612/68. They include the worker's spouse, descendants who are under the age of 21 and dependent relatives. There is no difficulty in concluding that the mother and daughter come within this definition in relation to Maria. However, as indicated above, Maria is not yet a worker within the

Community definition. The concern that those who are seeking employment and their dependants should not become a burden on another Member State would indicate that the rights of someone seeking employment could be terminated if they become such a burden. Therefore, if this is what is happening, the case of Maria and her family's rights are terminated and they could be deported.

The only way that Maria and her family can remain in the UK is if she can find employment. It is worth Maria or even her mother considering part time employment if full time employment is not available; however, if her mother obtained employment, it may not be so easy to prove that Maria and her daughter are dependent upon her. This is because it was held in the *Levin* case, mentioned above, that the term worker and its associated rights applied to those who only worked part time provided the work was 'real' work and not nominal or minimal. In *Kempf* (1986), a part time music teacher from Germany was working in The Netherlands and receiving supplementary benefits from the Dutch Government due to her low income from teaching. When she claimed a residence permit as a worker it was refused, even though such a permit is a recognition of the worker's rights under the Treaty and not a prerequisite for finding employment.

However, the Court held that a person who pursued a genuine and effective activity as an employed person, even on a part time basis, could have the status of a worker. In *Raulin* (1989), the ECJ said that the national court should take account of all the services actually performed, and the duration of the activities, when considering whether the work is genuine and effective. If Maria can gain this status, she will be granted a residence permit for at least five years and this will be automatically renewable. The rights and benefits associated with such a status, such as not to be discriminated against on the grounds of nationality with regard to education, social advantage, access to employment and training and housing, will also apply to her mother and daughter as long as she remains as a 'worker'. This is because their rights depend upon the national of another Member State pursuing an activity as an employed or self-employed person in the territory of another Member State.

Question 34

'The European Community is concerned with encouraging the freedom of economic activity within the Community associated with the employed, the self-employed and business organisations.'

Discuss.

Answer plan

This essay question allows you to demonstrate your knowledge and understanding of the wider perspective of the free movement of workers as well as the right of establishment and the right to provide services discussed in Chapter 9. However, this question is in this chapter because, as you will see, the free movement of workers forms the bulk of the answer. Depending upon your preparation, you could expand on the right of establishment, etc, and still provide a good answer to the question.

The main points you should cover are:

- Art 39 – free movement of workers;
- Art 43 – freedom of establishment;
- Art 49 – freedom to provide services;
- restrictions on mobility – not a general mobility right;
- power of derogation under the Treaty; and
- policy of the EC to remove barriers and widen the scope of free movement.

Answer

The main treaty establishing the European Community is the European Economic Treaty, which, as its title suggests, is predominantly concerned with economic activity. Although many areas of economic policy are covered by the Treaty, it does deal specifically with the economic activity of individuals with regard to the free movement of workers, the right of establishment and the right to provide services. The philosophy of a common market requires the removal of all obstacles to the free movement of the factors of production in the form of labour and enterprise. Thus, rather than provide an absolute freedom of migration, for example, the Treaty confines itself to specific economic situations although, as the Community has matured as an organisation, this has been relaxed to a certain extent, as recent directives illustrate.

One of the objects of the Community is to establish a 'common market in manpower', which would serve the purpose of moving labour or workers around the Community. Formalities at borders and points of entry are kept to a minimum. No visas are required from EC nationals, only an identity card or passport. Under Art 39, workers who are nationals of a Member State are free to move to another Member State to accept offers of employment actually made and to remain in a Member State for the purpose of carrying on employment. There is no definition of 'worker' in the Treaty, but subsequent secondary legislation and case law have provided a number of characteristics. A worker is someone who performs services for another during a certain period of time and under the direction of another in return for remuneration (*Lawrie-Blum* (1987)). It was also decided by the Court that it included those workers who are 'part time', as long as the work was 'real' work and not nominal or minimal (*Levin* (1982)). In addition, it was held in *Antonissen* (1991) that those individuals who move to another Member State to seek employment have a temporary right to remain in a Member State to search for work. This should be for a minimum of three months, although in the UK it is, in fact, six months. Having gained employment, a worker has a right to a residence permit in that Member State, valid for five years and automatically renewable. The freedom of movement of workers is mainly based on the principle of non-discrimination on the grounds of nationality, although it is possible for a Member State to derogate from this obligation under Art 39. Article 39 is applicable where the work is in a public service and the individual would be exercising discretion and authority affecting the State. However, it can be seen from the main provision of Art 39, and its extension by the case law indicated above, that it is confined to those who are seeking to take part in economic activity. If the worker loses his job voluntarily and is unable to find another, his residence permit may not be renewed and he may be deported if he is no longer involved in economic activity. This occurred in *Williams v Dutch Secretary of State* (1977), where a British subject was continuously unemployed in The Netherlands.

In addition to the worker, under Directive 68/360 members of the family, and other dependants, also obtain rights of entry and residence in the Member State as the principle of non-discrimination must be extended to them. This is an essential requirement, as it would otherwise make the practical implementation of mobility of labour meaningless. Those who can join the worker are defined by Art 10(1) of Regulation 1612/68. Family rights terminate with the primary rights of the worker, and also when a dependant ceases to be a member of the family. The death of the worker will not deprive members of his or her family of their right to remain in the Member State. If they have not acquired their own right to remain, they are given preferential treatment if the death of the worker is associated with employment, such as an occupational disease or an industrial accident.

Freedom of movement could prove illusory if, by moving from one Member State to another, the worker loses the rights acquired under social security regulations, notably those associated with the pension entitlement of the worker and his or her dependants. The Treaty has therefore provided for the adoption of a system ensuring that all employment periods are taken into account under the laws of several Member States where the beneficiary has worked. These periods will be added together for calculating the amount of any benefits and they will be paid to the beneficiary in whichever Member State he or she resides. Overall, therefore, freedom of movement for the worker means applying the same treatment to the migrant worker and his or her dependants as the nationals of the Member State of residence.

Although a worker is an individual, the right of establishment necessary to exercise a profession or to render a service is not confined to individuals, but also includes companies. In *Segers* (1986), the ECJ held that to allow a Member State in which a company carried on its business to treat that company in a different manner solely because its registered office was in another Member State was contrary to the Treaty. This was confirmed in the *Centros Ltd* case, where a company registered in England was refused recognition by the Danish Trade and Companies Board. There is no definition of the group of persons entitled to the right of establishment. The rules of entry and residence are broadly the same as for workers, discussed above. Article 43 contemplates a group of people who, in principle, pursue activities as self-employed persons or set up and manage undertakings within the meaning of Art 48. Such persons belong, as a rule, to recognised professions, whose status and membership are regulated by law. Therefore, the full enjoyment of the right of establishment depends upon the recognition of professional qualifications. Without this recognition, the mobility of this part of the 'common market in labour' would be severely restricted. Therefore, the European Commission has concentrated on this recognition of professions as the main barrier to such mobility. Initially, the Commission attempted to compare various professional qualifications and training in the Member States and aimed at harmonisation through directives. However, this was a very slow process with limited success. For example, the directive on recognition of qualified architects took over 13 years to reach agreement. There has been some success with a number of sectoral directives being adopted, including doctors, nurses, dentists and veterinary surgeons. The change in policy was reflected in the Mutual Recognition Professional Qualification Directive (89/48), which came into force in April 1991. Basically, this directive requires a Member State to recognise someone who has qualified to practise a profession in one Member State to be able to do so in another Member State. This right is subject to the power of the host Member State to require some additional training, but within specific limits of time and assessment. The underlying philosophy of the directive is that professional education and training may vary in detail between Member States, but that any fully trained professional in a given field is likely to have the same knowledge as that required of his counterpart in a different Member State.

To complement the right of establishment there is also the freedom to provide services under Arts 49–55. The provision of services is often connected with the exercise of a profession, and in this respect is inseparable from the right of establishment. The services are provided for remuneration or payment. The main difference is that the individual who is providing the service remains resident in another Member State, and temporarily pursues his activity where the service is provided. Again, the individual must be allowed to do this without discrimination and on the same conditions as the State imposes on its own nationals.

It can be seen from this discussion of the rights of workers, the self-employed and companies that the Treaty does give priority to the mobility of 'labour' and 'enterprise' for economic purposes. Although the European Court has held that Arts 39, 43 and 49 are based on the same principles as far as entry and residence and non-discrimination on the grounds of nationality are concerned, reference is often made in the judgments of the Court to 'economic activity'. However, in three directives adopted in 1990, there does seem to be a recognition that the scope of mobility needed to be widened. Directive 90/364 gives rights to persons of independent means and Directive 90/365 covers retired persons, whereas Directive 90/366 provides rights to students undertaking a vocational course at a university in another Member State for the duration of the course. These examples do not detract from the fact that generally, mobility is associated with economic activity.

Question 35

Alfonse is a German national who qualified as an accountant and who has been working in Germany, where he was trained. He recently applied for a job with the Wessex local authority in England, which had advertised for accountants. Although it had already filled the post, Wessex offered him an associate contract which amounted to two-thirds of a full time post. Alfonse wishes to accept this offer of employment, but he has been informed by the British immigration authorities that he cannot take up this post because:

(a) UK legislation requires that posts with local authorities must be filled by UK nationals only; and

(b) as the post is not full time it does not come within EC legislation and has to be based on UK law alone.

Advise Alfonse.

Answer plan

As Alfonse is an accountant, this question could have been worded differently, so that it came within the context of the right of establishment dealt with in Chapter 9. This illustrates the need to read any question, especially a problem question like this one, very carefully. The main points to cover in this question are:

- Art 39 and Regulation 1612/68 on the right of workers;
- what is a worker? – *Levin* and *Lawrie-Blum*; and
- restrictions under Art 39 and the *Belgium* case (1981).

Answer

Under EC law, there is a freedom of movement for workers to move around the Community to take up offers of employment. This is based upon Art 39 and the associated secondary legislation which has been issued to provide the detail necessary to identify the specific rights of the Community worker. The main question in this problem is whether Alfonse comes within this category of worker, and whether there are any specific characteristics of the post which could deprive him of the ability to exercise his rights.

Article 39 is quite clear in providing the right for workers who are EC nationals to accept offers of employment actually made. This is confirmed by Art 1 of Regulation 1612/68 on freedom of movement of workers within the Community, which refers to the right to 'take up an activity as an employed person'. Unfortunately, neither gives a definition of worker, but the ECJ has decided that the words should be given their ordinary meaning and should not be interpreted restrictively. However, the concept only covers pursuit of effective and genuine activities. In the *Levin* case (1982), the Court held that the concept of 'worker' is a Community concept and is not dependent for its meaning on the laws of the Member State. How does the Court decide if someone comes within the Community concept of worker? In *Lawrie-Blum* (1987), the Court suggested that the essential characteristics which should be identified in a 'worker' are that he performs services in a particular time period for and under the direction of another in return for remuneration. Obviously, Alfonse satisfies the basic requirement under Community law in that he is a national of a Member State, but does he come within the definition in *Lawrie-Blum*? From the facts given in the problem, it would seem that he is going to perform the service of an accountant for Wessex local authority, in return for which it is going to pay him a salary as remuneration. Does the fact that he is only employed on a two-thirds contract affect his position? In the *Levin* case mentioned above, the Court held that the term 'worker' applied even to those who worked to a limited extent, that is, part time, provided that the work was real. There has to be some economic activity on the part of the person who claims to be a worker. This was confirmed in *Kempf* (1986), where a music teacher was working part time in The Netherlands and applied for a residence permit. In normal circumstances all those who are workers exercising their rights under Art 39 have a right to such a residence permit, which must be valid for at least five years and automatically renewable. This permit is proof of the right granted by the Treaty itself and which exists independently of the document.

The definition of 'worker' in the Community sense rarely causes difficulty in practice, because if an economically active claimant under Art 39, like Alfonse, is not a worker he is probably self-employed, in which case, Art 43 or 49 come into play. Article 43 deals with the right of establishment, including the right to take up and pursue activities as a self-employed person or to set up a business. Article 49 deals with the freedom to provide services. The European Court has held that Arts 39, 43 and 49 are based on the same principles as far as entry and residence and non-discrimination on the grounds of nationality are concerned. Therefore, categorisation under Art 49, as opposed to Art 43 or 49, will rarely be crucial.

However, even if Alfonse does have a right to enter the UK to take up his post, albeit part time, does the second point mentioned by the immigration authorities raise any obstacles for him? Under Art 39, it is specifically recognised that Art 39 will not apply to employment in the public sector. In other words, it is possible for a Member State to discriminate in favour of its own nationals on the grounds of nationality for certain jobs. This appears to provide a wide discretion to Member States, but it has been given a very narrow interpretation by the ECJ. In *Sotgui v Deutsche Bundespost* (1974), Sotgui was employed as a postman. His employers, the German post office, paid an extra allowance to workers living apart from their families in Germany, but refused it to Sotgui, an Italian national working in Germany. The Court held that the exemption provided by Art 39 (then Art 48(4)) did not apply to all employment in the public service, as this was too wide a definition. Rather, it applied to those activities in the public service which were connected with the exercise of discretion or official authority involving the national interest. On the specific point of discrimination raised by *Sotgui*, the Court went on to say that Art 39 (then Art 48(4)) only applied to access to employment and did not permit discrimination once a person had been employed in that occupation.

In another case, *Commission v Belgium* (1981), which is similar to that facing Alfonse, the Court held that a Belgian law which stated that posts in the public service could be limited to Belgian nationals was declared to be contrary to Art 39 (then Art 48). As with the term 'worker', the concept of 'public service' is a Community concept and is not to be interpreted only on national terms. It should apply only to those exercising official authority, as it was intended to apply only to employees safeguarding the general interests of the State. Does this mean that Alfonse can take up his post? It would appear that he will not be in a position to exercise official authority. He will not have the status of a civil servant, although this was held by the Court, in *Lawrie-Blum*, not to mean that Art 39 (then Art 48(4)) applies.

To enter the UK to take up this offer of employment, all Alfonse needs is a valid passport or identity card and a letter from Wessex local authority offering him the job. If, as indicated in the problem, he is refused entry by the immigration officer, he is entitled to have access to the normal rights of appeal available under national law. If he is successful, as he should be, in obtaining entry to take up his post he is entitled to a residence permit, renewable automatically at the end of five years, and not to be discriminated against on the grounds of nationality with regard to conditions of employment, housing, social security, etc.

Question 36

Analyse TWO of the following cases which came before the ECJ, and explain their importance in the development of Community law:

(a) *Lawrie-Blum* – Case 66/85;

(b) *Rutili* – Case 36/75;

(c) *Bonsignore* – Case 67/74.

Answer plan

When approaching a question like this, the temptation is to produce too descriptive an answer. The facts are important, but are only one element of the answer. You should try to deal with the following:

- the facts, the legal points raised and the decision of the Court;

- what kind of case was it? A preliminary reference or a direct action? What Article of the Treaty was it based upon?; and

- the cases chosen for this type of question have usually played their part in developing or reinforcing European Court judgments – what part has this case played?

Answer

(a) Lawrie-Blum – Case 66/85

Deborah Lawrie-Blum was a British national who passed the first examination at the University of Freiburg to become a teacher at a *Gymnasium*. She was refused admission to the probationary service leading to the second examination, which qualifies successful candidates for appointment as teachers. The law of the *Land* Baden-Württemberg required the possession of German nationality for admission to the probationary service. Mrs Lawrie-Blum contended that this refusal on the grounds of nationality had infringed her rights under Art 39 (then Art 48), whereas the *Land* argued that a probationary teacher is not a 'worker' within the meaning of Art 48. During the proceedings which followed in the German court, a preliminary reference was made to the European Court under Art 234 (then Art 177).

The *Land* claimed that since a trainee teacher's activity falls under education policy, it is not an economic activity within Art 2 of the Treaty. The term 'worker' within the meaning of Art 39 (then Art 48) and Regulation 1612/68, they argued, covers only those persons whose relationship to their employer is governed by a contract subject to private law and not persons whose employment relationship is subject to public law. The period of preparatory service should be regarded as the last stage of the professional training of future teachers.

The European Commission took the view that the criterion for the application of Art 39 (then Art 48) is the existence of an employment relationship, regardless of the legal nature of that relationship and its purpose. The fact that the period of preparatory service is a compulsory stage in the professional development of a teacher, and that it is spent in the public service, is not relevant if the objective criteria for defining a 'worker' are satisfied. These criteria would include such things as the existence of a relationship of subordination vis à vis the employer, the actual provision of services by the employee and the payment of remuneration.

The ECJ said that the freedom of movement for workers was one of the fundamental principles of the Community. Therefore, the term 'worker' should not be left to be defined by the individual Member States, but should have a Community meaning. Given its fundamental importance, the Community concept of 'worker' must be given a broad interpretation. The essential feature of an employment relationship is that for a certain period of time a person performs services for and under the direction of another person, in return for which he receives remuneration.

Applying this concept to the facts of Mrs Lawrie-Blum's case, for the entire period of preparatory service she is under the direction and supervision of the school to which she is assigned. It is the school that determines the services to be performed by her and her working hours and it is the school's instructions that she must carry out and its rules which she must observe. The amounts she receives may be considered as remuneration for the services provided and for the duties involved in completing the period of preparatory service. Consequently, the three criteria for the existence of an employment relationship are fulfilled in this case.

The argument put forward by the *Land*, that services performed in education do not fall within the scope of the Treaty because they are not of an economic nature, was rejected. The Court said that all that is required for the application of Art 39 (then Art 48) is that the activity should be in the nature of work performed for remuneration, irrespective of the sphere in which it is carried out. The economic nature of someone's activities cannot be denied merely because their activities are governed by public law. The Court had already stated, in *Sotgui* (1974), that the nature of the legal relationship between employee and employer is immaterial as regards the application of Art 39 (then Art 48).

(b) Rutili – Case 36/75

Roland Rutili was an Italian national, although he had lived in France since birth. He had married a French woman and, until 1968, had held a privileged resident's permit. He was resident in the department of Meurthe-et-Moselle, where he worked and engaged in trade union activities. As a result of Rutili's alleged political actions during the parliamentary elections in March 1967 and the events of May and June 1968, and of his participation in a demonstration during the celebrations of 14 July 1968, the Ministry for the Interior made a deportation order against him. On 10 September 1968, an order was issued requiring Rutili to reside in the department of Puy-de-Dôme. In November 1968, the Minister for the Interior revoked the deportation and residence orders affecting Rutili, but decided to prohibit him from residing in particular departments. In January 1970, Rutili applied for a residence permit for a national of a Member State of the EC. In October 1970, following an appeal by Rutili, he was issued with a residence permit by the Prefect of Police valid for five years, but restricting his residence in line with the views of the Minister for the Interior. In December 1970, Rutili brought proceedings seeking the annulment of the decision limiting the territorial validity of his residence permit.

The *Tribunal Administratif*, Paris, decided to stay the proceedings under Art 234 (then Art 177), so that questions could be put to the ECJ. The first question concerned the interpretation of 'subject to limitations justified on grounds of public policy' in Art 39 (then Art 48). The Court said that this concerned both those legislative provisions adopted by each Member State to limit the freedom of movement and residence within its territory, and the individual decisions taken in application of such provisions. The object of the provisions of the Treaty and secondary legislation is to regulate the situation of individuals and to ensure their protection, thus the national courts must examine whether individual decisions are compatible with Community law. The second question asked for the precise meaning of the word 'justified'. The freedom of movement of workers is one of the fundamental principles of the Treaty, and therefore any derogation must be strictly interpreted so that its scope cannot be determined unilaterally by each Member State. Therefore, the word 'justified' seeks to limit the discretionary powers of Member States and to protect the rights of those who are seeking to exercise their rights under Art 39.

The duty imposed upon Member States is to base the measure adopted exclusively on the personal conduct of the individuals concerned, as required by Art 3 of Directive 64/221, and to refrain from adopting any measures which are not related to the requirements of public policy, or which adversely affect the exercise of trade union rights. They should immediately inform anyone against whom a restrictive measure has been adopted of the reasons on which the decision is based, so that they can consider an appeal.

In particular, measures restricting the rights of residence which are limited to part only of the national territory may not be imposed by a Member State on nationals of another Member State who are subject to Art 39, except in the case and circumstances in which such measures may be applied to nationals of the State concerned. Therefore, the judgment in *Rutili* reinforces the non-discrimination approach of the Treaty. A Member State does not have the power to restrict the movement of nationals of other Member States within its territory unless it has the power in similar circumstances to restrict its own nationals.

(c) Bonsignore – Case 67/74

Carmelo Angelo Bonsignore was an Italian national residing in Germany. He was convicted of a firearms offence, in that he was in unlawful possession of a firearm which accidentally caused the death of his brother by his careless handling of the firearm. The local German criminal court found him guilty of possession of the firearm and imposed a fine for breach of the firearms legislation. The court also found him guilty of causing death by negligence, but imposed no penalty on this count, considering that no purpose would be served in the circumstances, notably the mental suffering caused by the death of his brother. Following this criminal conviction, the Aliens Authority ordered that he be deported. Bonsignore appealed against this decision, during which a reference was made to the European Court under Art 234 (then Art 177).

The reference was required because the German court wished to know the interpretation of Art 3(1) and (2) of Directive 64/221, which dealt with the co-ordination of special measures concerning the movement and residence of foreign nationals which are justified on the grounds of public policy, public security or public health. These are the grounds available under Art 39 which allow a government of a Member State to derogate from their obligations under the Treaty.

The German court hearing the appeal was of the view that deportation was not justified because of the special circumstances of the case. There was no special preventive characteristic of Bonsignore in the case. The only reason could be to deport Bonsignore as a general preventive measure, as an example to others who may also be in illegal possession of firearms. The directive had been introduced into German law by a special Law on the Entry and Residence of Nationals of Member States of the European Community, passed in 1969. The German court wanted to ensure that the German legislation was applied in accordance with the requirements of Community law, hence its request for interpretation.

The first question refers to whether Art 3(1) and (2) of the directive is to be interpreted as excluding the deportation of a national of another Member State as a deterrent to other foreign nationals from committing criminal offences of the type committed by the person to be deported. The second question posed the alternative meaning of these Articles in the directive, namely, that the EC national to be deported will commit further offences if he remains in the Member State.

The ECJ said that according to Art 3(1) and (2) of Directive 64/221, measures taken on grounds of public policy or of public security shall be based exclusively on the personal conduct of the individual concerned and that previous criminal convictions shall not in themselves constitute grounds for the taking of such measures. These Articles have to be interpreted in the light of the objectives of the directive and the need to ensure the uniform application of Art 39, without discrimination between nationals and non-nationals of a Member State.

Article 3 of the directive provides that measures adopted on grounds of public policy and for the maintenance of public security against nationals of Member States cannot be justified on grounds outside the personal conduct of the individual involved. This has to be the situation where a government is seeking to depart from one of the fundamental principles of the Community, that is, the free movement of persons. Thus, we have the requirement that a deportation order may only be made for breaches of the peace and public security which might be committed by the individual concerned. Therefore, the outcome for Bonsignore was that the European Court said, in answer to the Art 234 (then Art 177) reference, that Directive 64/221 prevents the deportation of a national of another Member State if the purpose is solely to deter other aliens, that is, of a preventive nature.

CHAPTER 9

THE FREEDOM OF ESTABLISHMENT AND THE FREEDOM TO PROVIDE SERVICES

Introduction

Very often, these topics are joined with the free movement of workers, and therefore a good understanding of all three aspects should be obtained. This is especially true as the Court has held that the principles of non-discrimination, etc, are the same whether it is Art 39 (the free movement of workers), Art 43 (the freedom or right of establishment for the self-employed and companies) or Art 49 (the freedom to provide services). Problem questions are very popular in this area of Community law although, on law degrees, it is not uncommon to have an essay question on the freedom of establishment for lawyers.

Checklist

You should be familiar with the following areas:

- Art 43 and the freedom of establishment;

- Art 49 and the freedom to provide services;

- Art 50 and what constitutes a service;

- the right to receive services;

- derogation under Art 46 and Directive 64/221;

- Directive 73/148 on rights of entry and residence;

- Directive 75/34 on the right to remain after employment for the self-employed and their families;

- the special problems of 'professionals' and the Mutual Recognition Directive; and

- special measures to deal with companies operating within the Community.

Question 37

Pierre is a fully qualified engineer in France. As a result of attending the 'Engineering 2000 Fair' in Paris, he applied for a two year postgraduate course at a British university. He was accepted onto the course and arrived at Dover with Anne-Marie, his Canadian cohabitee. His luggage was searched and found to contain pornographic videos, which were confiscated. The immigration officer checked the Home Office computer, which indicated that the French police had reported that Pierre was a member of an anarchist organisation. On the basis of this information, the immigration officer refused them permission to enter the UK on the grounds that their exclusion would be conducive to the public good.

Advise Pierre on their rights, if any, under EU law.

Answer plan

This question deals with the mobility of students within the Community. It concentrates on the right of individuals to move to another Member State to receive services as against the provision in the Treaty which deals with the right to provide services. This provision should be discussed and applied, along with the following points:

- Arts 39, 43 and 49 to identify if Pierre is covered by any of these provisions;
- the case of *Luisi*, which identified rights of recipients of services;
- the meaning of vocational courses – *Gravier v City of Liège*;
- Directive 64/221 on derogation; and
- Directive 93/96 for students.

Answer

The EC Treaty has, as one of its basic freedoms, that of the ability of individuals to move between Member States in order to carry out certain activities. The Treaty specifies three situations, namely, the free movement of workers, the right of establishment and the freedom to provide services. As Pierre does not seek to establish a business in the UK, the Treaty provisions associated with establishment have no application to the problem. Is he a worker? The concept of worker is a Community concept and is not dependent for its meaning on the laws of any particular Member State. The essential characteristic of a worker, according to *Lawrie-Blum* (1986), is that he performs services during a particular time period for and under the direction of another in return for remuneration. This concept has been generously interpreted by the ECJ, in *Procureur du Roi v Royer* (1976), to include the right to enter another Member State in order to search for work. However, although he is a qualified engineer, Pierre is not seeking to enter the UK as a 'worker', but to take up his place on a two year postgraduate course. Article 39, specifying the rights of workers, does not provide any assistance to him. It is the last category associated with services which needs to be considered if the EC law is to provide any assistance to Pierre and Anne-Marie.

Articles 49 and 50 provide for the removal of restrictions on the freedom to provide services. More importantly for Pierre, they have been interpreted by the ECJ to embrace the freedom to receive services. This would include the postgraduate course which he wishes to take. It was stated by the Court, in *Luisi v Ministero del Tesoro* (1983), following the Commission's view in *Watson and Belman* (1976), that there was a freedom for the recipient of services to go to another Member State, without restriction, in order to receive a service there. Although the case involved the transfer of money out of Italy in breach of Italian currency law for the purpose of tourism and medical treatment, the principle in the judgment included persons travelling for the purpose of education. The right of residence exists during the period for which the service is provided, which, in Pierre's case, would be the two years' duration of the course. Any breach of this freedom would be *prima facie* a breach of Arts 49 and 50.

Would Pierre's course qualify under this right to receive services? As an economic orientated Treaty, the main concern would seem to be education or training of a vocational kind. However, the Court has given a wide definition to the meaning of vocational education. In *Gravier v City of Liège* (1984), it was held to include all forms of teaching which prepares for and leads directly to a particular profession, or which provides the necessary skills for such a profession. Although Pierre is already a qualified engineer, the postgraduate course he has applied for would seem to satisfy this definition, in that it deals with a specialist area of engineering skills. Thus, he may claim equal access, and on the same basis as nationals of the Member State, that is, UK nationals. This was confirmed in *Blaizot v University of Liège* (1987), which involved a university veterinary studies course. However, as with all the freedoms arising from the Treaty, there are exceptions where the Member State may derogate from their obligation under the Treaty. These are specifically those in Arts 46 and 55, which allow for derogation on the grounds of public policy, public security and public health. As there is no indication that Pierre offers any threat with regard to public health, it is public policy or public security which may be used by the UK Government to justify its actions. The public policy provision has been interpreted strictly by the European Court to ensure, as it stated in *Van Duyn v Home Office* (1975), that its scope is not unilaterally determined by the Member State without control by the European Community institutions. In *Rutili v Ministre de l'Intérieur* (1976), the Court held that restrictions on the movement of an EC national on the grounds of public policy could only be accepted where the behaviour of the individual constitutes a genuine and sufficiently serious threat to public policy.

Article 3(1) of Directive 64/221 states that any exclusion on the grounds of public policy or public security must be based exclusively on the personal conduct of the individual. Is Pierre's membership of an anarchist association sufficient personal conduct to exclude him? In *Van Duyn*, a Dutch national was refused entry to the UK to take up employment with the Church of Scientology because the UK regarded the activities of the Church as objectionable and socially harmful. The Court held that, although past association with an organisation does not count as personal conduct, present association does, and the activities in question must constitute a genuine and sufficiently serious threat to public policy affecting one of the fundamental interests of society. Do French anarchists pose such a threat, given that there are probably British anarchists? In *Van Duyn*, mentioned above, the Court allowed the UK to apply a stricter standard on an EC national than the one it applied to its own nationals, because the UK deemed that it was necessary. It would appear that, if Pierre is a member of such an organisation and the UK Government do believe that he constitutes a genuine and sufficiently serious threat to society, they can exclude him. If they do, it must be on the membership of the anarchist association, because the pornographic videos would not, in themselves, amount to a reason to exclude him. In the *Bonsignore* case (1975), it was accepted that the concept of personal conduct expresses the requirement that a deportation order may only be made for breaches of the peace and public security which might be committed by the individual concerned.

Under Art 6 of Directive 64/221, Pierre is entitled to know on which ground, that is, public policy or public security, the decision is based, unless this information contravenes State security. This allows the individual to prepare his defence. If the UK fails to comply with Art 6, it may lead to the quashing of a deportation order, as happened in *R v Secretary of State for the Home Office ex p Dannenberg* (1984). Under Art 8, Pierre is entitled to the same legal remedies in relation to a decision on entry. In the UK, an immigrant normally has a right of appeal against immigration decisions to a person called an adjudicator and then to the Immigration Appeal Tribunal. Such appeals cover issues of fact, law and the exercise of discretion, so the merits of the decision would be fully reviewed.

In June 1992, a directive specifically issued to cover the situation of students came into force. It was challenged by the European Parliament before the ECJ on the grounds that the co-operation procedure should have been used, rather than the Parliament just being consulted. As a result, that Directive, 90/366, was replaced by Directive 93/96, which only applies if the person concerned does not come within one of the categories in the free movement provisions of the Treaty. The directive is purely supplementary and the case law indicated above still applies to Pierre. What about Anne-Marie? She is a Canadian national and, as such, does not receive the benefits associated with the European Community, which are for EC nationals only. However, does her relationship with Pierre provide her with any rights of entry? If Pierre was allowed entry to take up his place on the postgraduate course, would she be able to enter with him? Perhaps because of the limited duration of a course, under Directive 90/366 there is a narrow definition which only includes the student's spouse and dependent children and not family members. If Anne-Marie was married to Pierre, there would be no problem, in that the nationality of the spouse does not need to be that of one of the Member States. However, she is his cohabitee, and is not included in the directive. In *Netherlands State v Reed* (1986), the Court held that the term 'spouse' included cohabitee. Although this case was concerned with the mobility of workers, it will not help Anne-Marie even if the Court applied its principles of interpretation across the mobility categories. The decision was on the basis of non-discrimination, in that the Dutch authorities were required to give Reed the right of residence, as they recognised the rights of cohabitees under Dutch law. Therefore, the judgment will not assist migrants in a similar situation unless the State they wish to enter has the same rule as the Dutch. The UK does not have such a rule.

It would seem that if the Court is satisfied that there are grounds for the UK Government to derogate from the Treaty, they will uphold the refusal to allow Pierre to enter the UK to take up his postgraduate course. If they are not satisfied, and Pierre is allowed to enter the UK as a student, he must be given a residence permit for the duration of the course. However, whatever happens to Pierre, it can be seen from the *Reed* case, above, that Anne-Marie will not be allowed to benefit from the rights given to him. She must seek a visa in her own right as a Canadian national.

Question 38

Critically discuss the development of EU law with regard to the right of a lawyer to practise in another Member State.

Answer plan

This essay question requires a discussion of the development of Community law on the right of establishment and the provision of services as they apply to lawyers. In particular, the following points should be raised:

* freedom of establishment under Arts 43–48;
* Directive 77/249 and the right to provide services;
* problems of lawyers and other professionals;
* the impact of the Mutual Recognition Directive.

Answer

A lawyer could be a 'worker', in the sense that he or she is employed within an organisation to manage its legal affairs, in which case, the normal rules associated with the free movement of workers would apply. However, generally speaking, the ability to practise as a lawyer, as a professional, is more complicated and involves issues about the right to provide services and the right of establishment. The Community principle of equal treatment is not always sufficient to ensure that the immigrant is able to practise a profession in another Member State. In the case of lawyers, it is obvious that recognition of their professional qualifications and admission to the appropriate professional organisation is also required and can cause problems. Generally, each Member State has remained free to regulate the exercise of the legal profession in its territory.

There is no directly applicable provision in the EC Treaty requiring Member States to recognise qualifications acquired in another Member State or obliging them to allow immigrants to practise a profession without the appropriate qualifications (*Auer (No 1)* (1979)). This seems reasonable, given that the services of such professionals have a big impact of those who seek their advice and services. However, Art 47 requires the Council to adopt directives on the mutual recognition of diplomas, certificates and other evidence of formal qualifications. Without a relevant directive, the migrant is likely to find that Community law is of limited assistance. The Commission had attempted to remedy the situation by promoting separate directives for each profession, such as medicine, dentistry, veterinary medicine and midwifery. The objective of these directives has been to make it easier for a person practising a profession in one Member State to practise that profession in another Member State. However, the important difference between these professions and lawyers is that, although the principles of medicine or dentistry are much the same in every Member State, those of law differ. It is therefore hardly surprising that the progress on facilitating the free movement of lawyers has been very slow. Directive 77/249 was specifically aimed at lawyers, but it is only concerned with the provision of services and not the right of establishment. It makes provision for lawyers to carry out their profession in another Member State on a temporary basis. 'Lawyer' under this directive is defined by a list of terms to reflect the diversity in the European Community. The function of the list is to indicate those practitioners who are able to benefit from the rights conferred by the directive and the activities to which it applies. Thus, anyone who is recognised as a 'lawyer' for the purpose of the directive can perform the work of a lawyer in another Member State, but only on a temporary basis. While performing this work, he or she must use the title of the home country, as it would appear in that country. Thus, a French lawyer must call himself *'avocat'*, even when he is working in the UK or Germany. This avoids any misunderstanding and indicates the specialism of the lawyer in the law of the appropriate Member State. In this capacity, the foreign lawyer can do all the work of a local lawyer, unless the national law of the Member State reserves certain activities for its national lawyers and on the proviso that he represents a client in court work in conjunction with a local lawyer. This has meant in the UK that such foreign lawyers cannot undertake probate or conveyancing work, which is reserved for UK lawyers.

It could be expected that, in time, the European Commission would issue a directive which would widen the scope of recognition for lawyers of one Member State to establish themselves and practise in another. However, recognising the time involved in such a process as producing specific directives, the Commission changed its strategy and concentrated on producing a general directive that would apply to all professions. This directive applies to the legal profession and is the Mutual Recognition Directive 89/48. Like all directives on establishment, Directive 89/48 benefits Community citizens with regard to qualifications awarded in a Member State. Under this directive, recognition is to be given to diplomas as defined by Art 1(a). There must be three essential characteristics for such 'diplomas'; it must be awarded by a competent authority in a Member State following the successful completion of a course lasting at least three years at a university or equivalent institution, plus professional training. Finally, such a 'diploma' must qualify the holder for the pursuit of a regulated profession in a Member State. The profession of a lawyer is in the list of regulated professions. Article 3 of the directive provides the basic rule that if a Member State requires a 'diploma' as a condition for exercising a regulated profession, it must accept a 'diploma' obtained in another Member State. In contrast to the situation where a lawyer is providing a 'service' of a temporary nature, when he or she is exercising the right of establishment, the lawyer is entitled to use the professional designation of the Member State in which he or she practises. Thus, a French *avocat* who establishes himself and practises in the UK can call himself a solicitor. Negotiations began within the EU legal organisations with regard to the Rights of Establishment Directive or 'the Lawyers Directive' 98/5, which is designed to facilitate the practice of a lawyer on a permanent basis in a Member State other than the one he or she obtained his or her qualification in. Having proved that he or she is already registered as a lawyer in another Member State, after three years as a lawyer in that Member State, he or she will have the right to gain admission to the legal profession of the host country and use the appropriate professional title. Thus, if he or she was an *avocat*, he could become a solicitor after that period elapsed.

This would seem to make it straightforward for a lawyer qualified in one Member State to practise in another. However, the directive does recognise that professional training varies between Member States and allows the Member State where the individual wishes to practise to set certain conditions. This may involve an adaptation period during which supervision by a qualified practitioner is required of the foreign national or an aptitude test of professional knowledge. In England, the test for foreign lawyers wishing to practise as solicitors is called the Qualified Lawyers Transfer Test. Having successfully completed this test, the normal rules concerning registration and admission to the appropriate professional body will apply. However, such registration or admission cannot be refused on any grounds contrary to Community law. As with any member of the legal profession, once registered or admitted, migrant lawyers must obey the rules of professional conduct laid down by the Member State in which they practise. Should these rules be incompatible with the Treaty's freedom of movement principles, they will not be applied. For example, a French rule requiring migrant doctors to give up their registration in their country of origin before being allowed to register in France was contrary to the Treaty. Although it happened before this general directive came into effect, the case of *Ordre des Avocats v Klopp* (1984) illustrates this point with regard to the legal profession. This case involved a French rule that an *avocat* cannot establish chambers in more than one place. Klopp was a German who qualified as a lawyer in Germany and opened an office there. He then re-qualified in France and applied for admission as an *avocat*, but his application was refused, because he was not prepared to give up his office in Germany. The Court held that such a requirement was contrary to the Treaty.

Question 39

'Company law is one of the most important and active areas in the harmonisation of the national laws of the Member States. The European Community's objective is to create a uniform system of company law.'

Discuss.

Answer plan

Although it is not very common to get examination questions on European Community policy towards company law, it does form part of the syllabus of most European law courses as part of the freedom of establishment. Where questions do arise, they are generally in the form of an essay question like this one. The best way to approach these questions is on the basis of freedom of establishment and the right to provide services, and the implications these have for the recognition of companies in the various Member States. The answer will use authority based on the Treaty, as there are very few cases on these aspects of company law. The main points to cover are:

- Art 43 and the right of establishment;
- Art 48 and the meaning of company;
- Art 44 and the need for safeguards;
- Arts 49 and 50 and the provision of services by companies;
- Art 293 and negotiations of conventions;
- directives adopted for harmonisation, with examples;
- European Economic Interest Groupings; and
- the European Company.

Answer

Although there are many developments associated with the rights of workers and the self-employed within the European Community, it must be remembered that companies play the predominant part in any modern economy. It is to be expected, therefore, that provision should be made for companies to move around the Community to take part in economic activities. The main provisions of the EC Treaty concerned with the right of establishment and the freedom to provide services apply to companies. However, one of the main problems encountered is that whereas individuals, whether as workers or self-employed, are uniform in their identity across the Community, this does not apply to companies. Member States have different requirements with regard to such matters as incorporation, registration and liability. If there is to be true mobility for companies, action has to be taken to make sure that these differences are not used to create barriers to the mobility of companies. This was reinforced in the build-up to the completion of the single market policy in 1992, when the European Commission said that such an internal market cannot exist, unless companies incorporated in one Member State are permitted to do business in another. The case of *Centros Ltd* (1999) confirmed this principle by requiring the Danish Trade and Companies Board to register a company set up, but not trading, in England.

The EC Treaty identifies two rights for companies, namely, establishment and provision of services. Under Art 43, companies have the right to establish themselves in another Member State by setting up agencies, branches or subsidiaries. Having so established themselves, the companies have the right not to be discriminated against and must be treated under the same conditions as those laid down by the Member State for its own nationals. What companies can benefit from this freedom? The same rule applies to companies as it does to individuals, who must be nationals of a Member State if they are to benefit from the freedom specified in the Treaty. Article 48 specifies that, as far as companies are concerned, they must be formed in accordance with the law of a Member State and have their registered office, central administration or principal place of business within the Community. The ECJ held, in the *Segers* case (1986), that to allow a Member State in which a company carried on its business to treat that company in a different manner solely because its registered office was in another Member State would render Art 48 valueless. Just as there is a requirement that workers and the self-employed should receive remuneration in order to satisfy the Treaty, so companies which are non-profit making do not come within the definition of Art 48. The remuneration requirement is repeated in Art 49, dealing with the right to provide services. This provision deals with a company established in one Member State providing services of an industrial, commercial or professional nature in another Member State. The main difference with services is that, in contrast to establishment, the company is entering another Member State only temporarily to pursue this activity.

As indicated above, companies should be able to establish themselves or provide services on the basis of non-discrimination on the grounds of nationality. They should also not be subject to any more burdensome rules in the host Member State than are absolutely necessary. The European Community has attempted to deal with this last point by seeking uniformity in the whole Community, or at least on the basis of 'equivalents'. Article 293 requires the Member States to negotiate conventions with each other in order to secure uniformity of recognition of business practices across the Community. The Article specifically mentions the mutual recognition of companies within the meaning of Art 48. As a result of this requirement, a Convention on the Mutual Recognition of Companies and Bodies Corporate was signed in 1968 by the six founder members of the EC. However, it is not in force, as it was not ratified by the Member States. Given this failure, but recognising the importance of company law, the policy of the EC has been to move forward on the basis of directives dealing with specific matters.

The company law of each Member State has developed through its own legal and political traditions, and hence there are wide variations, not only in terms, but also in concepts. It was thought necessary, if the freedom of establishment was to be a reality, that there should be a minimum safeguard to protect the shareholders or members of companies and others who enter into transactions with the company. This is specifically mentioned in Art 44. If companies in the EC are to deal across national boundaries, it is important that investors, customers and creditors are able to deal with confidence with enterprises from other Member States, whether directly or through their subsidiaries or agencies. The fact that over 13 directives have been proposed reflects the extensive programme of harmonisation of company law embarked upon by the European Community. Although not all of these directives have been adopted, those which have cover such technical matters as company capital, company accounts, appointment of auditors and disclosure of information. These are important, because companies established or providing services in different Member States facing the need to adjust to different regulatory regimes may lead to duplication of accounting, licensing and other requirements. This would act as a disincentive to penetrating other national markets. It may also reduce the opportunities for benefiting from economies of scale.

Another way of seeking to reduce the problems for companies operating in more than one Member State is to establish EC corporate structures. The first step was taken in this development with the establishment of European Economic Interest Groupings (EEIGs) by Regulation 2173/85. These EEIGs permit companies and others to co-operate within the Community on a cross-border basis, and thus provide a vehicle for joint ventures. EEIGs have the mixed characteristics of companies and partnership. They are not separate, in the sense that the companies are still liable for the debts of the EEIG, but they do have a separate legal capacity. Such groupings have to be registered, which in the UK is a requirement to register with the Registrar of Companies. An EEIG cannot have more than 500 employees, or offer any share participation to the public. Obviously, there are certain limitations with EEIGs, but they do provide a flexible vehicle for economic activity.

The ultimate aim of the Community is to have a new company formation which will have legal capacity throughout the Community. This is to be the European Company, or *Societas Europaea* (SE), which will be established by registration with the European Court in Luxembourg under a distinctive European Community company statute. Even though registration would be with the Court, the SE would be domiciled in a particular Member State. The intended role of the SE is to facilitate cross-border co-operation by means of large scale mergers and associations. It can be seen that this is perhaps the natural extension from the EEIG, which facilitates such ventures, but on a smaller scale. There have been some criticisms of the establishment of the SE, which has led to delay in the adoption of the necessary Community legislation. However, the Nice IGC in December 2000 reached a political agreement on the social aspects of the SE and in October 2001 the Council finally adopted the regulation and directive on the SE, which will enter into force in October 2004.

It can be seen from the points discussed above that the Treaty clearly identified the need to harmonise areas of company law if companies were to exercise the rights of establishment and provision of services. However, Community legislation has progressed slowly, as the national requirements of the Member States varied widely. The directives which have already been adopted have helped companies involved in cross-border activities, but the ultimate establishment of the European Company has not been achieved. The regulation allowing for EEIGs was a major advance, but is aimed at smaller joint ventures. The objective of the Community is to ensure that company law across the Community does not act as a barrier to economic activity by companies and provides safeguards for those who are doing business with them. To this end, the Community seeks to provide a minimum standard of uniformity in company law across the Member States.

Question 40

Analyse TWO of the following cases which came before the ECJ, and explain their importance in the development of Community law:

(a) *Reyners* – Case 2/74;

(b) *Van Binsbergen* – Case 33/74;

(c) *Walgrave and Koch* – Case 36/74.

Answer plan

When approaching a question like this, the temptation is to produce too descriptive an answer. The facts are important, but are only one element of the answer. You should deal with the following points:

* the facts, the legal points raised and the decision of the Court;
* what kind of case was it? A preliminary reference or a direct action? What Article of the Treaty was it based upon?; and
* the cases chosen for this type of question have usually played their part in developing or reinforcing European Court judgments – what part has this case played?

Answer

(a) Reyners – Case 2/74

Although born and bred in Belgium, Jean Reyners was of Dutch nationality. Although resident in Belgium, where he had been educated and been made *docteur en droit belge*, it had not been possible for him to be admitted to the practice of the profession of *avocat* in Belgium. The reason for this is that the Belgian *Code Judiciaire* provides that no one may hold the title of *avocat* or practise that profession unless he is a Belgian and holds the *docteur en droit*. Having previously obtained this qualification, it was the nationality requirement which was impeding Reyners. It was possible to obtain dispensation from the condition of nationality in cases determined by the King, on the advice of the General Council of the *Ordre des Avocats*. This was provided for in a decree of 1970, but was limited to the nationals of countries which themselves admitted Belgians to the profession. Unfortunately, the Netherlands Bar was only open to the Dutch.

Reyners had made a number of applications for dispensation from the nationality requirement, but they had all been refused. He finally applied to the *Conseil d'Etat* of Belgium, the highest public law court, to have this provision of the decree quashed on the grounds of its incompatibility with the EC Treaty. To enable it to decide the case, the court stayed the proceedings and a reference was made for a preliminary ruling under Art 234 (then Art 177). The main questions under the Art 177 procedure were whether Art 43 (then Art 52) on the right of establishment became directly applicable at the end of the transitional period and whether the 'official authority' exception in Art 45 (then Art 55) applied to *avocats*.

The governments of Member States were divided on the direct effect of Art 43 (then Art 52). Although the German Government supported the possibility of direct effect in its intervention, the governments of Belgium, Ireland, Luxembourg and the UK disagreed. They based their views on the fact that Art 43 (then Art 52) was wider and vaguer than the prohibition of non-discrimination on the grounds of nationality and the fact that it was to be enforced by directives left discretion to Member States. The view of the German Government was that the provisions which impose on Member States an obligation which they have to fulfil within a particular period become directly applicable when, on the expiration of this period, the obligation has not been fulfilled.

The Court held that the rule on equal treatment with nationals is one of the fundamental legal provisions of the Community. Therefore, if there is a set of legislative provisions effectively applied by the country of establishment to its own nationals, these are capable of being directly invoked by nationals of all the other Member States. The fact that the freedom of establishment should have been attained at the end of the transitional period is made easier by, but is not dependent on, the implementation of a programme of measures. The fact that the progression has not been made leaves the obligation itself intact beyond the end of the period provided for its fulfilment. After the expiry of the transitional period, the right of establishment is sanctioned by the Treaty itself with direct effect.

Article 45 provides for a derogation from the right of establishment when the activities which are involved in that State are connected, even occasionally, with the exercise of official authority. Given that the freedom of establishment and the rule on equal treatment are fundamental to the Community, the Court stated that Art 45 (then Art 55) cannot be interpreted so as to defeat the objective of the Treaty. It wanted to avoid the effectiveness of the Treaty being defeated by unilateral provisions of Member States. Although each Member State must be looked at individually, the professional activities of *avocats* do not constitute, as such, the exercise of official authority. For Art 45 to apply, there has to be a direct and specific connection with the exercise of official authority.

This decision does not mean that any citizen can simply move to another Member State and set up in business or a profession. Each Member State has its own rules which apply to its own nationals covering such matters as qualifications. However, if the professional or other qualification is already recognised in the host country as being equivalent, Art 43 forbids the refusal of permission on the grounds of nationality (*Patrick* (1978)) or a requirement that the arrival obtain the national qualification (*Thieffry* (1977)).

(b) Van Binsbergen – Case 33/74

Van Binsbergen was a Dutch national who wished to challenge a social security decision against him. He had authorised Kortman, a Dutch national established in The Netherlands, to act on his behalf and bring an appeal against the decision. Kortman was an experienced legal adviser and representative in social security matters. However, during the case, Kortman moved his home to Belgium, and it was from there that he corresponded with the Dutch court. The court concluded that Kortman was now practising from Belgium. Under a Dutch statute on procedure in social security cases, legal representation could only be provided by persons established in The Netherlands. They therefore said that he could no longer act for Van Binsbergen.

Kortman invoked Arts 49 and 50 (then Arts 59 and 60) providing for the progressive abolition, during the transitional period, of restrictions on freedom to provide services within the Community. The Dutch court made a preliminary reference to the European Court under Art 234 (then Art 177). There are some similarities with the *Reyners* case (2/74), only here it is a question of services rather than establishment. In fact, after *Reyners*, it should be quite straightforward to hold Arts 49 and 50 (then Arts 59 and 60) to have become directly effective at the end of the transitional period, at least as regards discrimination on the grounds of nationality.

The problem was to identify the discrimination involved in the case. Kortman, Van Binsbergen, the social security court and the domestic law in question were all Dutch. However, the fact that the Dutch law did disqualify any legal adviser of any country who was not established in The Netherlands was relevant. The establishment requirement is a restriction within Art 49, but does the Article have direct effect in the sense of providing a right which the national courts must enforce?

The European Court said that the restrictions to be abolished under Arts 49 and 50 (then Arts 59 and 60) included any requirements imposed upon the person providing the service on the basis of nationality or residence which do not apply to persons established within the Member State. This latter requirement of habitual residence could have the result of depriving Art 49 of all useful effect, as its object is to abolish such restrictions.

However, this has to be balanced against the possibility of the person providing the service taking advantage of his right to avoid professional rules of conduct which would be applied if he was established in that State. Therefore, a residence requirement could be imposed if the desired ends could not be achieved by less restrictive means. Such rules must be considered objectively and would be permissible provided they satisfied certain criteria. These are that they are non-discriminatory, objectively justified and not disproportionate.

Following the principles in *Reyners*, the Court held that Arts 49 and 50 (then Arts 59 and 60) did have direct effect. However, the importance of *Van Binsbergen* is that it shows that the ECJ were careful to limit the area in which Art 49 (then Art 59) works directly, namely, with restrictions based on nationality and residence.

(c) Walgrave and Koch – Case 36/74

Bruno Walgrave and Norbert Koch are both Dutch nationals who offer their services for remuneration to act as pacemakers on motorcycles in medium distance cycle races. They provide these services under agreement with the 'stayers', who cycle in the lee of the motorcycle, or the cycling associations or with sponsors. Competitions in which their services are requested include the world championships. Under the rules for the world championships to apply after 1973, the pacemaker must be of the same nationality as the stayer. Walgrave and Koch considered that this rule is incompatible with the EC Treaty, as it prevents a pacemaker of one Member State from selling his services to a stayer of another Member State. They therefore brought an action against the association Union Cycliste Internationale, which was the body that made the rule.

The national court made a reference to the European Court under Art 234 (then Art 177) relating to the interpretation of Arts 39, 49 (then Arts 48, 59) and 7 (now repealed). Article 39 (then Art 48) provides for the free movement of workers, whereas Art 49 (then Art 59) deals with the freedom to provide services. Article 7 is one of the fundamental principles of the Community, in that it prohibits any discrimination on the grounds of nationality. However, the rules in question were not made by a government of a Member State, but an international sporting federation, which is not subject to public law. Could the prohibition be applied to them? That was the important question raised by this case.

The practice of sport is subject to Community law only in so far as it constitutes an economic activity within Art 2. The Court stated that the activities referred to in Art 49 (then Art 59) are not to be distinguished in their nature from those in Art 39 (then Art 48) merely because of the form of the regulation covering employment. The prohibition of discrimination found in these Articles does not only apply to public authorities, but extends to rules of any other nature aimed at regulating gainful employment and the provision of services.

The abolition by Member States of obstacles to the freedom of movement for persons and the freedom to provide services are fundamental objectives of the Community contained in Art 3(c). This abolition would be compromised if barriers of national origin could be neutralised by obstacles resulting from autonomous associations or organisations which do not come under public law. Therefore, these Articles may be taken into account by the national court in judging the validity or the effects of a provision inserted in the rules of a sporting organisation. The *Bosman* case (1996) would be another example where the activities of professional sportsmen had been affected.

The national court had anticipated this possible answer, so it asked whether the fact that this was an international organisation made any difference. The key point for the Court was where the relationship governed by the rules was entered into or the place where they took effect. If these were within the territory of the Community, then the Community view on non-discrimination would apply. Thus, any races, for example, which took place in a Member State could not do so under rules prohibited by the Treaty.

CHAPTER 10

FREEDOM FROM DISCRIMINATION

Introduction

The main focus of freedom from discrimination is based on the economic aspect of employment and sex discrimination. However, you should look at Chapter 2, where the protection of fundamental rights was identified as one of the general principles of Community law. The general principle has a wider meaning than merely discrimination based upon sex. This chapter concentrates on the general principle of equal pay for equal work for men and women, laid down in Art 141, and the directives issued to provide the detail required for the full implementation of this principle. Generally, the questions asked on this topic are of an essay type, because of the wider knowledge of national employment law normally required for problem questions. Such questions are more likely to arise in employment or industrial law papers. However, it is possible for questions to be constructed in a way that deals specifically with Community law.

Checklist

Following on from the general principle of non-discrimination, you should understand the following points and the appropriate cases:

*   Art 141 on the principle of equal pay for equal work for men and women;
*   the meaning of 'pay' within Art 141;
*   the extent of the direct effect of Art 141;
*   Directive 75/117 on equal pay for work of equal value;
*   Directive 76/207 or the Equal Treatment Directive for men and women in employment;
*   Directive 79/7 with regard to equal treatment in matters of social security;
*   Directive 86/378 regarding equal treatment for occupational pension schemes; and
*   Directive 86/613 regarding equal treatment in self-employment;
*   Art 13 EC; and
*   Directives 2000/43 and 2000/78.

Question 41

'The European Union has widened the scope of sex equality to other areas of discrimination.'
Discuss.

Answer plan

This discussion question provides an opportunity to review the case law and recent changes in the Treaty with regard to sex equality. However, that discussion must go beyond the recital of cases such as *Defrenne* or *Marshall*. This may be the starting point but the essay should then be developed to include the following points:

* *Defrenne* judgment in 1976;
* scope of Art 141 (then Art 119) through the meaning of pay and worker;
* Equal Pay Directive 75/117 and Equal Treatment Directive 76/207;
* general principle of non-discrimination;
* Art 13 of the EC Treaty;
* Directives 2000/43 and 2000/78.

Answer

In Art 3 of the EC Treaty, the European Community lists the main activities which it will achieve at the same time as eliminating inequalities and promoting equality between men and women. This indicates the special status given by Community law to the principle of equality. This principle has been repeated in secondary legislation, mainly directives, and the case law of the European Court. In fact, it has principally been the judgments of the Court that have elevated the principle to its special status.

The main example given of this special status accorded to the principle of equality can be seen through the case law relating to equal treatment of men and women in terms and conditions of employment within the European Community. It is the cases associated with Art 141 which show this development clearly. Article 141 requires each Member State to ensure that men and women should receive equal pay for equal work. Equal pay, under this Article, refers not only to wage levels but also to any payment in kind in respect of remuneration for employment. In its judgment in the *Defrenne*

(No 2) case (1976), the Court held that Art 141 (then Art 119) has a double aim which covers both economic and social aspects of employment. It seeks to ensure that States which have implemented the equality principle do not suffer a competitive disadvantage and to achieve social progress. In 1978, whilst delivering its third judgment associated with Madame Defrenne's case, the Court expanded the principle of equal pay into a general fundamental right of equality which required the elimination of discrimination based on sex.

With regard to the application of the principle of equality in employment, it is not only Art 141 which is important, as a number of important directives have been adopted which have expanded the application of the principle. Article 141 itself refers expressly to pay but the ECJ has adopted a liberal interpretation to the question of what constitutes pay. In *Garland v BREL* (1982), the Court held that the grant of special travel facilities to former employees after retirement constituted pay, even in the absence of any contractual entitlement to such facilities.

In *Bilka-Kaufhaus v Weber von Harz* (1986), Weber was a female part time worker who was seeking to challenge her employer's occupational pension scheme. Although the scheme was non-contributory for full time employees, with the employer paying all the contributions, this was not the case with part timers. The Court held that the benefit constituted consideration paid by the employer to the employee in respect of her employment and thus came within Art 141 (then Art 119). In this case, the Court seemed to draw a distinction between contractual and statutory pension schemes. However, Art 141 was held to be applicable to a statutory social security benefit in *Rinner-Kuhn v FWW Spezial Gebeaudereiniging GmbH* (1989). This case also involved a part time employee who was employed as a cleaner. She challenged the German legislation which permitted employers to exclude workers who worked less than 10 hours per week from entitlement to sick pay. Despite statements in *Defrenne* and *Newstead v Dept of Transport* (1986) that social security schemes were outside the scope of Art 141, the Court held that sick pay fell within the Article. Therefore the German legislation was contrary to Art 141 (then Art 119).

It is not only the case law associated with Art 141 to which the principle of equality in employment has been applied. As indicated above, a number of directives have been adopted to implement or supplement Art 141. The Equal Pay Directive 75/117, for example, requires the elimination of all discrimination on the grounds of sex with regard to all aspects and conditions of remuneration. In *Jenkins v Kingsgate (Clothing Productions) Ltd* (1981) (then Art 119), the Court held that this directive restates the equal pay principle of Art 141 without altering its scope. Guidelines were provided in the later case of *Bilka-Kaufhaus*, mentioned above, to assist in identifying what might constitute objective justification for such differences in pay. The onus is on the employer to prove that the difference in treatment corresponded to a genuine need of the enterprise, that it was a suitable way to obtain the objective pursued by the business, and that it was necessary for that purpose. This could perhaps be described as the application of a principle similar to proportionality.

Another important directive was the Equal Treatment Directive (76/207). This directive dealt with access to employment, vocational training, working conditions and social security. In the UK, this directive has been used in the context of different retirement ages for men and women. The most important case in this respect was *Marshall v South West Hampshire Area Health Authority* (1986), where Marshall successfully challenged her employer's decision to force her to retire at an earlier age than male employees. The important factor in the case was acceptance by the Court that this directive had direct effect. Article 2 of the directive allows derogation from the equal treatment principle on specific grounds. This was raised in *Johnston v Chief Constable of the RUC* (1986) by the police employers as a defence to their refusal to renew Johnston's contract of employment due to the special requirements of policing in Northern Ireland and the need for the police to carry firearms. The Court held that there was no general public safety exception to the equal treatment principle available under the EC Treaty, and that it was for national courts to decide whether the conditions specified in Art 2 are satisfied. The directive has also been used by pregnant employees who have been discriminated against (*Dekker* (1991) and *Webb v EMO Air Cargo (UK) Ltd* (1994)).

Article 141(4) allows Member States to pursue a policy of positive or affirmative action in favour of the 'under-represented sex'. In *Kalanke v Bremen* (1995), the ECJ considered Art 2(4) of the Equal Treatment Directive. This Article concerns measures taken to promote equal opportunity for men and women, including removing existing inequalities which affect women's opportunities. However, the judgment in *Bremen* was greeted with dismay in several Member States, as it construed the provision very narrowly. The Commission issued a communication suggesting that the judgment in *Bremen* did not affect quota systems. The ECJ clarified the situation in *Marschall* (1997), which allows women to be given priority for promotion in the event of equal suitability, competence and professional performance. The potential weakness in the area of positive or affirmative action was recognised by the insertion in the Amsterdam Treaty of Art 141(4).

The case of *P v S* (1996) appeared to suggest a more general prohibition on discrimination embracing transsexuality; the ECJ judgment in *Grant v South-West Trains* (1998) quashed this suggestion. In the *Grant* case, the ECJ said that EC law did not currently cover discrimination on the basis of sexual orientation. The ECJ felt that it was not its function to bring about a positive change which was properly to be enacted by legislation (*D v Council* (2001)). However, there have been occasions when the ECJ has extended individual rights not to be discriminated against as a general principle of EC law. In *Sabbatini* (1971), the plaintiff used the general principle of non-discrimination against her employer, the European Parliament. Following this, the case of *Prais v Council* (1975) extended protection to discrimination based on religion. Both cases were brought against EC institutions and the principle needed wider application.

This perhaps led to the most important recent development when Art 13 (previously Art 6(a)) was introduced into the EC Treaty by the Amsterdam Treaty. Article 13 provides that the Community may take appropriate action to combat discrimination based on sex, racial or ethnic origin, religion or belief, disability, age or sexual orientation. There has been much activity in this field since then. In 2000, two directives were adopted. Directive 2000/43 implements the principles of equal treatment between persons irrespective of racial or ethnic origin, and Directive 2000/78 establishes a general framework for equal treatment in employment and occupation. The latter directive covers religion or belief, disability, age and sexual orientation. The Council now has the authority to take appropriate action to combat discrimination based on sex, racial or ethnic origin, religion or belief, disability, age or sexual orientation. Since the 1960s, the institutions of the EU have taken a wide view of categories of discrimination and this new Article reflects that range. When these directives become operative they will have a strong impact in some Member States.

Question 42

To what extent does Art 141 give workers in the Member States directly effective rights to equality, irrespective of sex?

Answer plan

This question covers the narrow area of Art 141, but it must be remembered that this Article is very important in the development of equal pay and non-discrimination on the grounds of sex. Particular reference should be made to the following cases:

- *Defrenne* (1976);
- *Macarthys v Smith* (1980);

- *Bilka-Kaufhaus v Weber von Harz* (1986);
- *Rinner-Kuhn* (1989); and
- *Enderby v Frenchay HA* (1994).

Answer

Article 141 requires each Member State to ensure the application of the principle that men and women should receive equal pay for equal work. Although this is an instruction to the Member States, by stating in the *Defrenne* case (1976) that the Article has direct effect, the Court has identified a right which can be enforced by the individual employee in the courts of the Member State. Under the principle of direct effect, three conditions have to be satisfied, namely, that the provision must be clear and unambiguous, it must be unconditional and it must take effect without further action by the EU or Member States. Once these conditions are met, the individual is not dependent upon the Member State or the institutions of the Community for the right granted by the Treaty or other source of Community law.

The principle of equal pay was said by the Court in *Defrenne* (1976) to form one of the foundations of the Community. Its role was seen as a way of achieving one of the social objectives of the Community, namely, the improvement of living and working conditions for men and women. This requires a levelling up of pay for women, rather than a levelling down of that for men. As was restated in *Enderby* (1994), the purpose is to remove obstacles which disadvantage women in employment. If this was to be achieved, the Community was conscious of the need to ensure that those States which had incorporated such equality principles were not disadvantaged in a competitive sense as against those States whose undertakings were not obliged to meet such an objective.

In *Defrenne v Sabena* (1976), the ECJ had upheld the direct effect of Art 141 (then Art 119). Madame Defrenne had been employed by the Belgian airline Sabena as an air hostess. She complained of being paid a lower salary than her male colleagues, although the work they did was the same. In an Art 234 (then Art 177) reference, the Belgian court asked if Art 141 could be relied upon before national courts. In its judgment, the court said that discrimination on the grounds of sex could be indirect and disguised discrimination or direct and overt discrimination. The latter type of discrimination was more easily identified and could be based solely upon the criteria of equal work and equal pay referred to in Art 141. In such cases, Art 141 was directly effective and gave use to individual rights which national courts must protect. It was necessary for additional measures to be taken with regard to indirect discrimination. This was achieved by the Equal Pay

Directive 75/117, which supplements Art 141. Article 1 of this directive provides for the elimination of all discrimination on the grounds of sex with regard to all aspects and conditions of remuneration. It must be remembered that Art 141 on its own is not sufficient to cover all aspects of equal pay, although this has not stopped the Court extending the scope of the Article through a number of very important judgments.

In the course of the Art 234 (then Art 177) reference in *Defrenne*, the UK Government and the European Commission submitted that Art 141 (then Art 119) would only have direct effect as between individuals employed by the State and not those employed by a private employer. In other words, they were claiming that it should only have vertical and not horizontal direct effect. The Court rejected this argument, claiming that Art 141 (then Art 119) is mandatory in nature and must extend not only to the action of public authorities, but to all contracts between individuals. This judgment cleared the way for individuals to challenge their employers directly on the basis of the EC Treaty in national courts, where they believed themselves to be victims of sex discrimination in matters of pay.

Article 141 states that men and women should receive equal pay for equal work. In *Macarthys Ltd v Wendy Smith* (1980), the Court held that a requirement of contemporaneity of employment is not to be read into the Article. Smith was paid £50 per week, whereas her male predecessor had received £60. Under UK legislation, the requirement was for the male and female workers to be doing the same job at the same time if a comparison was to be made. However, the ECJ held that the only issue was whether or not the work was 'equal' and it did not matter whether or not the man and woman whose work and pay were to be compared were employed at the same time in the undertaking or not.

Although it was initially thought that 'pay' in Art 141 was limited to the wages or salary received by the employee, it has been given a much wider interpretation by the European Court. For example, in *Garland v BREL* (1982), the special travel facilities granted to former employees on retirement were held to constitute pay, even if there was no contractual obligation to make such facilities available for those who had retired. Mrs Garland therefore had a right not to be discriminated against on the grounds of sex in comparison with a retired male employee.

There have been a number of cases involving pension schemes, including those where the claimant has been a part time employee. In *Bilka-Kaufhaus v Weber von Harz* (1986), Weber claimed that the pension scheme of her employer infringed Art 141 (then Art 119). Under the scheme, part timers had to be employed by the business for at least 15 out of the last 20 years, whereas full time employees benefited from the non-contributory scheme without any time requirement. As the contributions paid by the employer were to supplement existing social security schemes, they amounted to consideration paid by the employer to the employee within the meaning of Art 141 (then Art 119). Perhaps the most important case in pensions is the case of *Barber v Guardian Royal Exchange* (1990). Under the employer's scheme, the normal pensionable age for women was 57, and for men, 62. The Court held that, since the worker received these benefits from his employer as a result of his employment, they constituted 'pay' within Art 141 (then Art 119). The immediate impact of the *Barber* case has been that employers have been required to harmonise pension ages for men and women in contracted-out schemes. The limitation to contracted-out schemes reflects the judgment of the court that State pensions are not 'pay' within Art 141 (then Art 119). This was applied in *Roberts v Birds Eye Walls Ltd* (1992).

Sick pay has also been held by the Court to come within the meaning of Art 141. In the *Rinner-Kuhn* case, a part time office cleaner challenged the German legislation which permitted employers to exclude part time workers from entitlement to such pay. This discretion given to employers brought the payment of sick pay to part timers within Art 141 (then Art 119). Lastly, redundancy payments were held in the *Barber* case, mentioned above, to be pay within Art 141 (then Art 119), irrespective of whether payment is made under a contract of employment, on an *ex gratia* basis or under statute.

It can be seen from the cases above that Art 141 has been interpreted by the Court to give workers in the Member States directly effective rights to equality, irrespective of sex. Cases have been brought mainly by female workers, but males in the *Barber* case successfully used the Article to obtain equality with regard to redundancy and occupational pension payments. The direct effect of the Article has been limited by the Court, restricting it to direct discrimination, but with the support of the directives adopted on equality, notably the Equal Pay Directive, the Court has not limited the extensive application of the Article as a basic principle. This is illustrated by the way that the Court has given a wide interpretation to the meaning of 'pay' within Art 141.

Question 43

'Direct and indirect discrimination law in the Community is intended to remove sex-related pay discrimination.'
Critically discuss this statement, drawing on judgments of the ECJ.

Answer plan

This question deals with the general topic of discrimination, but offers the opportunity to display knowledge of recent cases. In this instance, one of the key cases is *Enderby v Frenchay HA* (1994). However, in addition to Art 141, you should make reference to the following cases:

* *Bilka-Kaufhaus v Weber von Harz* (1986);
* *Defrenne* (1976);
* *Nimz v Freie und Hansestadt Hamburg* (1992); and
* *Danfoss* (1989).

Answer

In the case of direct discrimination, sex is the cause of the less favourable pay or treatment, but there must also exist a causal connection between the sex of the worker and the lower pay. The allocation of particular wages or salary scales to particular jobs can result in direct discrimination. Since that form of direct pay discrimination is not expressly based on the sex of the worker, a female worker claiming equal pay encounters evidential problems if she has to prove the causal connection between her sex and the lower pay for particular types of jobs. Thus, when all the objective elements of discriminatory pay (work that is the same or of equal value, lower pay for a woman when compared with a man in the same undertaking) have been proved, there should be a rebuttable presumption of sex discrimination. It would be sufficient for the plaintiff to prove an example of the same (or equivalent) work by a man being better paid than that of a woman, leaving it for the employer to furnish counter-evidence, for example, by adducing objective grounds for the unequal pay which are not based on the sex of the recipient.

Indirect discrimination is a legal concept which enables cases of unequal treatment, for which there is an objective justification but which in fact results in the woman being disadvantaged, to be included as an instance of unlawful sex discrimination. In the case of *Enderby v Frenchay HA* (1994), Dr Enderby brought proceedings against her employer before an industrial tribunal, claiming that she was involved in work of equal value to that of a principal clinical psychologist and a grade 3 principal pharmacist. Her annual pay was £10,106, while those of employees in the other two professions, taken as comparators, were respectively £12,527 and £14,106. In the *Enderby* case, her professional group is characterised as a 'purely female profession'. Enderby's counsel put forward the argument that, in a purely female profession, the membership of that profession can have effects which are similar to a link with part time work. The fact that speech therapists are almost exclusively women is also at least partly due to the connection between the social role of women and work (that is, difficulties encountered by women in working full time – see *Bilka-Kaufhaus v Weber von Harz* (1986)). The opportunities of working part time and of flexible arrangements of working are particularly attractive to women.

Advocate General Lenz, in the *Enderby* case, stated that the purpose of a conceptual scheme is to comprehend methods by which women are placed at a disadvantage in their working lives and not to create additional obstacles to claims being made before the courts in respect of sex-related pay discrimination. In accordance with the result-orientated line taken by the ECJ in the past, a pragmatic approach ought to be pursued. The problem with UK legislation and legal tradition is that it does not readily allow for such an approach. However, Lenz warned that the historical and social context of a 'purely female profession' is most probably sex-related, and if an explanatory approach were accepted as sufficient justification, that would lead to the perpetuation of sexual roles in working life. Instead of the equality of treatment which is sought, there would be afforded a legal argument for maintaining the status quo.

Thus, a collective agreement, which, in these circumstances, includes rules applying exclusively to that professional group, may also represent rules specifically relating to women. In these proceedings, what is called for is a comparison between representative groups of employees, each doing work of equal value. If this comparison reveals that the group consisting principally of women suffered a significant disadvantage when compared with the male group comparator, a presumption of indirect sex discrimination will arise. In such circumstances, the employer, in order to avoid the charge of sex discrimination, would have to show that this was due to objectively justified factors unrelated to any discrimination on grounds of sex.

Thus, with both direct and indirect discrimination, the claimant can raise a rebuttable presumption of discrimination, in the first case with a specific comparison and in the other by a comparison of groups, which places the onus on the employer to adduce evidence in rebuttal of that presumption or to produce a justification. Article 141 requires the employer to justify objectively the difference in pay between job A and job B.

The principle of equal pay under Art 141, and repeated in Art 1 of Directive 75/117, has been held by the Court to be directly applicable (see *Defrenne* (1976)). It cannot be ignored by collective agreements, as it has effects on the relations between employer and employee. Moreover, it should not be open to an employer to conclude various collective agreements with different groups in order to limit the impact of the principle of equal pay, even if each agreement individually applies the principle. This applies in particular in the case of collective agreements within the same firm, where one element in the principle of equal pay is present in so far as the employer is the same.

What other reasons can be put forward by an employer to justify objectively the difference in pay? In some circumstances, the employer may be compelled by the state of the labour market to offer higher remuneration for members of a particular professional group in order to attract suitable applicants. The only question then is the extent to which the objective reason can serve to justify the difference in pay. In *Nimz* (1992), the Court held that a collective agreement which allows employers to maintain a distinction as regards overall pay between two categories of workers who are both performing the same type of work, but part time and full time, does constitute discrimination against female workers vis à vis male workers, if in fact a much lower percentage of men work on a part time basis than women. Such an agreement must therefore in principle be regarded as contrary to Art 119, unless the difference in treatment between the two categories of workers can be shown to be based on objectively justified factors unrelated to any discrimination on grounds of sex. In *Bilka-Kaufhaus* (1986), the employer argued that full time employees gained experience, and thus skills and abilities, more quickly than part timers working less than three-quarters of normal hours. However, the Court held that this was not sufficient to justify objectively the difference in treatment. However, it is important to remember that, when the national court is reviewing these factors, it is applying Community law. This requires them to take into account such general principles of Community law as proportionality, that is, whether and to what extent the shortage of candidates for a job and the need to attract them by higher pay constitutes an objectively justified economic ground for the difference in pay between the jobs in question.

In the *Enderby* judgment, the ECJ held that the shift of onus of proof takes place when that is necessary to avoid depriving workers who appear to be the victims of discrimination of any effective means of enforcing the principle of equal pay. There can be no doubt that the employer applied a system of pay which was not lacking in transparency, since the rates of pay of NHS speech therapists and pharmacists are decided by regular collective bargaining processes in which there is no evidence of discrimination as regards either of these two professions. However, if the pay of speech therapists is significantly lower than that of pharmacists, and if the former are almost exclusively women while the latter are predominantly men, there is a *prima facie* case of sex discrimination, at least where the two jobs in question are of equal value and the statistics describing that situation are valid. It is for the national court to assess whether it may take into account those statistics.

In the *Danfoss* case (1989), the employees' union produced statistics relating to the wages paid to 157 workers between 1982 and 1986 which showed that the average wage paid to men was 6.85% higher than that paid to women. The employers claimed that these differences were due to the application of criteria for additional payments based upon mobility, training and length of service. The ECJ held that the employer had to justify these criteria, with the exception of length of service.

As Art 141 is mandatory in nature, the prohibition of discrimination between male and female workers not only applies to the action of public authorities, but also extends to all collective agreements designed to regulate employment relationships and to contracts between individuals. In a successful action, the remedy available is to set aside that provision of the collective agreement which is contrary to Community law because of indirect discrimination. This can be done without requesting or awaiting its prior removal by collective bargaining or any other procedure, and to apply to members of the group disadvantaged by that discrimination the same arrangements as are applied to other employees, arrangements which, failing the correct application of Art 141 in national law, remain the only valid system of reference. There also remains the possibility of a *Francovich* action against the government.

Question 44

Analyse TWO of the following cases which came before the ECJ, and explain their importance in the development of Community law:

(a) *Defrenne (No 2)* – Case 43/75;

(b) *Marshall* – Case 152/84;

(c) *Barber* – Case 262/88.

Answer plan

When approaching a question like this, the temptation is to produce too descriptive an answer. The facts are important, but are only one element of the answer. You should deal with the following:

- the facts, the legal points raised and the decision of the Court;
- what kind of case was it? A preliminary reference or a direct action? What Article of the Treaty was it based upon?; and
- the cases chosen for this type of question have usually played their part in developing or reinforcing European Court judgments – what part has this case played?

Answer

(a) Defrenne (No 2) – Case 43/75

Madame Defrenne was employed as an air hostess by Sabena, a Belgian airline company. She claimed that, in paying their male stewards more than their air hostesses, even though they were performing identical tasks, Sabena was in breach of Art 141 (then Art 119). It was conceded by the employer that Defrenne did the same job as that done by male stewards, but, until 1966, she was paid less than them under the terms of a collective agreement negotiated between Sabena and the unions. She began her action in 1968, claiming the difference between her remuneration and that of men from 1963 to 1966. Under Belgian law, there is a five year limitation rule, so she was taking her claim as far back as she possibly could. She began her action in a Belgian labour court, which made a reference to the European Court under Art 234 (then Art 177), seeking the interpretation of Art 141 (then Art 119).

Article 141 provides that equal pay for work of equal value will be ensured during the first stage of the Community (ie, five years). This period expired at the end of 1961 without any action being taken by the Member States to implement Art 141 and the Commission had made a recommendation on the issue. As a result of this, the Member States adopted a Resolution which purported to give themselves more time, that is, extending this first stage. When this period, too, expired, the European Commission failed to use the procedure under Art 226 (then Art 169) against defaulting States, something it was criticised for by the Court. However, Madame Defrenne claimed that this failure on the part of the Member States did not affect her rights under Art 141 (then Art 119), because it had direct effect. The Member States and the Commission did not consider that the Article had, in fact, become directly effective at the end of the first stage, when the Member States had failed to fulfil their obligations under the Treaty.

The ECJ had found Articles of the Treaty to have direct effect before this case, as in *Van Gend en Loos* (1963), but, generally, this was in cases where the

Articles involved a cross-border or transnational element. In the case of *Van Duyn* (1975), Art 39 (then Art 48), which deals with discrimination on the grounds of nationality, was found to have direct effect. But, that concept of discrimination is straightforward when compared with Art 141 (then Art 119) which requires 'equal pay for equal work'. However, the Court identified that discrimination could be direct or indirect. With direct or overt discrimination it was possible for an individual to make a challenge without the need for further supplementary measures to identify what the term means. With regard to such actions, the Court held that Art 141 (then Art 119) was directly effective, because the criteria set for the principle of direct effect to apply were present.

It was necessary for directives to be issued to deal with the more disguised indirect discrimination, but Madame Defrenne was successful in her action for equal pay. As part of the social policy of the Community, the Court believed that the principle of Art 141 (then Art 119) was a fundamental right of Community citizens. This 'social' right was supported by the economic fear on the part of some Member States that the failure to have equal pay would lead to variations in business overheads, and thus competition between the Member States. However, the Court recognised the financial impact of its judgment that Art 141 (then Art 119) would have direct effect in both the public and the private sector. The Court limited its ruling by stating that anyone who had not already initiated an action in their Member State would not be able to claim 'back pay' in the way that Madame Defrenne had. All future cases would not be able to claim for a period dating back to before the judgment in this case.

(b) Marshall – Case 152/84

Miss Marshall was employed by Southampton Area Health Authority as a senior dietician until she reached the age of 62. When she reached this age, she was dismissed, even though she had expressed the wish to continue in employment until she was 65 years of age. The sole reason for her dismissal was that she was a woman who had passed the retirement age applied by the health authority to women. The authority's general policy was that its employees should retire when they reached the age at which State retirement pensions became payable. This was 60 for women and 65 for men. The authority was willing to waive its general policy for particular individuals in particular circumstances. This it had done for Miss Marshall by employing her for two more years after she reached 60. Marshall complained to an industrial tribunal against her dismissal, which she claimed was contrary to the Sex Discrimination Act 1975 and Directive 76/207, in that it unlawfully discriminated against her on the grounds of her sex.

The health authority claimed that, in laying down the retirement ages for its employees, it was merely reflecting the different retirement ages for State pensions. These differences in age were permitted by Art 1(2) of Directive 76/207. In addition, they argued that an EC directive could never impose obligations on individuals and could only have direct effect against a Member State in its capacity as a public authority, and not as an employer. The case reached the Court of Appeal, where a reference was made under Art 234 (then Art 177) to the ECJ. The Court of Appeal asked two questions on the interpretation of Directive 76/207. The European Court's answer was that the principle of equality of treatment was one of fundamental importance, and therefore Directive 76/207 was to be strictly interpreted. Thus, the exception to the prohibition of discrimination on the grounds of sex in relation to the granting of old age pension and retirement ages was in this category. Article 5(1) of Directive 76/207 was to be interpreted as meaning that a general policy dismissing women when they reached the State pension retirement age constituted discrimination on the grounds of sex, contrary to the directive.

Although the ECJ accepted the principle that a directive could not impose obligations on an individual, that is, horizontal direct effect, this was not true where the State was involved. It did not matter in what capacity the State was involved, in that it could be as an employer or as a public authority. In this case, Miss Marshall was able to invoke Directive 76/207 against her employer, the health authority, since this authority was an 'emanation of the State'. The main point was to stop a Member State taking advantage of its own failure to comply with Community law.

(c) Barber v Guardian Royal Exchange – Case 262/88

Barber was an employee of Guardian Royal Exchange (GRE). He was a member of a contracted-out pension scheme established and wholly financed by his employer. Under this scheme, the normal pensionable age was 62 for men and 57 for women. In the event of redundancy, the scheme provided for immediate payment of a pension to men aged 55 or women aged 50. Barber was made redundant at the age of 52, so he did not qualify immediately for a pension, but would receive a deferred pension payable when he reached the age of 62. He complained to an industrial tribunal, claiming unlawful discrimination on the grounds of sex. The tribunal dismissed his application, as did the Employment Appeal Tribunal. Barber appealed to the Court of Appeal, which made a reference to the European Court under Art 234 (then Art 177). The reference asked whether benefits paid to a redundant employee by his employer were subject to either Art 141 (then Art 119), dealing with equal pay, or the Equal Pay Directive 75/117 and the Equal Treatment Directive 76/207. The Court answered that Art 141 (then Art 119) did apply.

The previous case law of the European Court had been uncertain. In *Garland v BREL* (1982), the Court had held that certain benefits paid after retirement constituted pay. In *Worrington v Lloyds Bank Ltd* (1981), the Court rejected adjustments in gross pay designed to compensate for differential pension contributions as being incompatible with Art 141 (then Art 119). In *Bilka-Kaufhaus GmbH v Weber von Harz* (1986), it had held that a purely contractual pension paid by an employer came within Art 141 (then Art 119), whereas in *Burton v British Railways Board* (1982), the Court had held that a man denied access to a voluntary redundancy scheme on account of his age had not been a victim of a breach of Art 141 (then Art 119). In addition to this, the Community has always made it clear that State pensions are excluded from the scope of Art 141.

The reasoning of the *Barber* judgment was that the private, contracted-out occupational pension constituted consideration paid indirectly by the employer, and therefore fell within the scope of 'pay' within Art 141 (then Art 119). This also applied to any benefit paid on redundancy. Putting these two together, it meant that the pension and redundancy payments payable to Barber came within Art 141 (then Art 119). As there were different age qualifications for men and women under the pension scheme payable on redundancy, this offended against the principle of equal pay for men and women stated in Art 141 (then Art 119).

This was a very important judgment with far reaching implications for individual workers and the administration of occupational pension schemes. Both the Commission and the UK Government had mentioned to the Court in their interventions that this case would have financial consequences for these pension schemes. They asked the Court to limit the impact of its judgment, as the Court had done earlier in *Defrenne* (1976). This is what the Court actually did. The Court ruled that the direct effect of Art 141 (then Art 119) to such occupational pension schemes would generally only apply to cases arising after the date of the judgment in this case, with one exception. This was that cases already initiated, or where claims had already been raised under national law, could proceed on the basis of direct effect of Art 141 (then Art 119).

The reason given by the Court for this limitation of the impact of its judgment in *Barber* was that Directive 79/7 had authorised Member States to defer from the principle of equal treatment for men and women in certain matters, including contracted out occupational pension schemes. Thus the administrators of such schemes had been entitled to believe that they were not acting contrary to Art 141. In the interests of legal certainty, the retroactivity of this judgment would have severe effects on the financial balance of such schemes. Protocol 2 of the Maastricht Treaty reinforces this point by stating that, although there is full and immediate acceptance of the implications of the Barber judgment, problems have been created for employers, pension funds, insurance companies, etc. Therefore, the Protocol confirms that equal treatment in occupational schemes must be applied in respect of employment after 17 May 1990.

CHAPTER 11

EXTERNAL RELATIONS

Introduction

The external relations of the European Community include its ability to enter into agreements with third countries and international organisations. Therefore, the key point of this topic relates to the competence of the Community to enter such agreements. Generally speaking, the questions which occur on this topic are essay type, although on very rare occasions the direct effect of a treaty provision may appear in a problem question.

Checklist

Students should ensure that they understand the general point on the legal personality of the Community (Art 281) and the following points:

- the express external competence of the Community, including the common commercial policy (Arts 131–34), association agreements (Art 310) and agreements with international organisations (Arts 302–04);
- the procedure laid down in the Treaty for negotiating international agreements (Art 300), including the roles of the Council, Commission and the European Court;
- the implied external powers of the Community associated with the doctrine of parallelism;
- mixed agreements; and
- the direct effect of Treaty provisions.

Question 45

What are the express treaty making powers of the EU? Do individuals derive any rights from such treaties?

Answer plan

This essay question, the most common form of question on external relations, requires an answer which covers the following points:

- express treaty making powers, including the common commercial policy and association agreements;
- Opinion 1/75;
- Opinion 1/78;
- direct effect of Articles of treaties;
- *International Fruit Co;*
- *Bresciani;* and
- *Haegeman v Belgian State.*

Answer

This question raises two issues for consideration: Community competence and the ability of individuals to enforce any rights arising from these treaties. Express treaty making power is granted by the EC Treaty in two cases: commercial agreements (Art 133) and association agreements (Art 310). Article 300 lays down the general rules regarding the procedure to be followed where the treaty making power is exercised, but does not itself confer such powers on the Community. In addition, Arts 302–04 require the Community to co-operate with international organisations, and this is generally achieved by international agreements. The general rule is that all such international agreements are negotiated by the Commission and concluded by the Council.

The common commercial policy of the EC is a very important area of Community activity. Although it does not come within Pt 2 of the EC Treaty, which deals with the foundations of the Community, its appearance in Pt 3, dealing with the economic policy, reflects its importance. As the Community is based upon a customs union, it is necessary for not only a removal of internal barriers to trade, but also a common policy towards goods coming from outside the Community. This is where the common external tariff is required, as well as other measures related to the regulation of external influences of a commercial character on the internal market and its producers.

The common commercial policy is covered by Arts 131–34. It is Art 133 which gives an indication of the scope of the policy. It relates to tariff rates, trade agreements, export policy and measures to protect trade such as are necessary to deal with dumping or subsidies. The ECJ has stated that this list is not exhaustive, but merely examples of its scope. In Opinion 1/75 (Understanding on a Local Costs Standard), the Court stated that the commercial policy is made up of a combination and interaction of internal and external measures. It reflects a progressive development of a body of rules which come together to apply to the field of common commercial policy. In this Opinion, it was explicitly stated by the Court that the Community had exclusive power in this field of the common commercial policy. If this was not accepted, it would allow individual Member States to adopt positions on export credits which may differ from those of the Community and distort the institutional framework in which the common commercial policy should operate. Under Art 133, the Commission submits proposals to the Council for implementing the common commercial policy. If negotiations are required with third countries, these are authorised by the Council but undertaken by the Commission. Any agreement is concluded by the Council on behalf of the Community.

However, in its Opinion 1/78 on the International Agreement on Natural Rubber, the Court did recognise that in certain circumstances the participation of the Member States in an international agreement was necessary. This Opinion concerned an international agreement designed to achieve a balanced growth between the supply and demand for natural rubber. This required a guaranteed stable export earning for exporting countries, whilst ensuring supplies for importing countries at a fair price. In order to achieve this, it was decided to establish a buffer stock to even out fluctuations in the market for natural rubber. Although the subject matter of this agreement fell within the common commercial policy of Art 133, the financing of the buffer stock was to be provided by the Member State. If the financing had been provided by the Community, the Community would have exclusive power. Thus, as finance was to be provided directly by the Member States, they could participate in the agreement together with the Community.

Association agreements are governed by Art 310, which provides for such agreements with a non-Member State or an international organisation. Such agreements often act as preliminary to, or substitutes for, membership of the Community.

If the Community enters into agreements with third countries or international organisations, can these be invoked by individuals before their national courts? The effect of treaties on individuals within the European Community varies from one Member State to another, depending upon whether it is a monist or dualist State. For example, in Belgium, France, Greece, Luxembourg and The Netherlands, treaties can usually be invoked in national courts and are normally given priority over national laws, whereas in other Member States, such as the UK and Ireland, treaties cannot be invoked at all, but are considered to be purely a matter for the executive. In such countries, the content of such treaties can only be made binding as to individuals through separate legislation.

In the second *Haegeman* case (1974), the ECJ referred to the fact that treaties with third countries are concluded by an act of the Council and that their provisions form an integral part of Community law. The main principle which has to be considered in this respect is the direct effect of these agreements. In dealing with this question, there is no indication in the Treaty itself that such agreements may be directly effective, and the ECJ has not been wholly consistent in its approach. When deciding questions of direct effect, the Court is seeking to satisfy three requirements. These are: that a measure must be clear and unambiguous; it must be unconditional; and it must take effect without further action by the EC Member State. These apply to any measure which an applicant claims is directly effective.

In the *International Fruit Co* case (1972), the company claimed that certain EC regulations violated Art XI of the General Agreement on Tariffs and Trade (GATT). The Court had to decide whether the international agreement was capable of conferring rights on citizens of the Community which they can invoke before national courts. It was clear that the GATT agreement was binding upon the Community and thus its Member States. However, the general scheme and terms of the General Agreement were such that only the Contracting Parties or States could act if one of the other Contracting Parties acted contrary to the agreement. Therefore, the GATT agreement was not capable of conferring on citizens of the Community rights which they could invoke before national courts.

However, in the *Bresciani* case (1976), the Court accepted that an association agreement did confer rights on Community citizens which the national courts of the Community must protect. In this case, Bresciani was importing raw cowhides from Senegal, a State which came within an association agreement under the Yaounde Convention. Under Italian law, an inspection fee was charged, covering the cost of examinations and laboratory tests. This fee amounted to a charge having an equivalent effect to a customs duty and was prohibited under the Treaty. Also, in *Haegeman v Belgian State* (1974), the ECJ accepted that the association agreement with Greece was an act of the institutions of the Community and therefore within an Art 234 (then Art 177) preliminary reference for interpretation.

Therefore, there are a number of specific subject matters where the Treaty grants express treaty making powers to the Community, notably under the common commercial policy, the association policy and relationship agreements. This was confirmed in the 'open skies' cases concerning agreements made by some Member States and the USA (*Commission v UK* (2002)). In addition, following the *ERTA* case (1971), the external competence of the Community has been extended by the doctrine of parallelism, whereby an internal power may give rise to an external competence. Whatever the origins of the external power, the approach of the Court has not been consistent. The result has made the individual very dependent, on occasions, on the approach taken by the courts of the Member State towards the recognition of treaties with third countries.

Question 46

What is meant by the doctrine of parallelism? What has been its impact on the external competency of the EC?

Answer plan

The doctrine of parallelism is derived from the judgment in the *ERTA* case and, therefore, the answer requires this case to be dealt with and also the following points:

- legal personality of the Community under Art 281;
- express treaty making powers;
- *Cornelis Kramer* case;
- Opinion 1/75;
- Opinion 1/76;
- Opinion 1/78; and
- Opinion 1/92.

Answer

The doctrine of parallelism is associated with the external relations of the European Community. The Community was given its own legal personality, separate from its Member States, by Art 281. This meant that it had the power to enter into agreements with third countries or international organisations like the GATT. Having been given this authority by the Treaty, there are specific Articles of the Treaty which give express powers to enter into agreements on specific matters. For example, the Community may conclude agreements with third countries under Arts 131–34 on those matters which come within the common commercial policy enumerated in Art 133.

As far as the Member States were concerned, the Community only had those external powers which were expressly conferred by the Treaty. If there were no such express powers, they felt that none were to be implied. The Member States were rudely awakened when the ECJ gave its judgment in the

ERTA case (1971). This case was brought before the Court because of a dispute between the Council and the Commission over the division of powers and responsibilities in exercising the external powers of the EU. This agreement provided the power to regulate the maximum driving hours for lorry drivers. The governments of the Member States claimed that, as treaty making power had not been expressly granted to the Community, the competence for such agreements remained with them. The Commission had started proceedings under Art 230 (then Art 173) for the annulment of the Council's discussions resulting in a common position.

The Commission failed on the merits of the case because the negotiations for the European Road Transport Agreement were well advanced before the adoption of a Council Regulation on road transport. However, the ECJ laid down the general principle that the existence of Community common rules precludes Member States from undertaking obligations with third countries which affect those rules. The Member States objected to this idea, because they said that it ignored the political element of such international treaties. However, the Court had reached this conclusion based upon Art 281 (then Art 210) relating to all the objectives defined in Pt 1 of the Treaty. This means that each time the Community adopts provisions laying down common rules to implement a common policy envisaged by the Treaty, the Member States no longer have the right to undertake obligations with third countries which affect those rules. This applies regardless of whether the Member State is acting individually or collectively with other Member States. They have to operate within the framework of the Community. The result is that the Community has exclusive power in all external matters affecting the application of the Community legal system, as the internal measures are inseparable from the external aspect.

The adoption of internal rules is frequently referred to as conferring Community competence in external relations. In the *Cornelis Kramer* case (1976), proceedings had been instituted in the Dutch courts against fishermen accused of contravening laws limiting catches of certain fish. These laws had been adopted in accordance with a recommendation of the North East Atlantic Fisheries Commission, a body established by an international convention ratified by all EC States except for Italy and Luxembourg. The Dutch court asked, by way of an Art 234 (then Art 177) reference, whether the Community alone has authority to enter into commitments of the kind contained in the international convention. The Court held that the Community must enjoy the capacity to enter into international agreements over the whole field of Pt 1 of the Treaty. However, the Court did concede that transitional interim concurrent rights might be exercised by Member States until such time as the Community itself exercised its own functions. When this happened, the power came within the exclusive power of the Community. This case seems to apply the *ERTA* decision.

This was discussed in the Art 300 (then Art 228) Opinion 1/75 on Export Credits, where the Commission argued that the conclusion of the OECD Local Costs Understanding was a matter of exclusive Community competence. However, the Member States cited *ERTA*, and argued that this could only be true if there were corresponding internal rules. In its judgment, the Court did not deal with this point, but held that the Understanding came within the Community's commercial policy under Art 133 (then Arts 113 and 114) and was thus within an exclusive Community competence. The Court spoke of the impossibility of concurrent powers being exercised at the same time in regard to the subject matter.

In Opinion 1/76 (Laying Up Fund), the Court made it clear that the existence of rules was not necessarily the prerequisite for the existence of Community competence. The power to bind the Community with third countries flows from the implications from the provision of the treaties creating the internal power. Also, in Opinion 1/76, the Court held that the Community is entitled to co-operate with another country in setting up a public international organisation and in granting powers of decision to that organisation. However, the Court stated that the structural elements of the Community cannot be sacrificed by the competence of a new international organisation. This view was repeated in the ECJ's Opinion regarding the European Economic Area (EEA) in 1992. The Opinion of the Court (Opinion 1/92) was that the establishment of a joint EEA Court was incompatible with the Treaty of Rome 'and would lead to serious legal complications'.

Therefore, Community competence in external relations exists where there is an internal power to act, whether or not it has been exercised, and participation in an agreement is necessary. This is illustrated by the case brought by the Commission against some Member States that had entered into 'open skies' bilateral agreements with the USA (*Commission v UK* (2002)). An internal power is therefore paralleled or mirrored by an external competence. This is the basis of the doctrine of parallelism, which has greatly extended the external competence of the European Community. There have been complications on occasions where the agreement with third countries have been 'mixed' agreements. This is where there is some competence with the Community and some within the powers and responsibilities of the Member States. In Opinion 1/78 (National Rubber), the ECJ accepted participation by the Community and Member States in an agreement which was clearly within the Community's commercial policy. This reflected the pragmatic view often taken by the Court. Under the 'economic' clauses of the agreement, finance was to be provided by the Member States, hence their participation. However, if the finance was provided by the Community, it would have exclusive competence and the participation by the Member States would not be accepted.

Question 47

Analyse TWO of the following cases which came before the ECJ, and explain their importance in the development of Community law:

(a) *ERTA* – Case 22/70;

(b) *Cornelis Kramer* – Cases 3, 4 and 6/76;

(c) Opinion 1/75.

Answer plan

When approaching a question like this, the temptation is to produce too descriptive an answer. The facts are important, but are only one element of the answer. You should deal with the following points:

- the facts, the legal points raised and the decision of the Court;
- what kind of case was it? A preliminary reference or a direct action? What Article of the Treaty was it based upon?; and
- the cases chosen for this type of question have usually played their part in developing or reinforcing European Court judgments – what part has this case played?

Answer

(a) ERTA – Case 22/70

In January 1962, under the auspices of the United Nations Economic Commission for Europe, the European Agreement concerning the work of drivers of vehicles engaged in cross-border journeys (ERTA) was signed by five of the then six Member States of the Community. The Agreement never came into effect, owing to a lack of sufficient ratification. Subsequently, negotiations began again in 1967 to revise the Agreement. Meanwhile, work had been going on within the EU with regard to harmonisation of driving and rest periods of drivers of road transport vehicles, resulting in a 1969 regulation. At its meeting in 1970, the Council of Ministers discussed the attitude to be adopted towards the forthcoming ERTA negotiations. They agreed a common position, as required by the EC Treaty. However, the Commission disagreed with this procedure, because it felt that this was now a matter for the Community and not the individual Member States. The Commission brought this case before the European Court under Art 230 (then Art 173), seeking judicial review of the Council's common position and negotiation of the ERTA.

The main point of the case concerned who had competence with regard to external agreements on this policy area. If it was still with the Member States, then the Council of Ministers' actions would be within the Treaty. However, if it was now a Community competence, the Treaty specified how the negotiations should take place. The Council claimed that as the Community only had such powers as had been conferred on it, authority to enter into agreements with third countries cannot be assumed in the absence of an express provision of the Treaty. More specifically, Art 71 (then Art 75), which conferred upon the Community powers defined in wide terms, implementing the common transport policy, relates only to internal measures.

The ECJ, however, said that, in the absence of specific provisions of the Treaty relating to the negotiation and conclusion of international agreements in the sphere of transport policy, it is necessary to look to the general system of Community law in the sphere of relations with third countries. Article 281 (then Art 210) provides the Community with legal personality to establish links with third countries over the whole field of objectives defined in Pt 1 of the Treaty. Each time the Community, with a view to implementing a common policy envisaged by the Treaty, adopts provisions laying down common rules, the Member States no longer have the right, whether acting individually or collectively, to undertake obligations with third countries which affect these rules. This applies whatever form the internal rules may take. Once this happens, the Community alone is in a position to assume and carry out contractual obligations toward third countries affecting the whole sphere of application of the Community legal system. The Member States must operate within the institutional framework of the Community, by which the Commission negotiates and the Council concludes such international agreements.

Although, on the facts, the Court found that the Council had not exceeded its powers, the judgment was to have long term implications for the external competence of the Community. The case developed the idea of parallel internal and external Community competence.

(b) Cornelis Kramer – Cases 3, 4 and 6/76

Criminal proceedings had been brought against certain Dutch fishermen who were accused of having infringed the Dutch rules limiting the catches of sole and plaice. These rules had been adopted on the basis of the provisions of the North East Atlantic Fisheries Convention. The Dutch court made a preliminary reference to the European Court under Art 234 (then Art 177) on the external competence of the Community. In essence, the questions asked were on whether Member States retained the power to adopt measures such as those under the Convention, whether such measures are compatible with Community law and whether the Community had exclusive competence in this policy area.

As there was an absence of a specific provision in the Treaty authorising the Community to enter into international commitments in the sphere of conservation of fish, the Court looked to the general system of Community law in the sphere of external relations of the Community. The Court recited the traditional view that Art 281 (then Art 210) gave the Community legal personality, and therefore the capacity to enter into international commitments over the whole range of Community objectives. The Court said that, in this specific case, it must be recognised that authority to enter into particular international agreements may be express or implied from the provisions of the Treaty. The only way to ensure the conservation of fish, both effectively and equitably, was through a system of rules binding on all the States concerned, irrespective of whether they were members of the European Community. In these circumstances, it follows from the duties and powers which Community law has established internally that the Community has authority to enter into international commitments on fish conservation. However, having established that the Community has authority, the Court needed to look at whether the Community had assumed external responsibility.

The Community had not yet fully exercised its functions in fish conservation and therefore, when the Convention arose, the Member States had the power to assume commitments, such as the Convention. Having had the power to enter the Convention, the Member State now had the power to enforce it within the area of its jurisdiction. However, the Court pointed out quite clearly that the authority of the Member State was of only a transitional nature, until the Community had acted so as to assume exclusive competence in this policy area. This had to happen at the latest six years after accession as, by that time, the Council was required under Art 102 of the Act of Accession 1972 to introduce measures for fish conservation. Once this had happened, the Member States were under a duty to use all the political and legal means available to ensure the participation of the Community in the Convention and similar agreements.

(c) Opinion 1/75

Under Art 300 (then Art 228), the ECJ can be asked to give its opinion on the compatibility of proposed international agreements with the EC Treaty. This opinion by the Court was on a draft Understanding on a Local Cost Standard, drawn up under the auspices of the OECD. The key question was whether the Community had the power to conclude such an agreement and whether that power is exclusive.

The Treaty does include, in Arts 132 and 133, a commercial policy which covers both internal rules and the power to conclude agreements with third countries. The field of the common commercial policy necessarily covers systems of aid for exports, and more particularly, measures concerning credits for the financing of local costs linked to export operations. These were the main provisions of this draft Treaty. The Council had already adopted directives on credit insurance in 1970 and 1971. Therefore, the Court concluded that the subject matter of the Understanding on a Local Costs Standard was within the sphere of the common commercial policy, and thus within the ambit of the Community's powers.

The Court said that a commercial policy is, in fact, made up by the combination and interaction of internal and external measures, without priority being taken by one over the others. Sometimes, agreements are concluded in execution of a policy fixed in advance, sometimes that policy is defined by the agreements themselves. Such agreements may be outline agreements, the purpose of which is to lay down uniform principles. This was the case with the Understanding on Local Costs.

On the question of exclusive competency, the Court said that, given the Community's commercial policy, it would not be acceptable for Member States to exercise a concurrent power in either the internal or the international sphere. Article 133 (then Arts 113 and 114) shows clearly that the exercise of concurrent powers by Member States and the Community is impossible. To accept the contrary view would recognise that in relations with third countries, Member States may adopt positions which differ from those agreed by the Community through its institutions. The Court said that it was of little importance that the obligations and financial burdens inherent in the execution of the agreement envisaged by the Understanding are borne directly by the Member States.

The Member States argued before the Court that the conclusion of the Understanding was not a matter of exclusive Community competence based upon the decision in the *ERTA* case. They said that there were no corresponding internal rules, so there could not be any parallel external competence. However, the Court did not deal with this point in its judgment, but held that the Understanding fell within the Community's commercial policy. Following on from the *ERTA* case, this judgment added to the exclusive external powers of the Community.

CHAPTER 12

THE INTERNAL MARKET AND BEYOND

Introduction

The internal market will always be topical, as the EU is based upon a customs union; therefore, the problems encountered with the reality of such an organisation will go in and out of fashion. At the moment, the main questions are on the legal implications leading up to the completion of the internal market, the important cases on the freedoms associated with the Community and the Maastricht Treaty. The Treaty of Amsterdam and the introduction of a single currency outline the next stage in the development of the Community.

Generally, questions on this topic are essay type questions, simply because problems would usually have to be very complicated to encompass the topic. As this topic changes so rapidly, it is very important to read newspapers to follow the changing political and legal environment in which the Community operates.

Checklist

You should be familiar with the following:

- the background to the Single European Act 1986, notably the Commission's White Paper on the completion of the internal market;
- the Single European Act – Arts 18 and 95 on the internal market, the changes to the voting procedures in the Council of Ministers and the powers of the European Parliament;
- the Maastricht Treaty on Economic and Monetary Union, but more importantly on European Union; and
- the proposed changes to the institutional balance.

Question 48

Discuss the importance of the Treaty of Nice in the development of an enlarged European Union.

Answer plan

With the work of the Convention on the Future of Europe receiving a great deal of publicity and the impending enlargement of the EU, this type of discussion question is increasingly used to get students to discuss current issues. You need to include the following points:

- the events leading up the Inter-Governmental Conference (IGC) at Nice in December 2000;
- the background to the enlargement to 25 or 27 Member States;
- the impact on the main institutions of the EU, namely the European Parliament, Council and Commission;
- the Laeken Declaration and the work of the Convention.

Answer

As the IGC in 1996 failed to address the issues of institutional reform and enlargement of the EU, the resulting Treaty of Amsterdam in 1997 neglected these issues. The result was that these matters became more pressing for the next IGC that culminated in the Treaty of Nice, concluded in December 2000. The 15 Member States realised that with the enlargement to 25 or more States in the near future, it was imperative that the institutions were reformed, not only in their membership, but also in the way they operated. Also, if the present policies were continued in the Common Agricultural Policy or the Regional Development Funds, there would be serious financial implications following enlargement. This essay will concentrate on the institutional issues, as the future budgetary policy of the EU following enlargement is still to be resolved.

It was recognised that with the expansion of the EU from 15 to 25 Member States in 2004 and possibly 27 in 2007, the institutions needed to be reformed. Suggestions had been made by the 'Three Wise Men' in their report in the 1970s but there had never been the political will to take the initiatives needed to deal with the Commission and the Council of Ministers. Although the European Parliament had changed – especially since 1979, when direct elections were introduced – the European Commission had been ignored. Recent suggestions had raised doubts as to whether the Commission in its present form could work effectively to fulfil its responsibilities under Art 211.

The present Commission has 20 members; each Member State nominates one Commissioner but France, Germany, Italy, Spain and the UK nominate two. This was very convenient for the UK as it was allowed to nominate one person from the government, Neil Kinnock, and one from the main opposition party, Chris Patten. However, if the present system continues, we would have over 30 Commissioners following enlargement, and this at a time when some argue that it is difficult to find meaningful roles for the current 20. There would also be the difficulty of managing a Commission of that size despite the power given to the President of the Commission by the Nice Treaty, and the maintenance of the principle of collective responsibility. The agreement reached in Nice is for each Member State to be limited to one Commissioner from 2005 onwards. This postpones the difficult decision with regard to the size of the Commission because it is inclusive, in that all Member States have at least one Commissioner. This still raises the problem as to the roles or portfolios they may be given. However, from the next stage of enlargement, when there are 25 members, the size of the Commission will be smaller than the number of Member States. This reduction will be achieved by a selection process based on a rotation system with the principle of equality being paramount. This is likely to lead to challenges by disappointed Member States before the ECJ.

The European Parliament, as the main democratic institution of the Union, has to be able to accommodate elected representatives from the new Member States. The number of MEPs was increased with the unification of Germany and there are currently 626. There is also the factor that the Parliament's building has been newly refurbished at great expense and therefore cannot be increased in size without even more expense. The solution was to put a cap on the number of MEPs irrespective of any further enlargement. The IGC wanted to ensure appropriate representation of the peoples of the Member States and stated that the number of MEPs may not exceed 732. Therefore, as new Member States join, the number of MEPs for existing members will be decreased proportionately. However, the Nice Treaty has extended the co-decision procedure to seven more areas of policy This will give more authority to the European Parliament in these areas, although it does not extend to taxation or social security policies.

The Council generally takes decisions by a qualified majority, which requires a mixture of large and small Member States to agree on a particular issue. Article 205 lists the weighted votes for all Member States, with the larger countries having 10 votes and the smallest only two. Sixty-two votes are required in favour for any measure to be passed by this process. Many of the new Member States have small or average size populations and this will act to the detriment of the larger existing Member States. Therefore, it was agreed in the Nice Treaty to change the system of qualified majority voting. The new system is often referred to as the 'triple majority' as there are three aspects to it. Any decision must command the agreement of the majority of the overall number of Member States, it must have 169 out of the 237 weighted votes and, lastly, the votes in favour must represent 62% of the total population of the EU. This last requirement will only arise where a Member State so requests. There is also the issue of whether the existing rotation arrangement for the presidency of the Council every six months is workable within an enlarged Community.

With enlargement will come an increase in the number of cases coming to the Community Courts, generally from the new Member States. Given the workload that the ECJ is currently facing and the demands for a reduction in the time taken for preliminary rulings to be dealt with, reform is necessary. The Court of First Instance is to be given an increase in powers so that it can hear direct actions, and there is the possibility that the anomaly of staff cases will be given to a specialised chamber.

Although the Nice Treaty was concluded in December 2000, some linguistic problems had to be resolved, so the final version is dated February 2001. The next stage was the ratification of the various Member States, which proved a problem in only one such country. In Ireland, a referendum required by the Irish Constitution resulted in a 'No' vote in June 2001. This was finally reversed in another referendum in October 2002, and thus removed the last barrier to the implementation of the Nice Treaty. However, some matters were not settled at Nice. These include the delimitation of powers between the EU and the Member States, the simplification of the treaties, the roles of the national parliaments and the legal status of the Charter of Fundamental Rights. Following the Nice Treaty there was the Laeken Declaration in December 2001 which clarified these issues but which, more importantly, established the Convention on the Future of Europe to take the discussion further by including representatives drawn from all the stakeholders in the debate. As a discussion forum, the Convention brings together a wide range of views on a 'Constitution for Europe' and other issues such as a 'United States of Europe with an elected President'. It is anticipated that decisions will be taken at the 2004 IGC in Berlin.

Question 49

Discuss the importance of the Single European Act in achieving the single European market.

Answer plan

The main points that should be covered are:

*   background to the Single European Act (SEA);
*   new policy areas added by the SEA;
*   the importance of new Articles, including Arts 18 and 95 on the internal market; and
*   the impact of the SEA on Community institutions, notably the voting in the Council of Ministers and the powers of the European Parliament.

Answer

The Single European Act (SEA) came into force in 1987, following its ratification by the national Parliaments of all the Member States. The Act had been agreed at the Luxembourg meeting of the European Council in 1985. The European Council had assigned two objectives for the Inter-Governmental Conference given the task of drafting the SEA. These were the revision of the Rome Treaty and the drafting of a treaty on political co-operation allowing for the co-ordination of foreign policies and European security. As far as achieving the single European market is concerned, it is the first of these objectives which is the most important. The SEA introduced new policy objectives and changes to the Community's decision making process.

Five new policy objectives were added in the SEA. These were the internal market, monetary capacity, social policy, economic and social cohesion and research and technological development. Two important Articles were added to the Treaty of Rome to deal with the internal market. These are Art 18, introduced by Art 13 of the SEA, and Art 95, derived from Art 18 of the SEA. Article 18 set the aim of establishing the internal market by 31 December 1992. It also repeats the characteristics of such a market as an area without internal frontiers in which the free movement of goods, persons, services and capital is ensured in accordance with the provisions of the Treaty of Rome. The target date of 31 December 1992 was expressed as an aim and was not intended to be legally binding. In a declaration annexed to the Act, the signatory governments express their firm political will to take, before 1 January 1993, the decisions necessary to complete the internal market. However, a further declaration annexed to the Act also indicates that Member States can still derogate from their obligations under the Treaty in certain policy areas. It states that 'nothing in these provisions shall affect the right of a Member State to take such measures as they consider necessary for the purpose of controlling immigration from third countries, and to combat terrorism, crime, the traffic in drugs, and illicit trading in works of art and antiques'. Some critics of the SEA believe that this annex extends the power of Member States to derogate from their obligations beyond that already found in the original Treaty.

As well as introducing Art 18, the SEA also introduces Arts 19 and 20. Article 18 requires the Commission to report to the Council on progress made towards achieving the internal market by the end of 1992. Article 20 requires the Commission to take into account, when drawing up proposals to achieve the internal market, the fact that economies of some Member States vary in their development. This allows some derogation from the provisions of the internal market, although they must be temporary and cause the least possible disturbance to the functioning of the common market.

Another important provision is Art 18 of the SEA, which adds Art 95. This provided the means for enacting legislation to complete the internal market. The original Treaty facilitates, via the traditional consultative procedure, the issue of directives for the approximation of laws which directly affect the establishment or functioning of the common market. The new Art 95 was designed to achieve the objectives set out in Art 18 by allowing the co-operation procedure to be used to adopt the measures for approximation. This co-operation procedure is discussed in more detail later, but it is important to note here that measures in Art 95 are not restricted to directives. Although Art 95 is broader than the original provision, it specifically excludes fiscal provisions, those relating to the free movement of persons and those relating to the rights and interests of employed persons.

When formulating its proposals, certain guidelines are given to the Commission. It is required to take as a base a high level of protection in its proposals concerning health, safety, environmental protection and consumer protection. This was included to deal with the concern of some Member States, notably those of northern Europe, that the process of approximation would lead to a lowering of standards. Obviously, taking a high level of protection as a base line could cause some problems for certain Member States, especially those who were relatively new members of the Community. However, Art 95 allows a Member State to derogate from a harmonisation measure on the grounds found in Art 30 or relating to the protection of the environment or the working environment. Any Member State wishing to do this must inform the Commission, which is required to ensure that the Member State is not using the derogation as a means of arbitrary discrimination or a disguised restriction on trade between Member States. If the Member State is thought to be acting improperly, the Commission, using Art 226, or another Member State under Art 227, can bring the matter before the ECJ. In some instances, the harmonisation measure itself can include a safeguard clause authorising the Member State to take provisional measures based on Art 30, subject to a Community control procedure.

The SEA contained two major changes in the Community's decision making processes, designed to speed up the voting procedure in the Council of Ministers and to give increased powers to the European Parliament. The Act extends the system of qualified voting in the Council. The system of qualified voting is described in Art 205 and is based upon each Member State having a certain number of votes, weighted to reflect its population. For example, France, Germany, Italy and the UK, as the largest Member States, have 10 votes each, whereas Luxembourg, as the smallest, has two. A majority is constituted by 62 votes, requiring the agreement of both large and small Member States. This extension of qualified voting is for most of the new policy objectives introduced by the SEA. In the case of the internal market, provision is made for qualified majority voting for the new Art 95. There are certain sensitive areas concerning the internal market which still remain subject to the unanimity role.

A new version of Art 149 is introduced by Art 7 of the SEA, giving increased powers to the European Parliament in those situations where the Council acts by qualified majority voting. The effect of these changes is that the European Parliament now has the opportunity of pronouncing on the final decision of the Council instead of simply giving a consultative opinion on Community legislation. Once the Commission has formulated a proposal for the Council, the latter must reach a common position which is communicated to the European Parliament. The Parliament can then either approve the Council's decision, in which case the proposal is adopted, or else it can reject or amend it. Rejection or amendment must be carried by an absolute majority of the Parliament's members. In the case of rejection, the Council can only pass the proposal by unanimity. In the case of amendment, the proposal must be re-examined by the Commission within one month, taking into account the European Parliament's changes. The proposal is then sent back to the Council, which can adopt it by qualified majority voting, but can only amend it by unanimity. Those amendments from the Parliament which were not included by the Commission in the resubmitted proposal are forwarded to the Council, where they may be adopted by unanimity. If the Council does not act within three months or, with an extension, four months, then the proposal fails.

The SEA is not without its critics. Some have pointed to Arts 2 and 3 of the original Treaty of Rome as indicating the foundations of the common market. The SEA, they argue, merely repeats these Articles, but adds nothing to them. In fact, they argue, where it does add to the original Treaty, it is in the ability of Member States to avoid their obligations by allowing derogations. The wide meaning of a common market is substituted by a more limited internal market, ignoring all the achievements of the Community. However, there are others who argue that, as a result of enlargement and changing world circumstances, the Treaty of Rome needed to have a new impetus and focus to bring it back to its original objectives. The SEA was a moral and political commitment on the part of all the Member States to make a reality of the internal market by 1993. The SEA reaffirmed the ideal of a common market in Art 18 and provided a mechanism by Art 95 to achieve it. The foundations were laid in the SEA for many of the developments taken forward in the Maastricht and Amsterdam Treaties.

Question 50

Critically review the Maastricht Treaty in the development of the European Community.

Answer plan

The Maastricht Treaty recognised the need for reform in both institution and policy areas of the EU. This discussion question provides the opportunity to raise issues arising from the Inter-Governmental Conferences which were held to discuss developments. It is important with this type of question to know what is happening in the European Union, something which can be gleaned from good newspapers rather than textbooks. Your answer should cover the following points:

- background to the Maastricht Treaty;
- the meaning of 'European Economic and Monetary Union' and 'European Political Union';
- the need to deal with the democratic deficit in the Community and the measures implemented to achieve this;
- changes to the institutional balance, especially the co-decision procedure;
- the principle of subsidiarity;
- citizenship of the European Community; and
- developments in the Treaty of Amsterdam.

Answer

On 11 December 1991, the leaders of the 12 Member States agreed the text of a Treaty on European Union (TEU, or the Maastricht Treaty), 17 associated protocols and 33 declarations. The protocols are additional agreements between some, but not all, of the signatories. For example, the Protocol on Social Policy included all the Member States except the UK. The declarations do not have legal force, but outline the ways in which the provisions of the Treaty should be interpreted or implemented. The agreement was the culmination of long and arduous negotiations following the reports of two Inter-Governmental Conferences (IGCs) between the 12 Member States. One was on Economic and Monetary Union and the other was on Political Union.

The anticipated completion of the internal market required the Community to review future developments. In addition, there had been revolutionary changes in Eastern Europe, providing new opportunities, problems and the acceptance of enlargement of the EU from its present 15 Member States. Businesses within the EU were pressing for an end to fluctuating and uncertain exchange rates which imposed increasing problems for the movement of goods and services within the Community. The payment of commission and losses on the different buying and selling rates added to the problems encountered by businesses. A possible solution was a move towards European Monetary Union, with a single currency based upon the European Currency Unit (ECU) that could be used freely throughout the Community. These factors provided the catalyst for the establishment of the IGCs.

However, any move towards European Monetary Union would increase the powers of the Community. To offset this, there had to be a strengthening of the democratic accountability of the Community to balance this increased power. The increase in democratic accountability centred on the European Parliament and the concept of subsidiarity. The move towards European Union, a term which is given to the next stage in the process of integration between the 15 Member States, creates two inter-governmental bodies dealing with a common foreign and security policy and home affairs and justice.

The institutional revisions were mostly designed to improve the efficiency and democratic nature of the Community's institutional structures and decision making processes. The result has been an increase in the powers of the European Parliament and the complexity of the Community's decision making procedures. Different procedures apply to different areas of legislation. For example, with a proposal for environmental legislation from the Commission, there are four possible decision making procedures: co-operation procedure; co-decision; consultation with unanimity; and unanimous decision to vote by majority. The Treaty of Rome, in 1957, provided for the consultation procedure with a single Parliamentary reading, providing an opinion and unanimous or majority voting in the Council of Ministers. The co-operation procedure was introduced by the Single European Act 1986 (SEA) and gave greater involvement for the European Parliament when dealing with legislation on particular policies associated with the completion of the internal market.

The TEU introduced a new procedure called co-decision. For the first time, Parliament can prevent legislation being adopted, and in the Council of Ministers majority voting is required, with two exceptions where unanimity applies. Although this procedure is generally called co-decision, to differentiate it from the other procedures, the term does not appear in Art 251 of the Treaty. Co-decision has some of the elements of the co-operation procedure, but it goes further by giving the Parliament the power to veto a legislative proposal. The veto can only be exercised after the convening of a conciliation committee, comprising members of the Council or their representatives and an equal number of representatives of the European Parliament. This committee must approve a joint text within six weeks, which is followed by a further period of six weeks during which the Council and the Parliament have to adopt the proposal; otherwise it fails. The time period can be extended by common agreement of both the Council and the Parliament for a further two weeks. If the committee fails to agree, the Council may confirm its common opinion within six weeks, which would require the Parliament to reject the text by an absolute majority of its members to stop the proposal being finally adopted. This is what is referred to as Parliament's veto. Article 49 of the TEU also provides the Parliament with the power of veto with regard to the accession of new members. The Council has to obtain the assent of the European Parliament before acting.

A new institution was added to the list of Community institutions. Previously, there were four institutions: the European Parliament, the Council, the Commission and the ECJ. Now there is a fifth one, the Court of Auditors. Although the Court of Auditors has existed since 1977, its place in Art 7 indicates an upgrading of its status. This increased the influence of the Court of Auditors at a time when the completion of the internal market will bring added pressure on combating fraud and financial accountability for Community funds. A new advisory body was also added to the existing Economic and Social Committee. Under Arts 264 and 265, a Committee of the Regions has been established, to give opinions either in cases where they have been consulted by the Council or Commission or in cases where they consider it appropriate. Article 8 establishes a European System of Central

Banks and a European Central Bank to add to the existing European Investment Bank.

The TEU added Art 5 to the EC Treaty. This Article deals with the principle of subsidiarity. According to the words of the Article, the Community may take action 'only if and in so far as the objectives of the proposed action cannot be sufficiently achieved by the Member States and can therefore, by reason of the scale or effects of the proposed action, be better achieved by the Community'. The principle is strengthened by the inclusion in the Preamble to the Treaty of the objective of a closer European Union, where decisions are taken as closely as possible to the citizen in accordance with the principle of subsidiarity. It would appear that it is for the Commission to justify its chosen action when presenting a proposal, that is, why it is not leaving the action to be taken at another level, such as within a Member State. Thus the validity of a proposed Community measure may be successfully challenged on the grounds that it offends against the principle of subsidiarity. As Art 230 continues to give the European Court the power to hear actions for annulment, it will be necessary to wait until such an argument is brought before the judges.

The last major change introduced by the TEU concerns citizenship of the Union under Arts 17–21. Citizenship of the Union is mandatory for nationals of the Member States as there is no provision for opting out. Thus, citizenship of the Union has been grafted onto the body of the EC Treaty. This means that, as citizens of the Union, nationals of the Member States have, for example, the right to move and reside freely within the Community. They also have the right to vote and stand as a candidate in local and European Parliament elections in whichever Member State they reside. In addition, the European Parliament is required to appoint an Ombudsman to receive complaints from any citizen of the Union concerning maladministration in the activities of the Community institutions, with the exception of the Courts. In July 1994, the first legal attempt was made to identify the rights of a citizen of the Union when Gerry Adams challenged, in the High Court, the ban by the UK Government which prevented him addressing a group of MPs at Westminster. Generally, the rights of a citizen of the Union are stated with regard to movement between Member States, but here, the argument was about movement within the UK.

The TEU was finally ratified by all the parliaments of the Member States, although there were some problems in Germany, Denmark and the UK where there was opposition to its adoption. The Treaty is an attempt to deal with the challenges facing the Community. The 'democratic deficit' has been tackled by increasing the power of the Parliament and the addition of the Council of the Regions as an advisory body. At the same time, the Community has widened its scope of activities. Many of the additions to the original Treaty are not economic, representing the social and citizenship dimension of the Community. It is for this reason that the word 'economic' has been removed from the Treaty, so that it is now referred to as the EC or European Community Treaty. It would seem that the TEU was a natural extension to the Community, indicating its maturity and development towards the aims of its founders.

If the Community is to grow, more reforms involving its institutions are required. Unfortunately, the opportunity to deal with these reforms was not taken in the Treaty of Amsterdam 1997, although some changes were flagged up in the December 2000 IGC held in Nice. This IGC was held to deal with the issues associated with the growth to 27 Member States (25 in 2004). Some of the reforms will not come into operation until 2005, but at least reform of the Council and the Commission will take place. The Treaty of Nice, implemented in February 2003, is a natural extension of the Maastricht Treaty. Work is in progress in the Convention on the Future of Europe, which will report in time for the next IGC in 2004.

INDEX

Abuse of dominant
   position 112–15,
                     120, 123–27
Acte clair 88–92
Advocates General,
   appointment 8
   background 8
   duty. 8
   impartiality 8
   importance. 9
   independence 8
   judgment 8
   opinion. 9
   role 8
   status. 8
   term of office 8
Age discrimination. 175
Agreements,
   See International agreements
Annulment, European
   Court of Justice (ECJ) 25
Appeals,
   Court of First
      Instance, from 9, 12, 13
   European Court
      of Justice, to 9, 12, 13
Association agreements. . . . 190, 191, 192

Breach of EC law,
   See Direct actions
Budget,
   co-operation. 6
   common agricultural
      policy 5
   conciliation procedure 6
   European Parliament 5–6
   expenditure 5
   procedure. 5–6

CAP, *See* Common
   Agricultural Policy
Cassis de Dijon principle. 96, 103, 107

Certainty, principle of,
   European Court of
      Justice (ECJ) 9
CFI, *See* Court of
   First Instance
Co-decision procedure,
   conciliation committee. 5
   European Council. 5
   European Parliament 5, 7, 17
   introduction. 5
   rejection of proposals
      by European Parliament 5
Co-operation procedure,
   European Parliament 4–5
Comfort letters 118
Commercial agreements 190
Commission, *See* European
   Commission
Committee of Permanent
   Representatives 16
   agendas 11
   Commission proposals 11
   COREPER 1 11
   COREPER 2 11
   disagreements 11
   establishment. 11
   provisional agreement 11
   role 11
   workload 11
Common Agricultural
   Policy 15, 69, 202
   budget. 5
Common commercial policy. 190–91
Company law 161–64
Competition. 111–36
   See also Free movement
      of goods
   abuse of dominant
      position 112–15, 120,
                       123–27
   business secrets. 122
   clearance. 120
   comfort letters 118
   confidentiality 120

dawn raids.................... 121
definition 120
distribution 117
dominant position,
  abuse of.............. 112–15, 120,
                          123–27
duration of position
  in market 114
European Commission,
  powers of.............. 20, 119–23
exemptions................. 118, 120
fines................. 120, 121, 122
gentlemen's agreements 117
importance of policy 111
individual exemption............ 118
information powers 120, 121–22
interim measures 120, 123
market analysis................. 121
market share 114
Merger Directive............. 132–35
monopolies 117
national law and............. 112–15
policy 20, 111–36
predatory pricing 114
price fixing.................... 117
procedure for exercise
  of Commission powers 120
refusal to supply......... 115, 118–19
relevant market.............. 113–14
remedies..................... 119
restriction or distortion 121
restrictive trade
  practices 116–19, 120–21
selective distribution
  agreements............... 117–18
sensitive data.................. 122
significant market power......... 113
takeovers 113
United Brands............... 130–32
vertical integration........... 114–15
Conciliation committee,
  co-decision procedure 5
  European Commission 5
  European Parliament.............. 5
Consultation
  European Parliament.............. 4

Copyright, free movement
  of goods 103–04
COREPER,
  See Committee of Permanent
  Representatives
Council of Ministers................. 1
  decision making process 16–17
  European Parliament and 3, 17
  government ministers' role........ 16
  majority voting.................. 16
  membership.................... 15
  political institution, as 15–16
  powers 14–17
  Presidency 15
  qualified majority voting.......... 16
  role 15
  secretariat..................... 15
  veto........................ 16–17
  voting....................... 16–17
  workload 15
Court of First Instance........... 12–13
  administration.................. 12
  appeals to ECJ from 9, 12, 13
  attachment to ECJ................ 12
  categories of case before 12–13
  establishment.................. 9, 12
  facilities 12
  fines......................... 122
  judges........................ 12
  jurisdiction.................... 9, 12
  role 9, 12
  sittings 12
  treaty basis.................... 12
  waiting list.................... 13
Courts,
  Court of First Instance,
    See Court of First Instance
  European Court of Justice,
    See European Court of Justice
Customs union 103, 201

Damages, availability............ 64–67
Dassonville formula....... 95–96, 99, 101
Dawn raids 121

Decisions 23
   definition 29
   direct effect 42–43
   legal effects 42–43
Deportation,
   free movement
     of workers 149
Direct actions. 53–71, 85
   administrative stage. 54–55
   aim 55
   complaints 54
   direct and individual
     concern 58–59, 60,
                          68–69, 85–86
   duty of Commission. 54
   European Court
     of Justice (ECJ). 9–10
   formal proceedings. 55
   free movement of goods 56
   instigation of procedure 54
   judgment 55
   judicial stage 55
   penalties. 55
   Reasoned Opinion 55
   remedies. 54
   settlement. 55
   standing. 60–61, 62–63,
                             85, 86–87
Direct effect 39–43
   basic requirements 40
   categories of law
     capable of having 40
   criteria. 43, 44
   decisions. 42–43
   development 40
   directives 41–52, 65
   emanation of the State 47
   establishment of principle. 44
   horizontal effect 42, 50
   international agreements. 192
   prohibitions 40
   regulations. 30, 40, 49
   test. 43
   vertical 49, 50, 66

Directives. 23, 43–48
   definition 29, 44
   direct effect 41–52, 65
   emanation of the State 47
   European Parliament 3–4
   implementation. 41–42, 44
   indirect effect. 46–47
   interpretation of
     national legislation 47
   Marleasing principle 50, 51
   national courts,
     interpretation by 50, 51
   non-implementation. 64–67
   time limit for
     implementation. 41–42, 46
Disability discrimination. 175
Discrimination 171–87
   age. 175
   disability. 175
   free movement
     of workers 142, 147
   indirect. 179–80
   racial 175
   religious beliefs 175
   sex discrimination,
     See Equal pay;
     Sex discrimination
   sexual orientation 174–75
Dominant position,
   abuse of 112–15, 120,
                               123–27
Due process 28

EC Treaty,
   common commercial
     policy 190–91
   express treaty
     making powers 190–93
   role 23
ECJ, *See* European Court
   of Justice
Economic and Social
   Committee (ECOSOC) 13–14

Elections,
European Parliament 3
judges, ECJ 8
Emanation of the State 47
Enlargement,
European Commission 21
Equal pay 172–75, 176–82
See also Sex
discrimination
justifications for
differences 180–81
onus of proof 180, 181
part time workers 173
remedies 182
statistics 182
Equality 42, 172–75,
176–78
Establishment, right of,
See Freedom of
establishment
European Assembly 1
European Commission 1, 18–21
appointment of
Commissioners 3, 18, 21
civil service analogy 18
Commissioners,
appointment 3, 18, 21
background 18
independence 18
number 21
political office 18
portfolio 19
removal 18
responsibility 19
term of office 18
competition 20
competition powers 119–23
conciliation committee 5
duty 18
enlargement 21
European Parliament 3–5
external relations 19–20
'guardian of the Treaties' 19
independence of
Commissioners 18
legislative role 19
Merger Directive 132–35
mergers 20
powers 18–21
Presidency 3, 18–19
proposals for legislation 4
publications 1
reform proposals 20–21
removal of Commissioners 3, 18
resignation 3
role 18–21
subsidiarity 21
workload 21
European Company 164
European Council,
co-decision procedure 5
common position 4
Presidency 15
European Court of Justice 1, 7–10
Advocates General,
appointment 8
background 8
duty 8
impartiality 8
importance 9
independence 8
judgment 8
opinion 9
role 8
status 8
term of office 8
annulment 25
appeals from CFI to 9, 12–13
certainty, principle of 9
CFI, appeals from 9, 12, 13
chambers 9
characteristics 8
contextual interpretation 32
Court Registry 9
direct actions 9–10
See also Direct actions
enforcement of judgments 10
establishment 8, 12
facilities 12
free movement of goods 93–97
function 8

general principles of law 25–28
historical interpretation 33
influence on 9
interim measures 9
interpretation. 25, 30–33
judges,
    duration of office. 8
    election 8
    number 8
    renewal of office 8
judgment 8, 10
    enforcement 10
judicial review. 25
jurisdiction. 9
language. 9, 31
literal interpretation 32–33
national courts and. 9
number of cases before 9
precedent 9, 23
preliminary references 9–10
progress of cases 9
rules of interpretation 30–33
teleological approach
    to interpretation 31–32
workload 9, 12
European Economic
Interest Groupings
    (EEIGs) 163
European Parliament. 1–7
amendments 4–5
authority. 6–7
blocking legislation 4
budget. 5–6
characteristics 3
co-decision procedure 5, 7
co-operation procedure 4–5
common position 4
conciliation committee. 5
consultation 4
Council of Ministers and 3, 17
criticism 4
debates 4
deliberate obstruction
    of legislation by 4
democracy 2–7
directives 3–4

draft resolution 4
elections 3
European Commission 3–5
expenditure 5–6
history. 3
law-making power 3–4
membership. 3
opinion 4
powers 2–7
questions, parliamentary 3
regulations 3–4
report 4
sovereignty 49–50
standing committees 3
Exhaustion of rights,
free movement
    of goods 104, 105–06
External relations 189–99
    See also International
      agreements
association agreements 190–92
commercial agreements 190
Community competence 194–95
European Commission 19–20
meaning 189
parallelism, doctrine of 193–95

Fines,
competition 120, 121, 122
Court of First
    Instance (CFI). 122
Free movement of goods 93–110
    See also Competition
arbitrary
    discrimination 101, 103
barriers to trade. 94, 98–101, 103
basis of 94
Cassis de Dijon
    principle 96, 99–100,
                     103, 107
copyright 103–04
customs union 103
Dassonville formula 95–96,
                      99, 101
derogations 103

direct actions 56
European Court of
    Justice (ECJ) 93–97
exhaustion of rights 104, 105–06
fundamental freedom 93, 102
intellectual
    property rights 103–04
mandatory
    requirements 96–97, 99–101
marketing of goods
    in Member States. 97, 100
measures having
    equivalent effect to
        quantitative restrictions . . . 94–95,
                                            98–99
necessary measures 96–97,
                                            100–01
price differentials 104–05
proportionality 96
public policy/security 103
quantitative
    restrictions 94–95, 98–99
rule of reason. 96
trade marks 104–05

Free movement
    of workers 137–52, 154
    See also Freedom of
        establishment; Freedom
        to provide services
    accepting offers
        of employment 138, 145
    common market
        for labour 137, 141
    criminal record,
        persons with 150–52
    death of worker. 142
    dependants 139–40, 142
    deportation 149
    discrimination. 142, 147
    entry into UK. 138, 147
    family members 139–40, 142
    independent means,
        persons of. 144
    non-discrimination. 142
    part time employment 140, 142
    probationary workers 148–49

professions,
    recognition of. 143–44, 158–59
public policy
    exceptions. 149–50
public sector
    employment. 146–47
remaining in UK,
    requirements for 138
retired persons 144
right of establishment 141–44
searching for work 138–39, 142
self-employment. 143, 144
services,
    right to provide. 143–44
social security 139, 142–43
university students. 144
worker. 141–42, 145–46,
                                148–49, 154–55

Freedom of
    establishment. 143, 154
    See also Free movement
        of workers; Freedom to
        provide services
    companies 161–64
    lawyers. 158–60
    professions. 158–60

Freedom to provide
    services 143–44, 154,
                                        155–57
    See also Free movement
        of workers; Freedom of
        establishment
    companies 161–64
    duration of right
        of residence 155
    educational courses 155
    personal conduct, exclusion
        on grounds of 156
    postgraduate courses 155
    public policy/security 155–56
    services, freedom to receive 155
    students 157

GATT 20, 192
Gentlemen's agreements 117

Goods, *See* Free movement
of goods

Hearing, right to fair 28

Independent means,
persons of. 144
Institutions. 1–21
COREPER,
See Committee of
Permanent Representatives
Council of Ministers,
See Council of Ministers
Economic and Social
Committee (ECOSOC) 13–14
European Assembly 1
European Commission,
See European Commission
European Court of Justice,
See European Court of Justice
European Parliament,
See European Parliament
importance. 1
origins. 1
overview 1
purpose 1
Interim measures 9
competition 120, 123
Internal market 201–12
completion 201
customs union. 201
single currency 201
International agreements 75–76
association
agreements. 190, 191, 192
commercial 190
direct effect 192
GATT 20, 192
Member State participation. 191
Opinion 1/75. 198–99
relationship agreements 192
rubber 191, 195

Jenkins Commission. 56
Judges,
Court of First Instance (CFI) 12
European Court of
Justice (ECJ),
duration of office. 8
election 8
number 8
renewal of office 8
Judgment,
European Court
of Justice (ECJ). 8, 10
enforcement. 10
Judicial review,
European Court
of Justice (ECJ). 25

Language,
European Court
of Justice (ECJ). 9, 31
Lawyers,
freedom of
establishment. 158–60
meaning 159
recognition. 159
Legislation,
See Sources of law
Locus standi,
See Standing

Majority voting,
Council of Ministers. 16
Marleasing principle 50, 51
Merger Directive. 132–35
Mergers,
European Commission 20

National courts,
See also Preliminary
references; Preliminary
rulings
European Court of
Justice (ECJ) and 9

National law,
    direct effect 39–43
    EC law and................... 35–39
    supremacy of EC law 35–39, 49–50
Non-discrimination 26
    See also Discrimination

Parallelism, doctrine of 193–95
Parliament, European,
    See European Parliament
Penalties, direct actions 55
Precedent,
    European Court
    of Justice (ECJ)............... 9, 23
Predatory pricing 114
Preliminary references...... 9, 57, 73–92
    acte clair..................... 88–92
    decision to make................ 74
    role 75
    developments 75
    direct effect 75, 76
    discretion to refer 76, 78–80, 88
    effect........................ 87–88
    European Court of
    Justice (ECJ)................. 9–10
    extended jurisdiction 75
    framing questions................ 80
    guidelines.............. 78–79, 81–84
    impact....................... 75–76
    importance..................... 73
    judge *rapporteur*.................. 10
    obligation to refer 76–77, 78
    partnership, based on.......... 81–84
    procedure.................... 78–81
    progress 9–10
    purpose 75, 81–84
    refusal of request 81–84
    request 62, 81–84
    use of procedure................. 75
    written proceedings 9–10
Presidency,
    Council of Ministers.............. 15
    European Commission 3, 18–19
    European Council................ 15

Probationary workers,
    free movement
    of workers 148–49
Proportionality 25–26
    free movement of goods 96
Public sector employment,
    free movement
    of workers 146–47

Quantitative restrictions,
    free movement of goods 94

Race discrimination 175
Refusal to supply 115, 118–19
Regulations 23
    application..................... 29
    binding........................ 29
    challenging validity........ 29, 58–61,
                                63–64, 85–86
    decisions, as..................... 59
    definition 29, 58–59
    direct applicability 30, 40
    direct effect 30, 40, 49
    effects 30
    European Parliament............ 3–4
    formal requirements........... 29–30
    general application............... 29
    implementation.................. 30
    normative character 59
    true regulations............... 58–59
Religious discrimination 175
Remedies,
    competition 119
    damages..................... 64–67
    direct actions,
        See Direct actions
    equal pay 182
    preliminary references,
        See Preliminary references
    sex discrimination............... 182
Retired persons,
    free movement of workers 144

Self-employment,
free movement of workers 143

Services, freedom to provide,
See Freedom to provide services

Settlement,
direct actions 55

Sex discrimination.......... 50, 172–75,
179–82

See also Equal pay
collective agreements............ 180
comparators.................... 180
equality..................... 175–78
indirect..................... 179–80
positive action.................. 174
remedies...................... 182
sexual orientation 174–75
transsexuals 174–75

Single currency 201

Single European
Act 1986 204–08

Single market,
See Internal market

Social security,
free movement
of workers 139, 142–43

Societas Europaea (SE) 164

Sources of law.................. 23–33
administrative acts 23, 24
decisions,
See Decisions
directives,
See Directives
equality......................... 26
fundamental rights............ 27–28
general principles
of law 24–28
legitimate expectations 26–27
non-discrimination.............. 26
primary....................... 23

procedural rights 28
proportionality 25–26
regulations,
See Regulations
secondary...................... 23
treaties,
See International
agreements; Treaties

Standing,
direct actions 60–61, 62–63,
85, 86–87

Standing committees,
European Parliament.............. 3

Students....................... 157

Subsidiarity,
European Commission 21

Supremacy of EC law...... 35–39, 49–50

Takeovers....................... 113

Trade marks,
free movement of goods 104–05

Transsexuals 174–75

Treaties,
See also International agreements
enabling Act analogy 23
express treaty
making powers 189–93
importance...................... 23
parallellsm,
doctrine of 193–95
primary source of law 23

Voting,
Council of Ministers........... 16–17

Workers,
See Free movement of workers